D1553161

THE WAR
FOR
THE CITIES

ROBERT MOSS

THE WAR FOR THE CITIES

Coward, McCann & Geoghegan, Inc.

New York

First American Edition 1972
Copyright © 1972 by Robert Moss

Library of Congress Catalog Card Number: 72-76666
Printed in the United States of America

SBN 698-10449-8

Contents

6

Acknowledgements

Many people in all sorts of places contributed to this book. Some must remain anonymous because of their calling; among the others, I am grateful to Rosemary Allot, Major-General Richard Clutterbuck, Hedley Bull, Stephen Clissold, François Duchêne, Alistair Horne, Michael Leifer and Sir Robert Thompson for their ideas and advice; to Pablo Huneeus-Cox and Hernán Curbillos in Santiago; to Dick Noon in Bangkok and James Morgan in Kuala Lumpur; to Manning Clark, who first showed me the human face of history, and to Geoffrey Fairbairn, who first got me thinking about guerrillas. I owe a special debt of gratitude to Brian Crozier, for his constant encouragement and a pathfinding example that began with his book *The Rebels* more than a decade ago; to my friends and colleagues Brian Beedham and Gordon Lee (who waded through a rising tide of paper with unfailing good humour); and to my wife Katrina, who kept the raft afloat when it sometimes seemed in danger of sinking and, best of all, found time to bear me a daughter.

London
December 1971

THE WAR FOR THE CITIES

Introduction

The lookout gave the signal and the van swung out across the narrow one-way street, forcing the Ambassador's driver to brake suddenly. The guard and the chauffeur were taken by surprise as a 'fruit-vendor' on the pavement whipped a sten-gun out of his barrow and several armed men burst out of a villa across the road that had been rented a few days earlier. The Ambassador was tumbled into a stolen car and whisked away to a prepared hiding-place. That is more or less what happened to Burke Elbrick, the American ambassador to Brazil, in 1969, and to Geoffrey Jackson, the British ambassador to Uruguay, in 1971. The scenario for a typical political kidnapping is as simple as that. Like the hijacking of aircraft, this is one of the international crimes that are likely to remain familiar hazards of life in the 1970s, and it is very hard to stop kidnappings taking place without smothering prominent men with bodyguards and bullet-proof glass and walling them up in houses built like fortresses. To seize a diplomat or commandeer a plane is an easy way for a minority group to get its name into the headlines and capture an international audience—until the novelty wears off and the public comes to regard these crimes as something as routine and statistically predictable as the annual road-toll, if somehow more ominous.

But kidnapping and hijacking are only a minor part of the repertoire of the urban guerrilla. In the western industrial societies, as well as in Latin America, West Bengal and parts of the Middle East, urban guerrillas have proved the vulnerability of the modern city. The urban guerrilla uses primitive weapons against complex technology: Molotov cocktails against computer centres, dynamite (the favourite weapon of nineteenth-century anarchists) against bridges and power-stations. An American black power militant instructs his followers that it is possible to cause a delayed explosion in a big office-block by dropping kitchen matches into the air-conditioning system and also recommends scattering tacks and boards with protruding nails at major intersections during rush-hour traffic to cause spectacular collisions.[1] If the motivation is there, the technical possibilities are enormous. It might only take a small band of experienced saboteurs—sufficiently fanatical and enjoying the advantage of complete surprise—to disrupt the life of an industrial city for several weeks by striking at essential services and communications and by unleashing the kind of indiscriminate terrorism that would make people frightened to leave their homes.

But the technical possibilities are less important than the political repercussions. The urban guerrilla is above all a political partisan, for whom sabotage and assassination are psychological as much as military weapons. For the urban guerrilla, success or failure will hinge less on what happens on the field of battle than on his ability to convince the public that his violence is justified, to erode the morale of the forces of order, and to induce a 'climate of collapse' in government circles. Urban guerrilla? At first sight, the phrase seems to contradict itself. From the time of Clausewitz onwards, military analysts have been generally agreed that the first condition of guerrilla warfare is that the rebels should be able to range freely over the countryside and to fall back on to pockets of difficult, irregular terrain as their base-areas.[2] Most theorists (and practitioners) of guerrilla warfare have tended to agree with Fidel Castro that 'the city is a graveyard of revolutionaries and resources'.[3]

By definition, guerrilla warfare is the war of the weak against the strong—a campaign of harassment and attrition waged by inferior, lightly-equipped forces against conventional armies. The guiding principles of the 'war of the flea' are never to be caught defending a fixed position and never to attack without assuring a position of local superiority. Mao Tse-tung and Che Guevara both saw revolutionary warfare as a three-stage process: a preparatory phase leading through guerrilla operations to a war of movement in which the government forces would finally be annihilated. In Montevideo and Montreal, in Belfast and Rio de Janeiro, urban terrorism is in some ways the precise counterpart of rural guerrilla warfare. The 'people's wars' and rural uprisings of the decades since 1945 have given way in the 1970s to urban guerrilla operations in Latin America, Northern Ireland and Quebec, and to more diffuse forms of terrorist action in many western cities, in Istanbul, Teheran and Calcutta.

The phrase 'urban guerrilla' can be abused to apply to all sorts of people in all sorts of places, many of them romantic conspirators or nihilists without a strategy beyond the simple desire to see their names in print. Most of the terrorists in modern history, from the *Narodnaya Volya* in Tsarist Russia or the OAS in Algiers to the Turkish People's Liberation Army or the Weathermen in the United States have only managed to alienate public sympathy by using gangster-style techniques. What distinguishes the urban guerrilla from the terrorist is that he has a strategy for armed insurrection or political victory, however utopian it may seem.

The Brazilian guerrilla leader, Carlos Marighella, mapped out part of that strategy when he wrote that 'It is necessary to turn political crisis into armed conflict by performing violent actions that will force those in power to transform the political situation of the country into a military situation. That will alienate the masses, who, from then on, will revolt against the army and the police and blame them for this state of things.'[4] That is a scenario for civil war. It might be described as the strategy of militarisation. Most of the terrorist organisations discussed in this book, from Eoka in Cyprus and the IRA in Belfast to the Tupamaros in Montevideo, have set out to polarise public feeling in their countries by attempting to force the government to adopt repressive measures that will alienate moderates and erode popular faith in the legitimacy of the political system. It is one of the central arguments of this book that urban terrorists by themselves are unlikely to bring about revolution. On the other hand, the terrorist often acts as a political catalyst. His actions can change the political climate of a society and even help to break down the fabric of democracy—as was seen in Weimar Germany and is again taking place in Uruguay. The IRA in Northern Ireland helped to polarise the Catholic and Protestant communities, to cast the British army in a controversial role and to create a political situation where, by late 1971, the future of the province was in doubt.

It is the purpose of this book to explore the limits and the possibilities of urban guerrilla warfare. Chapters 1 and 2 are concerned with the origins of urban violence, the prospects for western industrial societies and the uses of terror as a political tool. There is a fundamental distinction that must be drawn between urban terrorists in western industrial societies and the would-be revolutionaries of the 'pre-industrial' cities of the third world, although it is important to remember that several Latin American countries are as highly urbanised as Britain or the United States. There is another basic distinction between the use of political terror in a colonial situation, where the aim is to persuade the occupying power that it has become too costly to hold on, and political violence in independent states, where the rebels will normally have to aim for a military victory. The strength or weakness of the terrorist is bound up with popular attitudes towards political violence. An extremist who places a bomb in the Rolls-Royce servicing centre in Paris to protest against British entry into the Common Market will not win much approval in a society that does not accept that this is a legitimate means of expressing dissent. On the other hand, there are two major groups in western societies that frequently fall outside the prevailing social consensus and may have different attitudes to violence: the more extreme elements of the New Left and ethnic, cultural and religious minorities.

The three historical case-studies in Chapter 2 are used to explore the uses of political terror in different situations: against autocracy, against colonial rule, and in defence of a threatened status quo. The Eoka campaign in Cyprus was one of the rare terrorist successes; but even so, the British decision to pull out of the island owed more to the gathering momentum of decolonisation throughout the third world and Eoka's support among the Greek Cypriot community than to terrorist operations in themselves. Chapter 3 examines the position in America and rejects the apocalyptic view that the United States is tottering between revolution and counter-revolution. The Black Panthers, the IRA and the FLQ in Quebec are singled out in Chapters 3–5 to examine the prospects for minority revolt; the problem for ghetto rebels in most societies is that if they press their campaign too far, they will be swamped by the majority groups. Chapter 6 looks at the pattern of insurgency in the third world, and the link between the mushroom-growth of the pre-industrial cities and political violence. As Fanon maintained, the slum-dwellers of third world cities may prove to be the new 'revolutionary class'.

Chapters 7–10 deal with Latin America, where the techniques of urban guerrilla warfare are generally most sophisticated and where in one country at least (Uruguay) urban guerrillas appear to stand a chance of carrying off an armed insurrection—unless revolution is headed off by electoral means or a foreign power decides to intervene. The failure of the rural guerrilla movements of the 1960s in Latin America is seen to be related to their own tactical errors and their distorted image of the Cuban revolution as well as to their failure to construct a political base or enlist significant outside support. Guatemala, Venezuela and Brazil provide contrasting models of how to cope, and how not to cope, with urban guerrillas. In Guatemala, 'counter-terror' was allowed to run amok and right-wing vigilante groups surpassed the rebels in brutality. In Venezuela, the serious threat of an armed insurrection was headed off by a combination of a vigorous military response and a dogged respect for the legal norms and the democratic process. As was seen in Venezuela, an election may help to steal the guerrillas' popular support. The Brazilian junta has rejected the Venezuelans' 'dual solution' in favour of a 'military solution' that seems to have broken the first wave of urban terrorism, but leaves many of its causes unresolved.

The book returns, finally, to two underlying questions. How far can urban guerrillas go? And what are the best ways of dealing with them? The past record of urban insurrections is undistinguished. Historical experience suggests that, even if an isolated urban uprising is possible, a government or a foreign army can suppress it so long as it preserves an outside base in which to regroup. The Paris Commune was destroyed by the French army (which was obligingly shunted out of the Prussian prisoner-of-war camps) and the conservative provinces. The Warsaw uprisings of 1943 and 1944 never stood a chance against a totalitarian régime fully prepared to use air power. The French army in Algiers showed how easy it is for a force unencumbered by legal restraints to recapture an occupied zone. Of course, there has never been a revolution in an advanced industrial society, and although the experience of France in May, 1968 makes it hazardous to peer too far into the future, there are reasons (discussed below) why that now looks more like a passing cloudburst than the start of the monsoon. Because of the modern technology of control, the complexity of western societies, and the fact that public opinion is largely on the side of the existing order, counter-revolution is a more likely prospect than revolution in the west. If either comes about, it will be because the extremists of both camps have managed to substitute the politics of catastrophe for the politics of consensus.

This is neither a 'how to do it' nor a 'how to bash them' book. Its aim is analytical rather than polemical. Its central concern is with revolutionary violence, and only marginally with official repression, the use of counter-revolutionary violence by private groups, or what it has become fashionable to call 'the violence of the system'. But it would be tendentious to talk about the guerrilla movement in Guatemala (for example) without mentioning the glaring social injustices and the short-sighted and self-seeking economic practices of foreign corporations like the United Fruit Company that explain its popular following. So a certain amount of social and political background has been sketched in throughout the book. It is argued in the next chapter that one cannot explain revolts merely by quoting poverty statistics, and that men do not rebel because they are deprived, but because they have become conscious that they are deprived. This argument, which is bound to be controversial, is not intended to minimise the appalling social injustice and the mounting pressure for social change that are obvious in many of the third world societies discussed in this book, or to deny the fact that armed rebellion is usually the symptom of a deep-seated social malaise. No one would quarrel with the idea that some governments are so corrupt or repressive that they deserve to be overthrown, or that violence is sometimes justified as a last resort for men who have no other avenue for protest. But many people fail to observe what de Tocqueville pointed out more than a century ago in his classic analysis of the French revolution: that, ironically, uprisings often begin at the moment when things are getting better, and there is a genuine possibility of peaceful reform.

I

The City and Revolution

It is striking that in western industrial societies, political violence has very little to do with the conventional Marxist idea of class struggle, and almost nothing to do with the class that was seen by Marx as the potential revolutionary force: the industrial working-class. It is now generally admitted that the liberal capitalist system has been able to meet labour demands for higher living standards and social security, although there is still the possibility of a revival of trade union militancy in conditions of economic stagnation and rising unemployment. At the same time, the fact that real political change is possible through the ballot-box and that there are few restrictions on the freedom of expression has encouraged the general belief that violence cannot be justified as a means of change in western countries. Even the traditional communist parties of western Europe have been slowly drawn into the prevailing social consensus, and there is more talk of 'convergence' than of revolution in the party headquarters in Paris and Rome.

But there is a ragged hole in the corner of this comfortable picture of civil peace. The present and potential advocates of political violence in the west come from two marginal social groups: from the body of alienated students and intellectuals whose dissent is ideological or emotional in nature and remote from the bread-and-butter issues that preoccupied the 'old' left; and from ethnic, cultural and religious minorities who do not share in the general affluence or are motivated by sectional chauvinism. The first group is often loosely described as the New Left. The nature of New Left protest obviously limits its popular appeal. 'The problem we are facing,' according to Herbert Marcuse, 'is the need for liberation not from a poor society, not from a disintegrating society, not even in most cases from a terroristic society, but from a society which develops to

17

a great extent the material and even cultural needs of man—a society
which, to use a slogan, delivers the goods to an ever larger part of
the population. And that implies, we are facing liberation from a
society where liberation is apparently without a mass basis.'[1]

New Left protest (which covers most cases of student protest not
immediately related to campus problems or national politics) is
basically either *qualitative* or *vicarious* in character. Qualitative
protest is an assault on bourgeois life-styles and social patterns. At
the aesthetic extreme, it is the culture of the hippie commune, and
the rejection of the acquisitive urge and a life built around a career
and a stable family relationship. At a political extreme, it gives rise
to various forms of anarchism, nihilism and to the violence of
America's 'radical bombers' and 'ecological guerrillas'.

The best example of vicarious protest was the wildfire spread of
the anti-Vietnam demonstrations in the late 1960s. The voters of
North Hull in England were probably perplexed to find themselves invited to support Mr Richard Gott on an anti-Vietnam
ticket. When was a British regiment last seen in Can Tho? There is
of course a popular New Left theory that, because the capitalist
economies are closely interlocked and the Americans are everywhere,
what is needed is a global revolution. But the theory does not explain
why students from Paris to Tokyo carried posters of a Latin American guerrilla (Che Guevara) aloft in 1968, or why student extremists
in America (the Weathermen) saw themselves as New York's
'Tupamaros'. That owed more to a romantic view of the guerrilla in
the jungle nurtured in academic hothouses, to the communications
revolution that has brought televised images of distant wars into
every suburban living-room, and to a new and dangerous theoretical
apology for violence.

Is student power a reality? Can New Left protest pose a genuine
threat to the ordering of western societies? The campus revolts of
1968, 'the year of the young rebels', inspired both alarm and exulta-
tion. When the paving-stones had been replaced and the slogans
washed off the walls, the student radicals were more or less back
where they started, tending the grass at the fringes of western
politics. *Les événements* of May are unlikely to prove, as one recent
writer has argued, the 'prelude to revolution' in France.[2] But what

happened in Paris demonstrated both the possibilities and the limits for student revolt. Daniel Cohn-Bendit, Alain Geismar and the other leaders would have been forgotten within a few weeks but for the response of young French workers to the campus revolt that started at Nanterre. It was the workers who downed tools and occupied their factories after May 14, in sympathy with the students, who made the Paris uprising different in kind from other campus revolts by dragging the hesitant trade union leaders towards the proclamation of the general strike.

But from that point the paths diverged. It is true that there were several thousand young workers who shared the revolutionary goals of the student radicals. But the men who strung up straw dummies labelled 'capitalism' from mock gallows in the factory yards they had taken over were in a tiny minority. The union leaders gave the signal for the general strike, and the vast majority of the workers joined in it, not because they were fired with enthusiasm by student slogans about a new and 'imaginative' society, but because they glimpsed the chance to secure immediate economic gains from an embattled government. They were bought off with pay rises that in no case amounted to more than 14 per cent—a modest figure by comparison with the recent level of wage claims in Britain. What made revolution in France in 1968 impossible was the factor that the New Left had never taken seriously: the lack of a class basis for the revolt, and above all the absence of a 'vanguard party', an organisation with sturdy roots in the labour movement *and* a coherent strategy for revolt.[3] The French Communist Party, as it transpired, was not prepared to assume that role. The French student rebels provided the trigger, but they could not provide the gun.

The position of the Italian Communist Party (PCI) is slightly more ambiguous, and PCI attitudes are likely to be influenced by the rising level of civil violence as well as by the shift to the right in favour of the Italian Social Movement (MSI) which registered some considerable gains in the administrative elections in June 1971. During the student troubles and wildcat strikes of 1968, the Italian communists seemed ready to ride the tiger of violent protest.[4] But from the end of the year, the faction that favoured a policy of 'convergence' with the 'advanced' middle-class parties and entrepreneurs had established its ascendancy within the party. In June 1969, the extremist *Il Manifesto* group was expelled from the party on the grounds that it had acted as a divisive force and undermined the communists' electoral support. The new policy of the PCI, according to Lucio Magri, one of the Manifesto rebels, was to bring about 'a convergence between the working class and the "advanced" wing of big capital, on a common economic programme for the elimination of parasitism and the development of social services, that will harmoniously reconcile the exigencies of productivity and the needs of workers within the system.'[5]

There are a number of reasons why Italy remains one of the most inherently unstable industrial societies. One is a history of uneven social and economic development that has left the South in a state of extreme backwardness and partly explains why primitive forms of group violence like banditism and regional popular riots coexist with forms of technological terrorism and student protest that have become almost universal in the west. Although it has been claimed that only four people died in Italy during the seven years that President Saragat was in office,[6] the frequency of rioting, prolonged strikes and student protest has engendered an atmosphere of *contestazione generale* in which the appeals of the far right for a return to Mussolini's 'corporate state' or a military coup as well as left-wing appeals for revolution gain wider audiences. The Manifesto group still hope to persuade the leaders of the PCI that Italy is headed towards political confrontation, and not any lasting form of 'convergence' between capitalist and communist. But for the moment, the PCI seems to have set its sails on a parliamentary course, and a Chilean-style coalition government is a more immediate prospect than a revolution of the streets or a military coup.

The gap between the New Left and the 'old' left parties and the union movement in France and Italy—the two western countries with the strongest communist parties—is characteristic of the industrial societies in general. In Japan, for example, student militants have remained isolated from organised workers, although left-wing railwaymen have joined in political strikes to protest against the Japanese–American alliance. Japan is admittedly in a rather special situation, since the intense nationalism and the ideal of devotion to duty that are built into the social system have discouraged radical protest in general, while the fragmented character of the trade unions has deterred attempts to stage countrywide political strikes.[7] In the United States, student militants are entirely divorced from the labour movement, and although there have been attempts to form a tactical alliance with black power groups, these have foundered on negro reluctance to join in anti-war demonstrations and suspicion of the motives and origins of white radicals.

New Left protest has rarely touched upon the everyday problems of the average man, and student radicals have failed to hitch their wagons to a broader national cause. It is interesting to observe, that as the campus left has rediscovered its basic isolation as a political force, there has been a tendency to move over to more violent forms of protest and to 'professionalise' the radical *groupuscules*. In Paris during the first half of 1971, for example, the police became accustomed to Saturday night punch-ups with student militants in the Latin Quarter. A student 'commando' would attract the attention of the police by starting a small fire in a sidestreet off the Boulevard St-Michel, or by provoking a small riot. These regular skirmishes affected the morale of the police and started a controversy over the nature of 'order' in French society, but they were wholly different from the May 1968 rallies, when the students were able to muster considerable popular support.

The way that Japanese student militants have equipped themselves for street-fighting is another example of the professionalisation of the far left. Since 1967, they have provided themselves with gloves and helmets and sometimes gas-masks as well. Student rioters in Tokyo were divided into a 'combat section' armed with stones and petrol-bombs and a 'defence section' equipped with long bamboo staves. They also practised more sophisticated street tactics. From the time of the protest rallies against the visit of Eisaku Sato, the prime minister, to America at the end of 1969, student rioters organised commando squads of five or six youths to stage diversionary assaults (by smashing windows, throwing fire-bombs and so on) to draw police away from the scene of the main demonstration.[8] In the United States, the professionalisation of student protest led to the formation of an urban terrorist group, the Weathermen, whose activities are discussed in a later chapter.

It would be dangerous to generalise about the future of radical student groups in western societies. But if it is true that terrorism is often the weapon of the weak, extremist groups that have despaired of engaging popular support through conventional political means may be tempted to take advantage of the vulnerability of the modern city to win cheap publicity in pursuit of a distant cause. The far more important point is that, to use Ronald Segal's phrase, the 'moral consensus' of western societies has been slowly eroded.[9] The New Left and the student militants represent elements who have rejected the traditional values of western societies and the general faith in parliamentary means of political change. In theory at least, they have also rejected the generally accepted idea (in western societies) that the government enjoys a monopoly of *legitimate* violence.

The same applies to the minority groups that have paradoxically displayed increased militancy in the age of what Marshall McLuhan calls 'the global village'. The Basque separatists who kidnapped the West German consul to San Sebastián in 1970, the Flemings who take to the streets to protest against the dominance of the French language in Belgium, and the French Canadian terrorists in Quebec who claim to be heading a revolt against 'Anglo-Saxon imperialism' are similar in the nature of their complaints. The resurgence of sectional feeling, of the *patria chica*, can be illustrated equally well by the stirrings of Scots and Welsh nationalists and Irish Catholics in Britain, and by the rise of radical movements among the negroes, Puerto Ricans and Mexican immigrants of the United States. The link between New Left protest and minority grievances in western societies is that both represent the opening of a *legitimacy gap* between the government and a sector of the population.

THE ROOTS OF REVOLT

Is it possible to generalise about the causes of urban revolts? It is clear that the reasons why men rebel in Guatemala City or Montreal are very different. This book is primarily concerned with the use of

terror by private groups for revolutionary ends, and only marginally
with official repression or the use of terror by non-governmental
groups for counter-revolutionary ends. But it would be perverse,
for example, to talk about the rise of urban guerrilla movements in
Guatemala or Brazil without mentioning the social injustice that
was at the root of revolt, the military coups that provided the
trigger, and the counter-terror that was used to put down the
uprisings.

It will be observed in many of the case-studies that follow that
there is a curious symbiotic relationship between extremists of both
camps. They feed on each other; they ape each others' tactics. They
have a common interest in breaking down the political consensus in
a democratic or reformist society and in opening the way for violent
and authoritarian solutions. Sir Horace Rumbold, an acute diplomatic observer of Weimar Germany, noted that the German
Communist party helped to finance Hitler's fledgling Nazis at a
moment when they were short of funds. It has been rumoured that
the Catholic and Republican IRA and the Protestant and Loyalist
Ulster Volunteer Force in Belfast have bought arms from the same
suppliers in eastern Europe.

As the character of violent protest in western societies suggests,
it would be wrong to imagine that men only rebel for the reasons that
were illuminated by a famous Mexican film that showed Zapata's
peasant uprising beginning with an angry man whose house had
been burned and whose wife had been savaged by a brutal landowner. To explain the origins of insurgencies, it is not enough to cite
poverty statistics, and it would be wrong to jump to the conclusion
that men only revolt when all the paths to peaceful change are
blocked. There is no direct connection between revolt and the
number of tractors per thousand of population or the number of
people whose names are on the electoral roll in a given country. If
that were the case, revolutions would be brought about by the most
downtrodden peasants in the most repressive police-states. The
facts are rather more complex and refractory.

It would be fair to generalise from past experience that the
societies that are least vulnerable to armed rebellion are those at the
political extremes: the most permissive and pluralistic, because they

are best able to remove the causes of revolt; and the most repressive
and totalitarian, because they are best able to suppress the first
stirrings of revolt. Urban guerrilla movements have not yet appeared
in South Africa or Russia, although the popular uprisings in Hungary
in 1956, in Czechoslovakia in 1968, and in Poland in 1970 showed
that communist systems are very fragile in the face of a challenge
from within once it has been allowed to emerge. But it is the transitional societies, those moving to the right or the left along the middle
band, towards industrialisation or towards economic recession, that
tend to be most vulnerable to political violence. The reason can be
put simply. As de Tocqueville observed of the French revolution,
getting his facts slightly wrong but his psychology right, men do not
revolt merely because they are poor and oppressed. They revolt
because they are aware of a gulf between their expectations and their
present conditions and of a possibility of crossing it at a single bound.

It is possible to make three general observations about the causes
of political violence in both the industrial and the pre-industrial
cities:

1 *The sense of relative deprivation*   One reason why primitive societies and 'new states' that are adjusting to new economic structures
and social institutions tend to be politically volatile is that people's
expectations rise faster than their actual living conditions. The
short-lived insurgency in Ceylon early in 1971 was in some respects
a classic example of the revolution of rising expectations. It presented the curious spectacle of a left-wing coalition government that
included communists and Trotskyists being outflanked on the left
by 'Guevarist' rebels led by the sons of peasants who had been to
university. It was a case of expectations of radical change out-
stripping what was actually offered by the reformers. It was also a
case of a society generating social unrest by offering tertiary education to more people than the economy could usefully employ.[10]

Following Samuel P. Huntington and Ted Robert Gurr,[11] it is
possible to outline four models of relative deprivation—the sense of
a gap between expectations and present conditions. The first is when
people's expectations rise, but their capabilities remain the same.
This is more or less what is happening to the second-generation
slum-dwellers of third world cities. The *favelado* (slum-dweller) on

the hillsides of Rio de Janeiro looks down on the modish affluence of the beachside apartment-blocks of Leme and Copacobana; he can glimpse a still more exciting world on a neighbour's television set. The spread of mass communications and the spectacular growth of third world cities are creating appetites that did not formerly exist. If they cannot be satisfied, the result may be an explosion of rioting and political violence.

The second kind of relative deprivation comes about when people's expectations outpace their rising capabilities. This was probably part of the explanation for the negro riots and ghetto revolts in the United States in the 1960s. The poverty of the ghettoes may have made some kind of social explosion inevitable; what was startling was the timing. The ghetto riots followed a period of rapid social and economic progress without precedent in black American experience.[12] To take a few random statistics, there was an 80 per cent rise in the number of black professional and technical workers between 1960 and 1967 (compared with a 30 per cent increase among whites). The figure was nearly as high for clerical workers and about 47 per cent for white collar workers in general. The number of blacks on the wrong side of the poverty line dropped from just under 11 million in 1964 to just over 8 million in 1967. Over the same period, the civil rights movement won a series of important victories and new anti-segregation laws were placed on the statute-books. Yet by the end of 1968, every major Northern city in the United States—irrespective of its record of social integration, its poverty levels or the behaviour of the local politics—had experienced a full-scale ghetto revolt. Some 200,000 black Americans are said to have taken part in riots between 1964 and 1968.[13]

These riots characteristically took the form of group assaults on property and policemen, triggered off by a precipitating incident like the controversial arrest of a negro or the news of the assassination of Martin Luther King in 1968.[14] It would be dangerous to over-generalise about the causes of the ghetto riots. The sense of frustration of those who had migrated to the cities from the Deep South in the post-war decades, to find themselves trapped in increasingly isolated islands of poverty no doubt played a part. So did the sheer force of example: the television image of neighbouring cities aflame. But it would seem that a general reason for the riots was the fact that the new reforms and the gains of the civil right programme had generated expectations that could not be satisfied immediately—leading to explosive frustrations and later to the rise of organised black militant groups that represent a potential urban guerrilla force.

The sense of relative deprivation also arises when a society comes upon hard times: expectations stay the same, but capabilities drop. There is a sad contemporary example in Uruguay, where the successes of the Tupamaros (analysed in Chapter 10) stem from the fact that a country once renowned for its liberal tradition and its welfare state institutions has entered a period of economic decline. Civil service salaries are held up; real wages tend to fall rather than rise; there is a chronic budget deficit. White-collar workers accustomed to a measure of social security almost unparalleled in Latin America are reluctant to tighten their belts, and those who offer a violent 'solution' gather popular support.

The fourth model of relative deprivation is for rising standards of living to keep in step with rising expectations over a limited period, and then suddenly drop behind. This is a classic revolutionary pattern that has been described by American social scientists as 'the J-curve phenomenon'.[15] It explains the rising militancy of the French bourgeoisie, peasants and city labourers over the decade leading up to the revolution of 1789.

2 *The appeal of violence*   If a widespread feeling of relative deprivation provides the basis for a mass uprising, it is equally important to consider the motivation of the rebel leaders. There is something in the apparent truism that 'it takes a rebel to rebel'.[16] Urban guerrilla warfare is essentially the work of tiny groups that regard themselves as a revolutionary élite. Terrorist organisations like the National Liberation Action (ALN) in Brazil, the Weathermen in America, and the FLQ in Quebec drew their recruits from similar social strata —above all, from alienated middle-class youth. It is worth considering the social origins of the 70 Brazilian prisoners who were released in exchange for the kidnapped Swiss ambassador, Giovanni Bucher, in January 1971. Of the 37 whose occupations were listed, 18 were students, 4 were civil servants, 3 were technicians, 3 army

defectors, and there was 1 priest.[17] Of course, there are familiar reasons why the bourgeois intellectual so often emerges as the leader of a revolt. One is that his class and education give him the chance to form a general view of society and elaborate a strategy for insurrection. In Latin America, one would have to take account of the heavily Marxist bent of the arts faculties of many of the state universities, and the appalling conditions under which many students have to work—bad teachers, shoddy textbooks, the lack of grants for education that forces most undergraduates to take part-time jobs.[18] In western societies, one might add the general sense of alienation and the boredom and apathy that are sometimes engendered by a long period of peace.

Most of the urban guerrillas studied in this book not only share a common range of terrorist techniques, but also a common faith in political violence—not just as a means of hastening social change, but as a cathartic force. Some of the popular theorists of revolution have encouraged the view that violence is more than a last resort; that it is also something that liberates the personality and creates 'true revolutionaries'. Frantz Fanon, the psychologist from Martinique who made himself the ideologist of the Algerian revolution, provided the most celebrated statement of this theory. 'At the level of individuals,' according to Fanon, 'violence is a cleansing force. It frees the native from his inferiority complex and from his despair and inaction; it makes him fearless and restores his self-respect.'[19] Many readers will have their doubts, but the New Left in western societies as well as Che Guevara and his heirs have often echoed Fanon. One might seize upon the following passage from a recent essay by John Gerassi as an example: 'The exhilaration that comes with street fighting,' writes Gerassi, 'is not, as Establishment (i.e. adaptation-oriented) psychiatrists insist, escapism, parental rejection, masochism, sadism, etc. On the contrary it is achieving selfhood, independence, the feeling that one is a man, taking pride in oneself and one's comrades. It is, just as Fanon said, an act of growing up, not of adolescent nihilism.'[20]

Gerassi's view that the rebel 'grows up' by throwing bombs or kicking people's heads in comes appropriately close to the stormtrooper's vision of life. The same image of violence as a kind of group

therapy is also to be found in the camp-fire literature of the proto-
fascist Freikorps in the Baltic provinces in the 1920s, and in the
paeons to war of the Italian poet d'Annunzio. It has something in
common with the classical anarchist argument that 'to destroy is to
create'. The real point is that the political tags matter less than the
psychological impulse. The glorification of action over intellect is
characteristic both of the prewar fascists and the postwar New
Left; those who share in it are less opposed to each other in personal
terms than to the gradualists, conservatives and 'wishy-washy'
liberals in the centre who believe in reason and reform.

There is clearly a tremendous difference between the argument
that men have a right to rebel under intolerable social and political
conditions (an argument that is not disputed in principle by modern
jurists) and the argument that violence liberates the personality. It is
no accident that men who exalt violence have so often turned out to
be more authoritarian and intolerant than the governments they set
out to overthrow. It is equally clear why rebel movements have so
often torn themselves apart through internal feuding and murderous
suspicion. Those committed to violence rarely comprehend rational
argument and honest dissent—and anyway, the constant danger
involved in underground operations makes it impossible to run the
risk of betrayal. The critic is branded as a traitor; he manages to
escape or he is shot. This book abounds with examples of this and
of 'revolutionary justice'.

What Fanon and Gerassi completely failed to spot is the corrupting effect of the systematic use of political violence, and its attraction
for people who never think twice about the rebels' stated goals.
Even the European resistance movements during the Second
World War attracted more than a few 'bad hats' who joined for the
fun of the fighting and the chance to operate as bandits while
posing as heroes. The IRA Provisionals in Northern Ireland have
drawn support from petty criminals in the Catholic slums and have
set up their own protection rackets as a way of raising 'party funds'.
The British army in the province reported occasions when the
Provisionals broke a man's back with an iron bar or kicked a
pregnant woman in the stomach in order to compel submission or
the payment of 'contributions'. The Moslem FLN in Algiers

recruited professional thugs like Ali-la-Pointe; the FLQ has enlisted drifters and corner pickpockets from the *hangars* (or gang-territories) of Montreal; and militant minority groups like the Black Panthers or the Young Lords in the United States have also channelled the energies of ghetto criminals for political ends.

It would be hasty to tar all guerrilla movements with the same brush, and it has been pointed out in any case that the founding impetus of contemporary urban guerrilla groups comes from young idealists and romantics: bourgeois students and intellectuals who believe in the need for a global revolution aimed primarily at the United States. But no terrorist group that resorts to bank-robbery and other forms of 'self-funding' can avoid the danger that its members will use a political label for merely criminal purposes. That is why recently even veterans of the Cuban revolution began to express their doubts about the methods of Latin American urban guerrillas.

The appeal of political violence is bound up with what might be called the rhetoric of vilification. When student radicals chant 'racist pigs' at the police; when the Black Panther newspaper says that the Panthers 'stood up in the bowels of fascist Amerikkka' with guns in their hands and told 'those murderous mad dogs who occupy our community like a foreign army' to get out; when Uruguay's urban guerrillas insist on describing a freely elected government as a 'corrupt dictatorship', the political rhetoric means something. Its psychological effect is to distort the speakers' view of the situation so that it seems there are only two possibilities: to fight the authorities or to join them, to overthrow the system or become its creature. The rhetoric of vilification is dangerous and pernicious because it is a positive incitement to violence (and counter-violence) as well as a way of transforming a complex situation into black-and-white stereotypes.

3 *The legitimacy gap*   No government bases its authority purely on force. Even the narrowest ruling élite must appear as a legitimate government to the men it counts on to ensure popular submission—the security forces. Legitimacy has been defined as 'the ability to evoke compliance short of coercion'.[21] Western democracies enjoy the highest level of legitimacy—to the point that, during periods of

domestic crisis, the majority of the population are willing to entrust the government with far greater powers than it normally enjoys under the constitution. A recent CBS public opinion poll in the United States, for example, showed that, in the face of rising political and criminal violence, 58 per cent of the people interviewed wanted to see the right of *habeas corpus* scrapped, 55 per cent approved of press censorship, and 54 per cent thought that it had become dangerous to allow the right of free speech.[22] A successful insurrection is impossible without considerable popular support, or at the least public neutrality. The strength of western societies in the face of political violence is precisely that most people regard the system as legitimate and that those who feel differently are in a small minority, and normally an isolated minority. It is when governments fail to solve major national problems that the legitimacy gap begins to widen. It is in this sense that urban guerrillas could act as a political catalyst in western societies as well as in the third world. A government confronted with mounting political violence (like Brian Faulkner's government in Northern Ireland) sometimes falls between two stools. On one side, there are the hardliners (and often the worried householder down the road) calling for tougher measures; on the other side, there are the liberals concerned for civil rights who protest against the government's moves without knowing how to head off the terrorists.

2

Terrorism as a Political Tool

It is a comfortable western illusion, and perhaps a characteristically British illusion, that political violence is something abnormal or that it has no place in democratic societies. It is true that in countries where real change is possible through the ballot-box, the use of violence for political ends is least justified and least likely to win any measure of public acceptance. Hotheads from the 'Angry Brigade' who place a bomb in a British cabinet minister's house and then announce that they intended to show their solidarity with trade unionists opposed to the Industrial Relations Bill will not get much of a hearing in a society that does not believe that it is legitimate for private groups to resort to political violence. But history can be forgotten quickly. The Nazis showed how terrorism can be used to erode the foundations of a democratic state. A sustained campaign of political violence has a corroding effect on any society. The government eventually comes under attack for failing to keep order in the streets; parliament is increasingly by-passed as a mere 'talking-shop'; force displaces reasoned debate and confrontation takes the place of consensus.

Of course, the collapse of Weimar democracy can be understood only as the result of a very singular set of circumstances, which included a desperate economic crisis, the lack of an entrenched parliamentary tradition, and the neuroses inspired by military defeat. But the rise of Hitler is the classic demonstration that democracies are not immune to the corrupting effects of political terrorism. And Hitler's methods are not the monopoly of the radical right. Contempt for democracy and faith in violent solutions are common to the extremists of both camps. It is enough to quote what was written recently by one of the founders of the Students for a Democratic Society in the United States: 'We have to give up any illusions about "peaceful" or "legal" means of change ... We are bringing Vietnam home. We are creating an America where it is necessary for the government to rule behind barbed wire, for the President to speak only at military bases, and where, finally, it will be necessary to fight back.'[1] Tom Hayden appears to believe that a cycle of terrorism and counter-terrorism will create the conditions for a second American civil war. That may be apocalyptic nonsense; but he is right at least to observe that a society changes character when it has to respond to the threat of political violence.

Repression rarely leads to revolution, but it can lead to the collapse of the social consensus and a loss of faith in democratic ideals. That is what has happened dramatically in one Latin American democracy, Uruguay, in the course of the campaign of selective terrorism that the Tupamaros have waged since 1968. Western societies are much more resilient; but a similar chain-reaction is imaginable even in advanced industrial countries, against a background of minority grievances and youthful disillusionment with the purpose and goals of the system. This makes it all the more important to consider the ways in which political terrorism can act as a catalyst, and the conditions under which terrorists can hope to achieve their ends.

Terrorism might be defined as the systematic use of intimidation for political purposes. That formula is broad enough to cover all sorts of varying situations. Terrorists can be classified according to their beliefs or their targets, but it is probably more useful to single out three *tactical* varieties of terrorism. *Repressive terror* is used by a government to keep its grip over the population or by a rebel movement as a means of eliminating rivals, coercing popular support, or maintaining conformity inside the organisation (in other words, bumping off 'traitors' and silencing critics). *Defensive terror* can be used by private groups like the American vigilantes to keep order or uphold the status quo; by patriots against a foreign invader; or by a community defending its traditional rights. *Offensive terror*, the kind that this book is largely concerned with, is used against a régime or a political system. Terrorist groups have fought to win national independence from a colonial government, to overthrow autocratic régimes, and to impose their ideologies (communist, fascist or anarchist) on democratic societies.

There is nothing specifically right-wing or left-wing about the repressive terror of police-states. Police-states come about when a government rules by repressive terror rather than popular consent, and when the security forces are allowed too much autonomy. But it is noteworthy that ideological régimes, and in particular post-revolutionary régimes, have been responsible for some of the worst repression. Lenin and Trotsky were both sceptical about the effectiveness of offensive terror when they were still merely plotters against the Tsarist régime, but they paved the way for Stalin by using 'mass terror' to get rid of their enemies after 1917. They had a good revolutionary precedent. Saint-Just, the radical Jacobin who showed plenty of dissenters the way to the guillotine before he was led there in his turn in 1794, once observed that 'Violence in itself is neither rational nor lawful, but there's no better way of making people respect reason and law'.[2]

Many postwar rebel movements have used repressive terrorism to eliminate what the Algerian National Liberation Front (FLN) called 'the party of the lukewarm' and to secure the obedience of the civil population. In colonial situations, the FLN, the Vietcong and the Eoka in Cyprus all used the assassination of pro-governmental officials and policemen as a means of removing alternative leadership. In general, it is only when a rebel movement has *already* established a firm grip on a significant section of the population that it can afford to use terror as a means of extorting shelter and supplies, of roping in new recruits and deterring potential defectors. At the outset, the terrorists are usually less concerned with intimidating the civil population than with demonstrating that the government and the security forces are vulnerable to attack.

The Vietcong perfected the system of 'repressive' terrorism in the course of an exceptionally protracted insurgency. In government-controlled areas in South Vietnam, Vietcong terrorism against neutral or anti-communist elements has normally taken the form of preliminary warnings, followed by kidnapping or assassination. The Americans claim that between 1966 and 1969, the Vietcong committed 18,031 political murders, as well as nearly 26,000 kidnappings (for indoctrination and other purposes). Terrorism in communist-held areas has ranged from oral intimidation and 'home surveillance' to 'thought reform' in special camps and execution.[3]

The other form of repressive terrorism—punishment of 'traitors' and dissidents—is common to all terrorist groups. In some situations, power-struggles and ideological debates inside rebel movements have claimed more lives than the campaign against the government forces. Since the split between the 'regular' and 'provisional' wings of the IRA at the end of 1969, for example, the two groups have staged a bloody gang-war for supremacy in Belfast. At one stage in 1970, the Regulars 'sentenced' eleven leaders of the Provisionals to death after a raid on their headquarters in the Falls Road. The sentences were cancelled after a truce was agreed on at the last moment. The constant internal feuding inside terrorist movements has an obvious psychological explanation in the constant fear of informers and betrayal and the basic intolerance of criticism of men committed to violence—and often to a rigid ideology as well.

Defensive terror has been used by French against Germans, by Poles against Russians, and by Armenian Dashnaks against Turks. The defence of the nation against a foreign invader is the most popular rallying-cry for any resistance movement. The Secret Army Organisation (OAS) in Algeria used defensive terror for a rather different purpose: the attempt to prevent the French government from granting independence. There is a long tradition of the use of violence by private groups to uphold the status quo in the United States. The National Commission on the Causes and Prevention of Violence agreed with the black power leader Rap Brown that 'violence is as American as cherry pie' and added that

> The historical and contemporary evidence of the United States suggests that popular support tends to sanction violence in support of the status quo: the use of public violence to maintain public order, the use of private violence to maintain popular conceptions of social order when government cannot or will not.[4]

There are plenty of examples throughout American history of the use of violence by private groups, with community support, for precisely those purposes. The original American vigilantes, like the South Carolina 'Regulators' (active between 1767 and 1769) were associated with the breakdown of law and order or the lack of public policing in a frontier society. After the Civil War, the Ku Klux Klan and other terrorist societies were formed to preserve white supremacy in the South. The Ku Klux Klan defined its original objective in unequivocal terms as 'The maintenance of the supremacy of the white man in the Republic by terror and intimidation'. Other secret societies, like the anti-Irish 'Know Nothings' of the 1850s or the racist 'White Caps' of the 1880s and 1890s used defensive terror against migrant or minority groups that they saw as a threat to the interests of white working men.[5]

In colonial situations, offensive terror was used to persuade the occupying power that it had become too costly to hold on. It was clearly impossible, for example, for the IRA in Dublin, or the Stern Gang and the Irgun Zvai Leumi in Palestine, or Eoka in Cyprus, to win a military victory over the British occupying forces. What each of those terrorist groups set out to do was to provoke a controversy in London and the outside world and to force the British to commit more and more of their resources to the campaign. They were all at least partially successful in persuading the British to withdraw, although the non-cooperation of the local population was probably a more important factor in Palestine and Cyprus.

Some of the Stern Gang's exploits were actually wholly counter-productive. The murder of Lord Moyne, the British Minister Resident in the Middle East, in Cairo in November 1944, inspired the Jewish Agency (under the moderate leadership of Ben Gurion) to launch an anti-terrorist campaign. It also had a considerable effect on Churchill, who had counted Moyne among his close friends, and led him to postpone his plans for Palestine indefinitely. The murder of Lord Moyne brought the Palestine terrorists enor-mous publicity, but it was of the most unfavourable kind, and the whole incident demonstrates the importance of careful selection of targets for the terrorist.[6] The IRA today believe themselves to be in a 'colonial' situation, and their strategy is similar to that of Eoka or the first Irish Republican Army. Their campaign of selective terrorism against the British forces stationed in Ulster is designed, first, to erode army morale and provoke repressive measures that will stir up controversy, and, second, to persuade the British that it has become too expensive to hold on. They are counting on a failure of the will at Westminster that would lead to the political decision to hand Northern Ireland over to Dublin.

Within an independent state, the use of offensive terror by a revolutionary movement is more complex. The government will not pack its bags and go away: the terrorists must aim either to trigger off an internal political crisis that will play into their hands or to pave the way for an armed insurrection. Terrorists do not make revolutions, but sometimes revolutionaries resort to terrorism. Terrorism fits into a broader strategy. It can be used as a political catalyst—as a means of initiating a vicious cycle of terror and counter-terror that will alienate popular support from the government. It is also characteristic both of the early and the declining phases of an insurgency: when a rebel movement is gathering strength, or when it has suffered heavy reverses.

Terrorism is always a dubious weapon. A good example of that was the reaction of the crowd in an Istanbul street in June 1971, after the Turkish police had managed to rescue a 14-year-old girl from her kidnappers. The terrorists, members of the Turkish People's Liberation Army, called out to the crowd in the street, 'We're doing this for you!' as they sniped at the police from an upstairs window. But the mob broke through police barricades in an effort to lynch the single terrorist who finally came out of the building alive.[7] That was a rather extreme example of the circumstances under which terrorist operations are wholly counterproductive. A schoolgirl who is seized as a hostage is bound to get more public sympathy than a greying middle-class businessman or a foreign diplomat. But the normal response to terrorist acts is revulsion. That is why the more successful contemporary urban guerrillas, in Latin America in particular, have gone to some pains to try to justify their crimes and have been very careful in selecting their targets. A terrorist group can never enlist popular support unless its leaders can manage to explain their operations as something more than nihilistic violence or random criminal assaults.

The central problem for an urban guerrilla movement is to make converts. Their battle is for minds, not bodies. The starting-point is to prove themselves a credible fighting force through successful operations and to publicise their political aims. That also explains the importance of *marksmanship*. In Latin America, urban guerrilla groups have singled out individuals and installations that they can publicly identify with what they regard as an oppressive political system. The Quebec Liberation Front (FLQ) in Montreal has bombed foreign businesses and barracks (but went disastrously astray when it murdered a French Canadian cabinet minister); the IRA in Belfast has specialised in selective terror against British troops. A campaign of selective assassination against soldiers and policemen can damage the morale of men in uniform—an essential prerequisite for any successful uprising.

But indiscriminate terror can also be used to effect. It is a central goal of all rebel movements to break down the existing social structures and promote a general feeling of nervousness, fear and disorientation. Conditions of general insecurity favour extremists in any society. The government comes under fire because it cannot provide adequate protection, and the people will finally be forced to side with whatever group is in a position to apply coercion or guarantee a measure of protection. Indiscriminate terror can also be used to embitter relations between two social groups. In Algiers, the FLN and later the OAS used random terror against members of the other racial group to dig an unbridgeable gap between the Arab and European populations.

Terrorist acts are often ambiguous. When a former Christian Democratic minister, Eduardo Pérez Zújovic, was murdered in May 1971, the Chilean press was full of rumours about his murderers. Some people suggested that the killing was a CIA plot to drive a wedge between President Salvador Allende's *Unidad Popular* coalition and the opposition Christian Democrats. Others said that it was the work of the Movement of the Revolutionary Left (Mir)—the former urban guerrillas who had supplied some of the members of the presidential bodyguard—and there were even dark rumours of government involvement. It transpired that the murderers belonged to the extreme left-wing People's Organised Vanguard (VOP), a splinter from the Mir.[8] Some of its leaders, including Arturo Rivera Calderón, had been released from jail by Allende shortly after he took office—despite heated protests from the magistrature and the conservative opposition. The VOP were trying to bring about a greater polarisation of political forces in Chile in the belief that armed struggle between the right and the left is inevitable. All they achieved was the destruction of their own organisation after a bloody gun-battle with the police.[9]

[The effectiveness of terror as a political weapon hinges on the popular response, which in turn will partly depend on how the government decides to tackle the situation. In a democratic society, the terrorists hope to place the government in the position where it will have to choose between overreacting and underreacting, between panic and weakness. The three historical case-studies that follow provide contrasting examples of the political uses of terror. Unlike most contemporary terrorist groups, the *Narodnaya Volya* in Tsarist Russia subscribed to a broadly democratic ideology and was acutely conscious of the moral dilemmas involved in the systematic use of violence—even though its enemy was autocracy. Eoka in Cyprus had considerable success in using terror against a colonial régime and in gaining control of the civil population. The FLN and the OAS in Algeria provide a striking example of the symbiotic relationship between political extremists, or how one brand of political violence encourages the other.

TSARIST RUSSIA: TERROR AGAINST AUTOCRACY

Russian revolutionary groups used terrorism in a systematic attempt to weaken the Tsarist state and create the conditions for an armed uprising over a period of more than thirty years (1879–1911). The exploits of the *Narodnaya Volya* ('People's Will'), the Social Revolutionaries and the lesser groups that paved the way for them are interesting both as a test-case of the impact of terrorism on the structures of an autocratic state and as an example of the political and moral dilemmas that confront a movement that resorts to the systematic use of terror. The Russian terrorists bequeathed a literature of doubt and self-justification that has not been paralleled by any later terrorist movement.

Terrorism in Tsarist Russia characteristically took the form of selective assassination. The targets were either key policy-makers or policemen and other officials who had become notorious for their brutality or their advocacy of repressive policies. The more idealistic leaders of the early terrorist cells thought of selective assassination as a means of 'warning off' members of the government hierarchy who sought to abuse their powers. The favourite target was of course the Tsar, and the *Narodnaya Volya* group staged six unsuccessful attempts on the life of Alexander II before he was finally killed by a bomb in 1881. The weakness of these tactics was that the terrorists were inclined to stake everything on a single throw. Each of their triumphs was bought at a tremendous cost, since each murder was followed by a massive police manhunt. At the same time, the terrorists isolated themselves from the liberal circles and workers' organisations of St Petersburg and Moscow to the point that they failed completely to communicate their political goals to other actual or potential opposition groups. Some of the assassination attempts were merely the work of dedicated exiles who had slipped back across the border from their refuges in Paris or Geneva.

Assassination had been commonly used throughout Russian history as a means of attempting a palace revolution or of removing competitors and family rivals. In the 1860s and the 1870s, a number of isolated assassins used it as a form of protest against the Tsarist system. In 1866, a terrorist called Karakosov tried unsuccessfully to kill the Tsar. In 1878, Vera Zazulich, an idealistic young woman who later became one of the mentors of the *Narodnaya Volya* group, shot and wounded General Trepof, the prefect of police in St Petersburg. Her eloquent defence of her crime against a man who had become notorious for his brutal treatment of political prisoners impressed the jury and the press, and she was acquitted—a rare but decisive propaganda victory for the Russian terrorists. Later in the same year, Stepniak stabbed to death the chief of the secret police, General Mezentieff. In 1879, the governor of Kharkov was struck down by another assassin, and there were more attempts on the Tsar. It was Stepniak, one of the most colourful and elusive figures in the Tsarist underground, who later supplied one of the most coherent descriptions of the terrorist strategy. He conceded that terrorism could not overthrow the state, but he argued that it could be made the key element in a campaign of attrition that would weaken the government, isolate its leaders, and force it to divert much of its energies to the arid duties of self-defence:

In a struggle against an invisible, impalpable, omnipresent enemy, the strong is vanquished not by arms of his own kind, but by the continuous exhaustion of his own strength, which ultimately exhausts him, more than he would be exhausted by defeat . . . The Terrorists cannot overthrow the government, cannot drive it from St Petersburg and Russia; but having compelled it, for many years running, to neglect everything and do nothing but struggle with them . . . they will render its position untenable.[10]

At this stage, the terrorists still lacked a centralised organisation; the shootings and bombings were sporadic. One of the earliest and most tragicomic attempts to found a terrorist organisation was Sergei Nechayev's *Narodnaya Kasprova* ('The People's Vengeance') which also described itself as 'The Society of the Axe'. Nechayev was one of history's revolutionary charlatans, adept at building insubstantial legends around himself, and is remembered not for anything he did, but for the curious fascination he exercised over two of his great contemporaries, Dostoyevsky and Bakunin. Nechayev was the model for Peter Verkhovensky, the half-crazed and wholly unscrupulous protagonist of Dostoyevsky's novel, *The Devils*, and like his fictional counterpart, he was perfectly prepared to practise blackmail, common theft and murder in the name of a hypothetical revolution. He even swindled his incorrigibly improvident host in Switzerland, Michael Bakunin, that shaggy mastodon of anarchist history who had supplied him with his political credentials as a member of an imaginary 'World Revolutionary Alliance' and helped him to write a series of pamphlets that quickly became notorious. Bakunin found in Nechayev (who first arrived in Geneva in 1869, recounting fictitious stories of how he had just broken out of the Peter and Paul fortress) a fanatic who shared his own unreasoning enthusiasm for violence. 'Let us put our trust,' Bakunin once wrote, 'in the eternal spirit which destroys and annihilates only because it is the unsearchable and eternally creative source of all life. The urge to destroy is also a creative urge.'[11]

But the *Revolutionary Catechism* that they concocted together reflects Nechayev's spirit, if it shows traces of Bakunin's hand. The portrait of the ideal terrorist and the description of his methods that is presented in that document has something in common with

Guevara or Debray in its élitism and its chillingly mechanistic view of the way in which revolution could be brought about. The *Catechism* exalted assassination as the instrument of political change. It instructed that revolutionaries should group themselves in clandestine cells, and infiltrate into all the branches of the Tsarist police. They should be guided always by a black-list of the targets for selective assassination, and Nechayev–Bakunin advised that it might be best to concentrate on eliminating the moderates rather than the hardliners in the régime, since 'the fact that those that are left are noted for their perversity or unpopularity may be useful in stimulating popular rebellion'. The *Catechism* presented a classic version of an argument that has become familiar to all political extremists: that by provoking increased repression and adding to the poverty and misery of the country, the terrorists would pave the way for a popular uprising. As for the terrorist himself, the *Catechism* described an ideal type who would be exceptional only for his inhumanity. The revolutionary, according to Nechayev–Bakunin, 'despises and hates present-day social morality in all its forms . . . All soft and enervating feelings of friendship, love, gratitude, even honour, must be stifled in him by an icy passion for the revolutionary cause . . . Day and night he must have only one thought, one aim—merciless destruction.'[12]

How did this perverted logic work out in practice? Nechayev returned to Russia, where he had some success in organising terrorist cells among radical students. But the first, and only, political murder that can be credited to him was the clumsy execution of one of his own recruits, a student named Ivanov. Nechayev had evidently quarrelled with him over a tactical issue, and wanted to compromise the other members of Ivanov's cell by involving them in the murder. When the details of the killing were published, there was a general wave of revulsion against Nechayev and his methods. Although he escaped to Switzerland, he was extradited and thrown into prison, where he died from tuberculosis ten years later. Nechayev represented a significant deviation from the mainstream of terrorist activity in Tsarist Russia. The leaders of the terrorist organisations that later emerged subscribed to a broadly democratic ideology and were always acutely conscious of the moral dilemmas associated with the use of political violence. Kropotkin summarised the general attitude when he wrote, in criticism of Nechayev, that 'a morally developed individuality must be the foundation of every organisation'.[13] It is worth observing that, in his anti-democratic attitudes, his élitism and his adulation of violence, Nechayev is a much more contemporary figure than the terrorist leaders who succeeded him—much more in tune with many of the latter-day urban guerrillas. He was also a supreme example of the corrupting effects of the systematic use of political violence.

The creation of the *Narodnaya Volya* organisation followed the failure of the 'migration to the people' (an attempt by middle-class liberals to make contact with the peasants and awaken them to politics) launched by the Narodniks, or Populists, in the early 1870s. The peasants were not visibly eager to be awakened, and the Tsarist police were vigilant: Stepniak claimed that 2,884 political arrests were made between 1873 and 1879.

In 1879, after a heated debate that caused a rift in the movement, the Populists decided to form a clandestine organisation to practise 'Central Terror'; the *Narodnaya Volya* was founded, and sentence of death was passed on the Tsar. As Vera Figner, one of the many women associated with the terrorists, later put it, 'It would seem odd to attack the servants without laying hands on the master.'[14] Like Stepniak, the leaders of the new organisation saw terrorism as a means of sowing doubt and uncertainty in the government camp. Under the guidance of A. D. Mikhailov, a leader who was celebrated for his devotion to efficiency and was reputed to have memorised the addresses of 300 houses in the capital that had double entrances, the *Narodnaya Volya* set about its work much more methodically than any earlier terrorist group.[15] They drew their support from students and young liberals, many of them (like Sophia Petrovskaya, the daughter of a former governor of St Petersburg) scions of the aristocracy.

Their repeated attempts on the life of the Tsar forced him to closet himself in secrecy, to change his bedroom nightly and surround himself with bodyguards. In 1880, after one unsuccessful assassination attempt, the terrorists offered to halt their campaign if the Tsar agreed to a programme of social reform and the adoption of a parliamentary system. Perhaps he should have agreed to the deal. On 1 March 1881, the assassin Grinievetsky made sure of his target by walking up to Alexander II's carriage with his bomb, and was killed by the same blast that ended the Tsar's life. But it was a pyrrhic victory for the organisation. Within a week, nearly all the remaining leaders of *Narodnaya Volya* had been rounded up by the police (the organisation was already reeling from the shock of earlier raids). Of the 36 original members of the central committee, 18 were sentenced to death (5 of them were actually executed). The *Narodnaya Volya* had mustered its energies to make a single decisive blow; but the blow that killed the Tsar also destroyed the original organisation.

It is the ideology of the 'People's Will' that commands most attention today. The dominant tendency was radical-democratic, although there was always a minority of nihilists and 'professional terrorists' in the Nechayev tradition. The Narodnik terrorists argued that they had been forced to practise murder because the Tsarist régime had closed all possibilities of peaceful reform. Their leaders even promised that, if they ever saw signs of 'even the possibility of an honest government' they would then 'oppose terrorism, as we are now opposed to it in free nations'.[16] Their political goal was the attainment of the basic freedoms entrenched in the American Declaration of Rights, and their comment on the assassination of President Garfield in 1881 serves to differentiate them clearly from later terrorist movements that aim at the overthrow of democracy:

> In a land where the citizens are free to express their ideas, and where the will of the people does not merely make the law but appoints the person who is to carry the law into effect ... political assassination is the manifestation of a despotic tendency identical with that to whose destruction in Russia we have devoted ourselves.[17]

The real successors to the *Narodnaya Volya* were the members of the combat section of the Social Revolutionary Party. The Social Revolutionaries announced in 1902 that terrorism was 'inevitable' in Russia, while also insisting that this technique had to be coordinated with a broader insurrectionary strategy. Their misfortune was

that by this stage the Tsarist secret police, the Okhrana, had perfected their techniques: their elaborate filing systems and their
network of secret agents were the envy of the political police in other
European autocracies. Victor Serge claimed that by 1912 the
Okhrana had at least 17 agents inside the Social Revolutionary Party,
20 inside the Social Democratic Party, and another dozen amongst
student groups.[18]

If it is impossible to be sure about total numbers, the role of Evno
Azev—perhaps the most successful and certainly the most mysterious
double agent in Russian history—is notorious. He had been on the
payroll of the Okhrana since 1893, when he was invited to take over
the leadership of the Social Revolutionary combat section after the
capture of its original chief in 1903. In the following year, he arranged
the murder of his own employer: Plehve, the minister of the interior.
That extraordinary piece of duplicity raised the whole question of the
ambiguity of the role of the double agent. It is impossible to tell
where Azev's true loyalties lay. Like many others who played the
dangerous game of underground intrigue, he seemed to delight in
betrayal for its own sake, and shortly before his death in exile in
Berlin, he was considering an offer to sell his services to the German
police.

The Social Revolutionaries called a halt to their terrorist campaign
when Tsar Nicholas II agreed to summon a *Duma* (parliament) after
the uprisings of 1905. It is significant that the terrorists played only a
very secondary part in the 1905 disturbances; they were cut off from
the real vehicles of popular unrest. Their constant internal debates
(revived during the wave of attacks on policemen that was launched
in 1906–7) reached fever-pitch when a Paris exile and littérateur
called Bourtzev finally disclosed in 1908 that Azev was a double agent.
After some intensive soul-searching, the Social Revolutionary leaders
concluded that they had submitted to the 'hypnotic influence' of a
traitor and been misled into 'exalting' terror as a political strategy.
The last important victim of the Russian terrorists was Stolypin, the
prime minister who was killed in 1911, in the middle of a calm between
two storms in which it seemed that the Tsarist system was stronger
than ever. The Social Revolutionaries resorted to selective assassination again after the October Revolution, to combat Bolshevik

repression, turning back upon their past at the moment when they ceased to have a future.

Ultimately, history passed the Russian terrorists by. Other men sprang up at the head of the 1905 uprisings and the February and October revolutions of 1917 (although the Social Revolutionaries found a brief place in the sun in the months before October). And there is no sign that the series of dramatic assassinations that came off weakened the Tsarist state *as a system of government*, although the elimination of prominent individuals in a highly centralised state was bound to have some effect on policy. But it was not the murder of Alexander II, of Plehve, or of Stolypin (the prime minister who knew best how to juggle with repression and reform) that finally knocked the supports from the rickety tenement of Romanov power. The February Revolution owed more to the disillusionment, hunger and frustration of a people ordered to fight a losing battle against the German army; to mutiny in the barracks and dissension in the high command; and to the secret intrigues of German diplomacy.[19] Lenin had already made up his mind, several months before Tsar Nicholas II gave up his throne, that terrorism had proved bankrupt as a revolutionary technique in Russia.

> Individual terroristic acts [he observed in a letter to an Austrian friend] are impractical as a means of political strife. It is only a mass movement that can be considered to be a real political struggle. Individual terroristic acts can be, and must be, helpful only when they are directly linked with the mass movement. In Russia the terrorists (against whom we have always fought) made a number of such attempts, but in December, 1905, when the cause had at last reached the point of being a mass movement, a rising, and when it was necessary to help the masses to use force, then the terrorists were not there to do it.[20]

CYPRUS: TERROR AGAINST COLONIAL RULE

The four-year campaign waged by Eoka (the National Organisation of Cypriot Fighters) between 1955 and 1959 against the British government was one of the most outstanding examples of the successful use of terror against a colonial régime, although the Cypriot terrorists failed to achieve their original political goal: *enosis*, or union with Greece.

It was always abundantly clear that no rebel movement could hope for a military victory in an island half the size of Wales with a population of just over half a million, that could easily be isolated from sympathetic groups abroad by a naval blockade. Eoka's strategy was rather to arouse public opinion in Britain and the United Nations and induce the 'psychology of withdrawal'. The 'Preliminary General Plan' drawn up in Athens two years before the start of the campaign defined the objective in the following terms:

> To arouse international public opinion, especially among the allies of Greece, by deeds of heroism and self-sacrifice which will focus attention on Cyprus until our aims are achieved. The British must be continuously harried and beset until they are obliged by international diplomacy exercised through the United Nations to examine the Cyprus problem and settle it in accordance with the desires of the Cypriot people and the whole Greek nation.[21]

This was to be achieved through a programme of systematic sabotage of military posts and government installations, through selective terrorism against the security forces, and through organised passive resistance on the part of the civil population. General George Grivas, the author of the plan, also insisted from the beginning that it would be necessary to take measures to ensure the obedience of a people that he privately regarded as politically apathetic. 'Care will be taken,' he warned in phraseology that was to become notorious, 'to punish severely any Cypriots who work for the enemy or act against our interests.'[22] The key to Eoka's success was that it was able to establish a tight grip over the Greek Cypriot population. That was possible partly because there was widespread sympathy for the cause that Eoka represented, and also because the terrorists enjoyed the full support of the church presided over by Makarios III, archbishop of Cyprus and Ethnarch of the Cypriot people. But in the final analysis, Eoka was able to command obedience because it could hold the threat of summary execution over a population that the colonial authorities, deprived of a reliable local police force from an early stage in the campaign, were powerless to protect. The techniques of intimidation employed by Eoka ranged from oral warnings or ostracism by a village community to beatings and assassinations.

The way they destroyed the network of local government was a sample of their methods. On 28 October 1955, Archbishop Makarios called for the resignation of all Greek Cypriot village *mukhtars*, or headmen. Only about a fifth of the men in office had complied by the end of the year, so Eoka picked out three headmen noted for their pro-British sympathies and shot them. There was no further problem with the *mukhtars*: within a month, more than 80 per cent had stepped down. A similar, but much bloodier, campaign was launched to break down the police force. The measure of Eoka's success in coaxing and coercing Greek Cypriot support was that, at the end of 1958, the British forces were compelled to sack all their Greek Cypriot employees after a series of terrorist attacks engineered from inside military bases.

By that time, the spectacle of mobs of schoolchildren throwing stones at British troops had become familiar to every English newspaper reader. General Grivas commented in retrospect that 'I know of no other movement, organisation or army that has so actively employed boys and girls of school age in the front line. And yet there is every reason to do so: young people love danger; they must take risks to prove their worth.'[23] Schoolchildren were enlisted into Grivas' original guerrilla squads, and staged some deadly acts of sabotage as well as participating in mass demonstrations and keeping up constant pressure on the British troops by heckling and stone-throwing. Grivas picked his recruits wisely, and it is no accident that the IRA in Belfast has also made use of children in the rioting and street-battles. Western public opinion is unused to the idea that boys as well as men can be guerrillas; and the image of British paratroops confronting Greek Cypriot children had a jarring effect in London.

The plans for the Eoka campaign were drawn up in Athens in the early 1950s in the course of negotiations between Grivas, Makarios, and sympathetic Greek politicians. *Enosis* was an old cause, and Marshal Papagos pledged the support of the Greek government in 1955. There is evidence that the Greek government gave steady support to Eoka throughout the campaign, although Grivas was never satisfied with the attempts that were made to smuggle arms through and ended with the feeling that Greek diplomacy (and

Makarios) had betrayed him. Grivas himself had a considerable military background. A deeply traditional Greek Cypriot obsessed with the legends of ancient Greece and the wild dreams of a Greek empire in the eastern Mediterranean that floated around prewar Athens, he joined the Greek army at the age of seventeen and led the right-wing resistance movement 'Xhi' after the German occupation. His lifelong hatred of the communists was reinforced by the extraordinary attitude that the Greek Communist Party later took during the Eoka campaign. The communists were one of the few important local political groups to stand aloof from the campaign, and their leader was the first man to divulge (in a broadcast from Moscow clearly intended for British ears) that Grivas was leading terrorist operations in Cyprus.

Grivas left for Cyprus to organise Eoka in October 1954. On the face of it, the terrain was not promising. The island was small, and the network of roads radiating across it from Nicosia, the capital, provided easy transport for the security forces. Even the wild Troodos Mountains in the western part of the island were criss-crossed by roads. Grivas decided that the terrorists should operate in two sections, one based in the mountains and making use of friendly monasteries, the other working in the towns. Starting with some 80 men, he built up a force that by February 1956, mustered 53 mountain guerrillas (divided into 7 squads), 220 urban terrorists (47 squads), and a reserve force of 750 men in the villages.

Their remarkable capacity for survival throughout the course of the campaign was based on the sympathy of the Greek community, the gaps in British intelligence, and Grivas' unquestioned military acumen. By dividing his men into penny packets, he lessened the chances of discovery in the massive sweep operations that were later mounted by the British. Grivas observed that 'From the guerrillas' point of view, it is positively dangerous to increase the size of groups beyond a certain point. I call this the saturation point. It is determined by the nature of the terrain, the skill of the fighters, their requirements in food and supplies, the tactics employed and the need to keep down casualties.' [24]

Grivas also made cunning use of diversionary tactics. The terrorists would initially choose their targets in areas where they were weak, so that the searches that were bound to follow would have minimal effect. In the course of the campaign, Eoka set an example to later urban guerrillas in the secrets of survival under urban conditions. Hiding in secret cellars and concrete foxholes, Eoka's urban cadres eluded persistent army searches—except on the rare but important occasions when an informer gave the game away. And Grivas, the greatest prize of all, outfoxed his pursuers for fully four years, much of them spent in suburban cottages in Nicosia or the southern port of Limassol.

The signal for the first wave of terrorist attacks came after the United Nations, in December 1954, rejected the Greek appeal for the Cypriots to be given the right of self-determination. The British government was not yet prepared to accept that Cyprus should ever be given independence. The Minister of State for Colonies, Henry Hopkinson, had remarked in July 1954, that Cyprus belonged to a class of territories which 'owing to their particular circumstances, can never expect to be fully independent'.[25] His statement was partly geared to domestic politics and the emotions of the Conservative right-wing, but it reflected the prevailing view that the island was strategically vital to Britain. The Eoka campaign, as well as the shock that followed the Suez débâcle in 1956 and the increasing pace of decolonisation in the third world generally, persuaded British opinion in the course of the coming years of the need to reappraise Hopkinson's view of British interests in Cyprus.

The first Eoka attacks, in the early hours of 1 April 1955, took the island by surprise. Bombs were hurled into government buildings, power stations, police posts, and the Wolseley Barracks in Nicosia. The most spectacular explosion was at the government radio station in the capital, where saboteurs destroyed broadcasting equipment worth £60,000 and blew the roof off the building. The only casualty of the first night of terrorist attacks was one of Grivas' own men, who was electrocuted when he rashly threw a damp rope over high tension wires in an attempt to damage the power supply. But Grivas had already instructed his squads to seek out 'targets of opportunity', and on Empire Day a bomb was placed near the seat of the Governor, Sir Robert Armitage, in the Pallas Cinema. The bomb exploded five minutes after he and his party had left the building. In June, there were a series of attacks on police stations and bars frequented by British troops, and this time the bombs were packed with shrapnel to cause maximal casualties.

On June 28, Grivas informed his men that 'The aim of our next offensive will be to terrorise the police and to paralyse the administration, both in the towns and in the countryside... Disillusionment will spread through the Police Force so rapidly that most of them, if they do not actually help us, will turn a blind eye to our activities.'[26] This was to be brought about by murdering 'over-zealous' policemen as publicly as possible, and by picking off patrols moving along country roads to discourage the police from advancing outside the towns. Warnings were issued to Greek Cypriot policemen to resign from the force: 'Do not try to block our path or you will stain it with your blood.'

But it was the murder of a Special Branch constable, Michael Poullis, in broad daylight in the heart of Nicosia on August 28 that had the most shattering effect on the morale of the security forces. He was shot, in full view of the hundreds of people who had just emerged from a Communist party meeting, by a three-man Eoka murder squad who afterwards managed to make a clean getaway. The Poullis killing showed policemen just how exposed they were, and it was followed by a flood of resignations from the force. In October, Eoka launched the 'Forward to Victory' campaign that again made policemen and police posts the prime targets.

By the end of 1955, the terrorist infrastructure was virtually complete. There was close co-operation between the guerrillas in the Troodos and Kyrenia ranges (Grivas had constructed a temporary headquarters consisting of seven dugouts and nicknamed 'the Castle' on a ridge overlooking the Adelphi forest in the Troodos ranges) and the teams of saboteurs and execution squads in the towns. But at the end of the year, the British took two important steps. The first was to appoint a new Governor. Armitage's replacement was Field-Marshal Sir John Harding, who had just retired as Chief of the Imperial General Staff. For the British to appoint their leading soldier, a man of enormous experience and leadership capacity, to take charge in Cyprus, was a measure of how serious the situation had become. Harding reorganised the security arrangements and, after some initial reverses, managed to score a few decisive hits against Eoka. The second step was to set up a tripartite conference, grouping together the British, Greek and Turkish governments, in which the British acknowledged that the Turks had rights to protect in Cyprus. This was the prelude to the final diplomatic settlement that gave the island independence but not *enosis*, and by bringing in the Turks at this early stage British diplomacy sidestepped the rebel leaders and their friends in Athens.

Harding integrated his security forces under a new chief of staff, with a network of District Security Committees (triumvirates including the district commissioner, the army unit commander, and the senior police officer) across the island. The state of the local police—terrorised, exhausted and overstretched, with a fair sprinkling of Eoka agents among their number—made it inevitable that the army would have to take over many normal police functions. The so-called 'Q' units, composed of Eoka renegades and Cypriot loyalists on the model of the 'counter-gangs' that the British had organised in Kenya, were set up as part of the intelligence system.[27] According to Grivas, Greek Cypriots living in London were flown back to Cyprus to work as British agents, mixing with villagers or taking jobs in coffee-shops where they could pick up gossip.[28] The successful use of informers enabled the British to round up several Eoka squads in 1956 and 1957, including a group of six guerrillas led by George Matsis who had been operating in the Pitsillia mountains. But Eoka reprisals against informers who failed to get on the first plane out of Cyprus were usually unerring, and the British never managed to rival the terrorists' own intelligence system. Top-level British security conferences were regularly taped by a Greek Cypriot Special Branch sergeant who belonged to Eoka.

Harding organised a series of sweeps and hunt-and-kill operations, ranging from lightning swoops on suburban streets to the deployment of 10,000 troops to encircle a mountain redoubt. Confronted with helicopters, Auster aircraft, police dogs and searchlights, Grivas remarked caustically that 'One does not use a tank to catch field-mice—a cat will do the job better'. The British staged a massive manhunt in the Troodos ranges in May 1956 that was primarily designed to catch Grivas, but after twelve days of hide-and-seek, the rebel leader slipped through the net and drove to Limassol. That particular operation did lead to the capture of three Eoka squads, but the policy of lighting fires to flush out guerrillas led to the deaths of twenty-one British soldiers in a sheet of flame.

The growing strength of the terrorist organisation drove the British to adopt progressively tougher political measures. Eoka operations were closely co-ordinated with mass demonstrations and strike action (including sympathy rallies in Greece). After the terrorist offensive in October–November 1955, a state of emergency was declared, the police carried blank detention orders, and the army conducted mass interrogation and mass searches. In March 1956, Harding took a further step that became highly controversial by exiling Archbishop Makarios to the Seychelles after the break-down of negotiations for a peace settlement. Makarios was working hand-in-glove with Eoka, but his removal meant that Grivas assumed the political command as well as the military leadership of the rebels, and the upshot was a more ruthless and bloodier terrorist offensive. Harding's own valet, Neofytus Sofocleus, tried to engineer his death by planting a bomb under his mattress. But Harding left his windows open that night, and the lower temperature affected the time pencil on the bomb so that it failed to explode. The incident led to the dismissal of all Greek Cypriot employees at Government House.

Left to his own devices, Grivas launched another offensive on October 31. The month that followed was remembered as 'Black November', because more than 400 acts of political violence took place. Eoka used electronically-detonated mines on a large scale for the first time (mines that could be detonated from a distance clearly reduced the danger of detection for the person who laid them) and there were frequent street killings as the murder squads picked off the British soldiers returning from the Suez campaign. Three British police sergeants were fired on in broad daylight in Ledra Street in Nicosia, and two of them were killed. Harding achieved a measure of revenge in the following year, largely through improved intelligence and the fact that the end of the Suez operation freed more troops for duty on the island. The 2nd Parachute Batallion claimed that they eliminated twenty-one Eoka terrorists in January 1957, and two of Grivas' favourite lieutenants, Gregoris Axfentiou and Mikos Drakos, were killed in the following months. A tighter watch was kept on arms smugglers, and Athens radio (the main propaganda vehicle for Eoka) was effectively jammed.

But the arrival of a new Governor, Sir Hugh Foot, at the end of 1957 was presaged by a dramatic act of sabotage carried out by Greek Cypriot technicians employed at Akrotiri air base: they wrecked several jet aircraft and caused total damage estimated at £4½ million. Foot encountered the general hostility of the Greek Cypriot community, symbolised by the boycott of British goods that started in March 1958. After some liberal opening gestures, Foot was compelled to bring back the emergency regulations (including execution for carrying arms). There was increasing criticism of the army's behaviour, but many of the 'atrocity' stories were exaggerated by those friendly to Eoka. For example, General Grivas made great play of the Avgorou 'massacre' of mid-1957, when two Greek Cypriots were killed during a riot. The inquiry disclosed that one of the men had been shot after he had hit an officer in the face with a brick; and that a woman had been killed by a flying stone.

One of the rare occasions when the army clearly did overreact followed a terrorist outrage in Famagusta, when Mrs Mary Cutliffe (the mother of five and the wife of a British sergeant) was shot in the back while shopping by an Eoka murder squad. The two British regiments in the area swept through the town, dragging the male Greek population out of their homes without excessive delicacy. A *Daily Telegraph* correspondent reported that he was shocked to find 'rooms full of bloody and bandaged Greek Cypriots lying on floors in Famagusta hospital'.

There was a rising crescendo of selective assassinations through 1958, and Eoka showed signs of increasing technical ingenuity (the widespread use of pressure mines, for example) and of having tightened its grip over the Greek community to the point where it could operate quite openly without risk of being given away. Eoka saboteurs sometimes went about their work as coolly and publicly as television repair-men. On 25 October 1958, for example, the terrorists managed to blow up two truckloads of soldiers that had just pulled up outside Yiallousia police station. There were twenty army casualties. A schoolboy-saboteur had crawled along a storm drain on two successive nights to lay mines beside the road, and the cable connected the charges to a house around the corner. The boy spent a total of seven hours in the drain, and Grivas comments that 'It was an unusual aspect of this operation that almost the entire village knew what was going to happen. Several people saw young Modestos clambering out of the storm-drain at dawn and everyone was warned to keep away from the post-office across the yard when the trucks arrived.'[29]

Eoka's hold over the Greek Cypriot population was cemented by the communal violence that began in May 1956, with the murder of Turkish policemen by terrorists. That was the trigger for a chain-sequence of communal rioting and savage butchery on both sides: in two months in mid-1957, 56 Greeks and 53 Turks were reported killed. The communal trouble was one of the factors that conditioned the final diplomatic settlement for Cyprus that was achieved in London in February 1959, in the course of talks between the British, Greek and Turkish governments; Archbishop Makarios; and the Turkish Cypriot leader Dr Kutchuk. The settlement was achieved over Grivas' head, and the irony was that the military section of the Cypriot rebels that had done so much to focus world attention on the island (and to make the British ask themselves whether it was really worth holding on) was left out at the last. Makarios got independence; the British held on to their military bases; the Turkish Cypriots got 30 per cent representation in parliament and the stationing of Turkish troops (as well as Greeks and British) on the island. Grivas received only a number of empty honorifics and a plane ride back to Athens. On 16 August 1960, Cyprus gained formal independence, but the original goal of *enosis* had been lost somewhere along the line.

Eoka's triumph was thus a highly equivocal success. The Cypriot terrorists were able to tie up vastly superior British forces over four years and to engineer an almost complete breach between the colonial authorities and the Greek Cypriot population. But it cannot be said that they actually pushed the British out; rather, they acted as a catalyst in the political process by which the British government came to accept the notion of a reduced role in the world and to redefine its strategic interests in Cyprus.

ALGERIA: THE MIRROR-EFFECT

It was one of the multiple tragedies of the Algerian insurrection (1954–62) that it spawned not one but several varieties of political terrorism. In the last months of French rule, when Moslems and Europeans were being machine-gunned from moving cars in the winding streets of Algiers, or blown up by plastic bombs in cafés and bazaars, it became impossible to predict whether the next outrage would be the work of the National Liberation Front (FLN), the Secret Army Organisation (OAS), or the *barbouzes* (a paramilitary group organised with police backing to out-terrorise the OAS). Confused spectators spoke not only of terrorism and counter-terrorism, but of counter-counterterrorism as well.

Nothing could better illustrate the symbiotic relationship between political extremists. Like the IRA and the Protestant Ulster Volunteer Force in Northern Ireland, or the urban guerrillas and the police 'death squads' in Brazil, the FLN and the OAS fed on each other. The OAS, a sinister apparatus that sucked in all the desperate men and threadbare political creeds of *Algérie française*, was in many ways the mirror-image of the Moslem FLN. The OAS crowded the whole repertoire of the FLN into the last violent months of French rule: murder, bombings, communal slaughter, terrorism in metropolitan France, the attempt to launch an uprising in Algiers, guerrilla operations in the mountains. But the curious resemblance between the FLN and the OAS was a matter of temperament as well as tactics. One OAS militant later remarked that 'I was undoubtedly closer to the communist, in thought and attitude, than to the decadent intellectual who sides with the left or the capitalist who pretends he has a social conscience.'[30] The political extremes seem to rub noses.

Even the name of the OAS bore a striking similarity to that of the military wing of Messali Hadj's Movement for the Triumph of Democratic Liberties (MTLD): the Secret Organisation (OS). That was where most of the original leaders of the FLN served their political apprenticeship. After the rift between the moderates and the extremists in Messali's movement in 1954, a group of activists led by Ben Bella, Belkacem Krim and Ben Boulaid broke away to form the Revolutionary Committee for Action and Unity (CRUA), which quickly changed its name to the FLN.

The FLN's campaign against the French began on 1 November 1954, with a wave of bombings, ambushes, arson and attacks on police posts. Terrorism played an important part throughout the FLN campaign. It was used for three main purposes: to eliminate pro-French and moderate Moslem leaders and to tighten the terrorists' hold over the Algerian population; to disrupt the life of the towns and to pave the way for an uprising in Algiers; and to carry the war to Paris and make metropolitan Frenchmen conscious of the strength of the organisation.

In the first years of FLN operations, the murder of uncooperative village chiefs and threats against Moslem deputies became common-place. The FLN soon became locked in an underground duel with Messali Hadj's new political vehicle, the Algerian National Movement (MNA). Messali's adherents were virtually wiped out in the coastal belt of Algeria, but they were in a much stronger position among the Algerian migrant community in France, and the real battle between the two factions was quickly transferred to the other side of the Mediterranean. In 1957, four leaders of the Messalist trade union organisation (USTA) were murdered in succession.[31]

Simultaneously, the FLN was working to consolidate its hold over the Arab quarters in Algiers, in preparation for a major urban offensive. By mid-1956 the terrorists were securely in command of the 80,000 Moslems living in the rabbit-warren of slums that made up the Casbah. An FLN leader named Ramdane Abbane managed to convince his chiefs of the virtues of an all-out terrorist campaign in Algiers. 'Is it better for our cause to kill ten of our enemies in a remote village,' he asked rhetorically, 'where this will not cause comment, or to kill only one man in Algiers, where the American press will get hold of the story the next day?' He concluded that 'If we are going to take risks, we must ensure that people learn about our struggle.'[32]

The man who was to succeed Ramdane Abbane as the FLN chief

in Algiers early in 1957, Yacef Saadi, was placed in charge of the explosives section. He organised the manufacture of schneiderite in backyard factories, and set up a tightly compartmentalised apparatus to handle transport, intelligence and sabotage.[33] From mid-1956 the terrorists moved from isolated assaults on police stations to selective killings of individual Europeans. On September 30, the campaign assumed a more sinister character when two bombs were exploded in a milkbar in the Place de l'Isly and a café in the Rue Michelet: three *pieds noirs* (European settlers) were killed, and forty-six injured.

This was the prelude to a wave of indiscriminate attacks designed to polarise the Moslem and European communities and provoke the kind of backlash that would make compromise impossible. The favourite targets for the bombings were crowded buses, sidewalk cafés and other European meeting-places. In the single month of December, there were about 120 terrorist attacks in Algiers. The police were visibly incapable of keeping order in the streets, and on 7 January 1957, the army was called in. General Massu and the 10th Paratroop Division assumed the responsibility for the security of Algiers, and they carried out their task with ruthless efficiency. By the end of February, most of the FLN leaders in Algiers had been forced to seek refuge in Tunisia. The secrets of the *paras'* rapid triumph soon became public knowledge in Paris.

Massu got his intelligence through mass interrogation and the systematic use of torture. He managed to build up an effective net-work of informers, and the presence of a man hiding his face behind a blanket became familiar at identity parades. Renegades from the FLN were conscripted into mobile commando units that went into action in the Arab quarters beside paratroop squads. Massu also enforced the principle of collective responsibility by installing the *îlot* system, under which the head of a family was made accountable for the behaviour of his relations, another was made responsible for the tenants in a building, another for a whole street or city block, and so on up the scale.

The FLN infrastructure in the Casbah was wrecked, and the terrorists only managed to creep back to rebuild it at the very end of the war. It would seem that urban terrorism in 1956–7 was almost

wholly counterproductive for the FLN—although the methods that
the army employed to win the Battle of Algiers were fiercely controversial in Paris. But although FLN terrorism failed against the French,
it was a crucial means of ensuring the obedience of the Algerians.

The French army was ordered to wage a second Battle of Algiers
in 1962, against a very different enemy. The men who joined forces
to form the OAS early in 1961 were an odd conglomerate: they
included self-styled revolutionaries who modelled themselves on the
Spanish Falange, dissident army officers and frustrated putschists,
and settlers who were more interested in trying to hold on to their
orange groves or grocers' shops than in joining in an ideological
crusade.[34] What these men shared with the generals who tried to
stage a coup in Algiers in April 1961, was a sense of betrayal: the
embittered belief that General de Gaulle and the *pathos* (their
contemptuous label for metropolitan Frenchmen) had sold them
down the river.

The army leaders clung to the conviction that the war had been
nearly won by 1960. In purely military terms, they were probably
not far wrong; but then it was doubtful whether a purely military
victory was tenable. There was a fundamental contradiction between
the goal of 'integration' that the intelligent apologists for *Algérie
française* continued to stand by and the idea of holding Algeria by
military force.[35] Yet General Maurice Challe, the man who placed
himself at the head of the April putsch, had claimed when he stepped
down as Commander-in-Chief a year earlier that during his fifteen
months in command, half of the FLN forces had been killed or
captured, terrorist acts had dwindled by 50 per cent, and the rebels
had been increasingly cut off from their outside sources of support
in Tunisia, Morocco and Egypt.

When he seized command in Algiers for his brief few days in
1961, he dreamed of a series of lightning victories over the FLN to
follow up his earlier successful offensives and persuade the government in Paris that it was possible to hold on to Algeria. If General
de Gaulle refused to be persuaded, Challe was ready to start a
'Spanish' war by dropping paratroops in Paris. But he hesitated
and stumbled. Challe's camarilla in Algiers simply crumbled away,
his regiments defected, and the aftermath was a purge of the officer

corps by an infuriated de Gaulle who proceeded to press on with the negotiations with the FLN.

The OAS had already turned out in the streets of Algiers in 1961, uninvited, and General Raoul Salan, the organisation's nominal leader, had flown in from Madrid. After the failure of Challe's paratroops and retired generals, the irregulars took over. The strategy of the OAS was never very clear. Unlike earlier right-wing terrorist groups in Algeria, it came to control at least 60 per cent of the settler population; if the campaign of the FLN deserves to be described as 'people's war', then perhaps this was the rival 'people's war' of the *pieds noirs*. The only policy platform that the OAS leaders could agree on was the maintenance of *Algérie française*, and that became something of an anachronism as it emerged that their immediate enemies were not the Moslem insurgents but the French government and that the army they had always counted on for at worst sympathy and at best active support was prepared to fire on them in the streets.

Jean-Jacques Susini, the neo-fascist idealogue of the group, dreamed of another Budapest uprising; a revolution of the streets. Colonel Yves Godard, his perennial rival, hardly seemed to think beyond the guerrilla techniques he had learned from the rebels he had fought in Indochina and Algeria. There were initially some wild hopes of direct support from Spain, Portugal or the United States; these were quickly disappointed. There were also hopes of building up a strong support group in Paris. Although it had become clear to almost everyone by September 1960, that General de Gaulle had made up his mind to pave the way for Algerian independence, there were still many important public men of diverse political leanings who remained emotionally attached to the cause of *Algérie française*. They ranged from Guy Mollet, the Socialist leader, to Georges Bidault and Jacques Soustelle on the right.

But Soustelle and Bidault were among the tiny handful of well-known politicians who dared to make any public defence of the OAS. The military intrigues of 1960 and 1961 had identified the cause of *Algérie française* in the minds of many Gaullists and liberal Frenchmen with Caesarism and hostility to democracy and de Gaulle; the astonishingly ill-conceived series of terrorist attacks that the OAS proceeded to launch in Paris now tended to equate it with blind savagery. There was general embarrassment at the methods employed by the OAS among sympathetic politicians; and the terrorists managed to make Mollet's position virtually impossible by murdering a series of Algerian Socialist leaders. In any case, when it came to the test of a crucial vote in the National Assembly, General de Gaulle was able to command an overwhelming majority. The general had doggedly set his course towards a negotiated settlement with the FLN at Evian; as it turned out, OAS terrorism merely served to bring the date of the agreement forward.[36]

The first OAS killings were carried out by the 'Delta' squads, organised by Lieutenant Roger Degueldre, a legionnaire who had risen from the ranks and was rumoured to have had links with the pro-Nazi Rexists in Belgium during the Second World War. The first important victim was Police Inspector Roger Gavoury, who was stabbed to death on 31 May 1961. Like the FLN, the OAS obtained much of their finance through 'expropriation'; after their efforts to get money from the European community through the collecting-box had fallen short of the mark, they stole $160,000 from the Merchant Marine Retirement Fund in 1961.

The favourite targets for selective terrorism in Algiers and Oran were policemen and European liberals, but from the start of the OAS campaign there was also plenty of indiscriminate terror against Moslems that mounted in ferocity as the hopelessness of the situation became apparent. They were remarkably successful in picking off the leaders of the government's counter-terrorist operations (including Major René Post, who was murdered by a Corsican gangster after plotting to capture Susini in October 1961) and in destroying the *barbouzes*—the Gaullist fanatics and Vietnamese mercenaries who were sent into the streets of Algiers to pay back the OAS in its own coin.

The strength of the OAS was that it was able to command such wide support from the *pieds noirs*. It was the strongest of all in the poorer working-class white areas like Bab-el-Oued in Algiers (whose population had tended to vote communist in more peaceful times). The real dividing-line between Algerian settlers in the last days was probably between those who could afford to pack their bags and get out and those who would lose everything unless they stayed. The OAS threatened murderous reprisals against middle-class settlers who tried to get their money out of the country and against airline companies who sold tickets to fleeing *pieds noirs*. They did manage to inhibit movement, but they never seriously interfered with the flight of funds, and in the long run they made the general exodus of settlers inevitable.

The OAS demonstrated its popular support at the end of 1961 with a series of noisy *Algérie française* rallies, but on December 13, for the first time in their experience, the *pieds noirs* were outshouted by the Moslems who poured into the streets to stage a counter-demonstration. Early in January 1962, the OAS issued a directive instructing all Europeans *and Algerians* (there were a handful of loyalists and ex-army auxiliaries in the OAS) to join the organisation, which would develop into a cross between the French Resistance and the Israeli Haganah. This decree laid the basis for the attempt at a mass uprising later in the year.

While the terror had been mounting in Algiers, the Paris branch of the OAS, under erratic and divided leadership, had staged a series of uncoordinated *plastiquages* (bombings with plastic explosives). There were eighteen explosions in four hours on the night of 18 January 1962. Unlike FLN terrorism in Paris, which had been aimed at individual policemen and their Moslem rivals, the OAS bombings were so indiscriminate that they inspired public revulsion in Paris and silenced many of the organisation's friends in high places—especially after a four-year-old girl was killed in an explosion that had been intended for André Malraux. Mutual fear of the OAS may have driven General de Gaulle and the FLN leaders towards an earlier settlement at Evian. At any rate, the General gave up many of his original demands (for a separate French province in the Sahara, for example) and the Evian accords were signed on 18 March 1962. There was to be an immediate ceasefire, and a referendum to provide Algerians with the opportunity for self-determination of their future was to be held within three months. French settlers were given the right to retain dual citizenship for three years after independence.

Now the problems of strategy for the OAS became acute. They

had failed to halt the drift towards independence; on the contrary, de Gaulle's desire to get rid of them once and for all probably accelerated it. A faction had already arisen inside the OAS that argued that the terrorists should abandon their ideal of *Algérie française* and try for something less: a partition of the country into an Arab interior and a European coastal zone. But for the founders of the OAS, it was all or nothing, and some of the leaders of the pro-partition lobby paid for their doubts with their lives. The immediate response to the Evian agreement was twofold: a campaign of mass terror against Moslems that started on March 21 when the OAS fired their only mortar into the crowded Place du Gouvernement in Algiers; and an attempt at self-government in the OAS stronghold of Bab-el-Oued. What Jacques Achard, the OAS leader in Bab-el-Oued, was planning when he issued an ultimatum to the security forces to get out of his district by March 22 looked suicidal. But at this stage, the OAS still could not believe that the army would fire on them in a street-battle.

They were disastrously mistaken. After terrorists in Bab-el-Oued had ambushed patrols, troops and police moved in with tanks, armoured scout cars and helicopters. The whole district was cordoned off for six days while a massive search operation was mounted. It was finally reduced to sullen submission. The army had used methods akin to those employed during the first Battle of Algiers against the FLN. In the weeks that followed, the increasing brutality of the troops was as obvious as the mounting volume of terrorist violence: Moslem soldiers fired on an unarmed mob in the Rue d'Isly later in March, killing at least forty people.

Defected in Algiers, the OAS tried to set up a rural guerrilla base in the Ouarsenis hills, but Said Boualem, the chief of the Beni-Boudouane tribe who had promised to back them, changed his mind and they were easily encircled by vastly superior military forces using aircraft. General de Gaulle proved he had won the battle in Paris when he gained an overwhelming majority in a plebiscite on Algeria's future on April 8. There was nothing left for the OAS, which was battering itself to pieces against the iron wall of the French army, except an orgy of senseless violence: an attempt to ravage what they were clearly losing.

One analyst has commented that in this downward process, the
OAS passed through all the phases that the French army's doctrine
of 'revolutionary warfare' prescribed for a declining guerrilla force:
'inability to regularise operations, return to guerrilla warfare, and
then to terror.'[37] The one glimmer of hope that remained was that
somehow the OAS might be able to defer the referendum that was
due to be held in Algeria on July 1. They hoped to achieve that end
by provoking the FLN into retaliating in kind (so far, the Moslem
terrorists had been content to stand back and watch their traditional
enemies—the settlers and the security forces—tear each other to
shreds). After *pied noir* teenagers ran amok with automatic weapons
early in May, dealing out death to whatever Moslems they encountered, the FLN decided on revenge, and the violence of
Algiers again became three-sided from May 14.

As it became clear that nothing would shake General de Gaulle's
resolve to go ahead with the referendum, the intelligent men in the
OAS began to pack their bags or sat down with FLN spokesmen
like Abderrahmane Fares in the hope of hammering out some
compromise over the division of power in the cities after the country
became independent. For a few weeks in June, it even looked as if a
bargain was possible, but when Ben Bella was released he vetoed all
ideas of a settlement. All that was left was 'Operation Apocalypse':
flames leaping into the sky as the OAS set fire to oil storage tankers,
schools and universities, while *pieds noirs* standing beside their
trunks at the wharves cheered hysterically.

The OAS—and French Algeria—died like a man dragged reluc-
tantly to the gallows, kicking so hard that the rope has to be tied
around his neck for a second time. What was the effect of their
terrorist campaign? One OAS militant claimed, almost certainly
unfairly, that the French government had thrown more into the
fight against the European terrorists than they had ever expended
on the struggle with the FLN. Although they saw themselves as 'the
last obstacles between France and peace at any price', they probably
helped to bring a settlement between de Gaulle and the FLN closer.
They succeeded only in their policy of 'all or nothing'. The violence
of the last months led to total segregation of Europeans and Algerians in the towns, and made the mass flight of settlers inevitable.

THE FAULTY WEAPON

The record of the terrorist campaigns in Tsarist Russia, Cyprus and Algeria shows that terrorism is a faulty weapon that often misfires. Even the Russian terrorists, with their hopes of an American-style democracy, discovered how the means usurp the ends. And in military terms, their isolated assassinations were scarcely more than pinpricks. Even General Grivas, one of the most successful colonial rebels, had his qualified victory stolen from him by the politicians at the last moment. He was able to set the process of decolonisation in motion, but he was unable to control the final political consequences. What must be borne in mind in comparing Cyprus and Algeria with contemporary urban guerrilla situations is that, while the military problems may be similar, the political context is completely different. The government and the army of an independent state will not simply go away (although Batista flew off to his foreign bank accounts when he saw Castro's rebel army advancing on Havana). If an urban guerrilla campaign is to progress beyond terrorist harassment, it must be combined with forms of political agitation and mass organisation that will make an armed uprising possible.

One of the weaknesses of most contemporary urban guerrilla groups is that they lack this broader base and wider perspective. The leaders who have tried to define a strategy have focused on short-term tactical problems. Carlos Marighella, for example, defines the two immediate objectives of the urban guerrilla as the assassination of politicians and members of the security forces, and the theft or destruction of 'government resources and those belonging to the big capitalists and imperialists'. [38] For a long-range strategy, it is necessary to turn back to an earlier period of urban violence, to the decade following the Bolshevik revolution, when the Comintern plotted armed insurrection throughout western Europe and China. The attempt to repeat the October risings in Petrograd and Moscow led to a whole series of failed rebellions in places like Hamburg and Reval, Canton and Shanghai. In a classic study of armed insurrection, the Comintern endorsed Lenin's view that 'a revolution is impossible without a revolutionary situation' and his three-point definition of the 'symptoms' of a revolutionary situation:

1 When it is impossible for the ruling classes to maintain their rule without any change; when there is a crisis, in one form or another, among the 'upper classes', a crisis in the policy of the ruling class, leading to a fissure through which the discontent and indignation of the oppressed classes burst forth. For a revolution to take place, it is usually insufficient for the 'lower classes not to want' to live in the old way; it is also necessary for 'the upper classes to be unable' to live in the old way;
2 When the suffering and want of the oppressed classes have grown more acute than usual;
3 When, as a consequence of the above causes, there is a considerable increase in the activity of the masses, who uncomplainingly allow themselves to be robbed in 'peace-time', but, in turbulent times, are drawn both by all the circumstances of the crisis *and by the 'upper classes' themselves* into independent historical action.[39]

The Comintern added its own conclusions about the preconditions for a successful urban uprising: the need to subvert and demoralise the armed forces; to build up a strong clandestine military organisation and a system of workers' councils to prepare for a general strike; to have a carefully thought-out plan of action, taking into account the deployment of the government forces and the possibility of intervention from outside the city; and above all to ensure 'that the masses are drawn into the conflict at the same time as the military organisation moves into action'.[40] In the eyes of the Comintern, urban revolution would finally be brought about through the combination of a general strike and an armed insurrection.

Today, it makes more sense to read Lenin or the communist theorists of the 1920s in order to understand the likely pattern of urban guerrilla operations than to read Mao Tse-tung, General Giap, or even Che Guevara. The reason why most of the urban guerrilla groups discussed in this book are likely to remain isolated terrorists becomes apparent when one considers Lenin's conditions for revolution or the Comintern's insistence on the need for central political direction and a mass base.

3

Under Western Eyes

'Whether American decisively moves to the right or to the left,' in the view of Eldridge Cleaver, the Black Panther leader, 'is the fundamental political problem in the world today.'[1] Few people would dispute that. The question is whether urban terrorism is likely to shift the internal political balance of the United States in any decisive way. By most conventional standards, America is a violent society—far more so than any other advanced industrial society. That can be judged by the fact that there are now more than 90 million firearms in the United States, and that more than half of the nation's 60 million householders own at least one gun.[2]

But although the level of political violence is high by western standards, it is low in relation to the far higher level of criminal violence. Between 1965 and 1968, for example, 214 people were killed and some 9,000 were injured as a result of political terrorism, political protest, and ghetto riots. Most of the deaths took place during the ghetto riots.[3] The startling thing is that the number was not far greater when one considers that more than 12,000 murders and more than a quarter of a million aggravated assaults take place in the United States annually, and that according to recent FBI figures, an American citizen now stands a 1 in 36 chance of being the victim of a serious crime in a given year.[4]

The link between the basic crime rate and the possibility of greater political violence is that both are closely related to race. More than 50 per cent of the violent crimes in the United States are committed by non-whites. There are obvious socio-economic and psychological reasons for that. There is also the rising danger that some of the random violence of the robber with a gun will be harnessed by urban guerrilla groups for political ends. Militant groups like the Young Lords of Chicago, a Puerto Rican revolutionary society that began as a street-gang in the slums, have already brought about this transformation. The Black Panthers drew most of their recruits from the criminals of the ghettoes—those that knew how to use guns and wanted to use them. Bobby Seale, the Panthers' chairman, complained that he had had 'problems with a lot of people who come in and use the Party as a base for criminal activity which the Party never endorsed or had anything to do with.'[5] Support for political violence in the United States comes from radical students and conscripts alienated from the system and from right-wing extremists like the Ku Klux Klan or the Minutemen who are prepared to use terror in defence of white supremacy or against a largely illusory communist bogey. But the real danger lies in the grievances of the ethnic minorities.

For several years, America has been dreaming an incendiary nightmare. While black power mavericks and less temperate New Left theorists have promised to 'bring home the Vietnam war', a military analyst has observed that the modern American city provided ideal terrain for guerrilla fighters. 'Vietnam's jungles,' he observes, 'have no elevators and stairwells in their treetops, but city buildings do—and a multitude of vacant rooms to which to flee. No jungle's tree branches are as secure. The degree of security for city guerrillas is almost too imposing to suggest.'[6] He is almost certainly wrong. America's cities are vulnerable to political sabotage, and the black ghettoes might provide the initial sanctuary for a minority revolt, but the real battlefield of the urban guerrilla is in men's minds. The overwhelming majority of the American population are not willing to sanction political violence for revolutionary ends, as the public opinion polls analysed below suggest. On the contrary, a continued escalation of revolutionary violence in America might well drive the country to the right; in the United States, as in other western societies, counter-revolution is both physically and psychologically more likely than revolution. But the choice is a remote one. The two-party system has proved remarkably durable in the United States, and it is not going to be overthrown by a handful of fanatics with Molotov cocktails. Those who talk of America as a 'new' society forget that, in terms of continuity of government, it is the second oldest country in the world—second only to Britain. In the short term, at any rate, the Americans have the instruments to contain communal unrest and the history of the two most prominent urban guerrilla groups (if the term can be applied at all to the Weathermen and the Black Panthers) was brief and undistinguished.

At the same time, the threat of political sabotage to industrial production and the normal functioning of American cities should not be underrated. According to one of the disciples of Robert Williams, the black revolutionary, 'What we must understand is that Charlie's system runs like an IBM machine. But an IBM machine has a weakness, and that weakness is complexity. Put something in the wrong place in an IBM machine and it's finished for a long time.'[7] And a significant upsurge in political violence in America might have global repercussions by imposing constraints on foreign policy and sowing dissent in the ranks of the armed forces. There are signs that this process is already taking place. It is the purpose of this chapter, first, to consider the case-histories of the Weathermen and the Black Panthers, and, second, to examine the limits of minority revolt in the United States and the implications of political violence for the system as a whole.

POLITICS AS PATHOLOGY

The Weathermen, like Charles Manson and his coven of murderers, belong to the pathology rather than the politics of contemporary America. Bernadine Dohrn, the nihilistic amazon who rose to lead the organisation, made that as clear as anyone could possibly have done when she told a Weatherman 'war council' at the end of 1969, after the news of the Tate murders had been announced, 'Dig it, first they killed those pigs, then they ate dinner in the same room with them, then they even shoved a fork into a victim's stomach! Wild!' It was reported that at the same meeting, they adopted as their salute a raised hand with four fingers spread, symbolising Manson's fork.[8] And yet the Weathermen have been described as the practitioners of 'a yoga of perfection'[9] by one sympathetic but critical New Left theorist, and as 'wild and wonderful kids' by one of the doyens of American radical journalism.[10]

As those comments suggest, the Weathermen may be crazed, but the really alarming thing is that they have not always been seen that way. Middle-class America was shocked by the appearance of these youthful urban terrorists who promised to wage war upon society; it had good reason to be. For the Weathermen were an ulcer that had grown up inside the soft centre of American society. The explosion of a hundred sticks of dynamite, some of it packed into lead-pipe bombs, in a Greenwich village townhouse on 6 March 1970 was heavy with symbolism. The blast tore apart a heavily ornate mansion valued at $250,000, the home of a wealthy radio proprietor and former advertising executive who was also the father of a Weatherwoman. It killed three of her friends, Ted Gold, Diana Oughton and Terry Robbins, who had been using the house as a bomb factory.

All of them were the children of affluence.[11] Ted Gold came from an upper-West-Side family of Jewish liberals; Diana Oughton was the daughter of a wealthy Illinois *restaurateur*. Their parents remembered them as dutiful children; their professors, as model or at least middling students who had drifted into the civil rights movement and then into radical organisations like Students for a Democratic Society (SDS). Both groups were at a loss to explain what had gone wrong. Some people talked of the malevolent influence of Weatherman leaders like Mark Rudd, always ready to accuse doubters of cowardice, of the 'compensation' factor in the case of young men like Gold, who was painfully conscious of his shortness and sought release in action, and above all of the general guilt-feeling of privileged students exposed for the first time to the poverty of the ghettoes.

This was characteristic of the American New Left in general. Its 'post-scarcity' origins and its total alienation from the American working-class meant that it was cut off from the traditional sources of left-wing militancy. The roots of the new radicalism lay instead in a vicarious self-identification with black militants and foreign revolutionaries and a wholly destructive urge to tear down the fabric of American society. In the case of the Weathermen, this led to a campaign of terror and to private rituals that resembled a Black Mass designed to exalt everything that ran contrary to traditional morality: orgy in place of monogamy, the drug culture in place of reason, evil (incarnated by Charles Manson) in place of good.

The one major achievement of the Weathermen was to divide and
eventually destroy the radical student movement from which they
emerged. Founded in 1960, SDS gathered support as the anti-
Vietnam-war campaign intensified. It was originally conceived as a
radical lobby within the Democratic Party, but after the Berkeley
revolt in 1964, it moved rapidly further to the left and took up the
cause of 'student power'. In 1966, it joined forces with a Maoist
group, the Progressive Labor Party. By 1968, when SDS spearheaded a campaign against university research institutes working
on government contracts, its leaders claimed to have recruited
35,000 members. The figure may have been inflated, but draft
resistance and growing disenchantment with the Vietnam war, as
well as the example of campus revolts in other countries, had promoted student radicalism in America. In 1965, there were radical
student organisations on 25 per cent of American campuses; three
years later, the figure had climbed to 46 per cent.[12] But SDS was
already falling apart. The leaders agreed that the organisation should
look for mass support outside the universities. But while the
Progressive Laborites maintained that this should be done by
appealing to the interests of American industrial labour, another
faction—that later gave birth to the Weathermen—insisted that
revolution could only be brought about through a coalition between
black power groups, third world rebels, and white radicals. It was
this faction that won in June 1969, when (by characteristically un-
democratic methods) it expelled the Progressive Labor faction from
SDS without taking a vote.

During the June meeting, the first Weatherman manifesto was
made public. It took its title from a line in a Bob Dylan song, 'You
don't need a Weatherman to know which way the wind blows'. This
document reflected a view of revolution in which the white American
community as a whole was regarded as an essentially conservative
force. The Weathermen regarded themselves merely as white
auxiliaries in a global war in which the front-line soldiers would be
coloured men:

> The goal is the destruction of US imperialism and the achieve-
> ment of a classless world: world communism. Winning state power
> in the US will occur as the result of the military forces of the US

overextending themselves around the world and being defeated piecemeal; struggle within the US will be a vital part of this process, but when the revolution triumphs in the US it will have been made by the people of the whole world. For socialism to be defined in national terms within so extreme and historical an oppressor nation as this is only imperialist national chauvinism.[13]

According to this view, the American radical left would perform a kind of collective throat-cutting exercise. It would forfeit any chance of winning a following among white Americans in order to tear down American society in the dimly-defined interests of foreign peoples and minority groups. It was a doctrine unlikely to win support except among the handful of youthful nihilists who relished the idea of national and class suicide.

That became clear when the Weathermen entered their 'street-fighting' phase later in 1969. On October 8, on a grey, drizzling afternoon, a few hundred Weathermen rallied round Vietcong flags in Chicago's Lincoln Park to commemorate the deaths of Che Guevara and the Vietnamese communist, Nguyen Van Troi. It was an obscure pageant to passers-by, but it turned out to be a violent one. On the first of their 'Days of Rage', the Weathermen roved around the affluent 'Gold Coast' district of Chicago, smashing car-windows and shop-fronts and lighting fires. They caused more than $1 million worth of damage—little enough by comparison with the negro rioters on whom they modelled themselves, but quite enough to provoke the arrest of some 300 demonstrators by the end of the week.

Dressed up in helmets and combat boots, the Weathermen also set out to provoke the 4,600 police and National Guardsmen who had been called out to contain them. Hatred of the police was central to the limited ideology of the Weathermen. It was as if they could only define their cause by conjuring up a bogey of repression to hurl themselves against. One of the student-demonstrators on October 8 later explained his reason for participating in the riots in the following terms: 'You hate the pigs so much you want to kill them. We may lose militarily, but by smashing pigs we will win in the eyes of the workers.'[14] In fact, what the people watching television saw was a disciplined police force (in sharp contrast to the police brutality during the riots in Chicago the previous October) confronting a handful of savage provocateurs.

The relationship between the police and militant groups is examined in more detail below. But it is worth noting how the attitude of the Weathermen towards the police confirmed their upper-middle-class origins as well as their doctrinaire arrogance and calculated tactic of confrontation. In one of their manifestoes, the Weathermen described the police as 'sweaty working-class barbarians' and observed that, by identifying the police with the system as a whole, militants could use them as the 'glue that holds the movement together'. [15]

The march on Chicago showed the full extent of the Weathermen's lack of support. There was an even poorer turnout for the second march on Saturday, October 11. Weatherman attempts at political agitation up to this point had been very sketchy. In Detroit, for example, the 'Motor City Collective' had staged impromptu lectures on the beach, invaded classrooms (including a university examination room where final-year sociology students were far from pleased to be interrupted) and circulated pamphlets at drive-in cinemas.[16] There were also close contacts with the Black Panthers—although the Panthers became cooler as they came to realise that the Weathermen were heading down a blind alley.

The Weathermen decided to abandon legal political activities altogether during their 'war council' held in Flint, Michigan, in December 1969. The decision to go underground was influenced by the fact that twelve leading Weathermen had been indicted on major felony charges resulting from the Chicago 'Days of Rage'. The 'war council' was almost a parody of the Weatherman's style: the Giant Ballroom in Flint was decked out with posters of Ho Chi Minh and Guevara, with a huge cardboard machine-gun dangling from the ceiling. One of the Weathermen at the meeting suggested that they should change their name to Vandals, after the barbarian tribe that invaded Rome. A Weatherwoman who later left the organisation commented on the 'near-orgy state' to which the members had descended: the talks sessions were punctuated by heavy drug-taking and indiscriminate sex. The Weathermen agreed on a terrorist strategy designed to create 'strategic armed chaos' in the major cities and 'a context in which mass public action happens'. These targets were not defined in any rational way. Members of the group were to be given *carte blanche* to undertake terrorist actions as the opportunity arose: 'Armed struggle starts when someone starts it.' The collectives in which the Weathermen had lived during 1969 were to be broken up into cells, or 'affinity groups' of three or four people. 'Our political objective,' according to one statement, 'is the destruction of honkiness.'[17] In hip vernacular, this appeared to mean the end of the way of life of the families from which the Weathermen had sprung.

All this made a mockery of Bernadine Dohrn's later claim that 'we are adapting the classic guerrilla strategy of the Viet Cong and the urban guerrilla strategy of the Tupamaros to our own situation here in the most technically advanced country in the world.'[18] The degree of understanding of genuine revolutionary theory among the Weathermen is perhaps best conveyed by a few verses from one of their songs (sung to the tune of 'Maria'):

> The most beautiful sound I ever heard
> Kim Il Sung
> Kim Il Sung, Kim Il Sung, Kim Il Sung
> The most beautiful sound in all the world
> Kim Il Sung . . .
> Say it soft and there's rice fields flowing
> Say it loud and there's people's war growing . . .
> I'll never stop saying Kim Il Sung[19]

In the year that followed, the Weathermen claimed responsibility for the bombing of the New York City police headquarters on June 9, and the bombing of a New York branch of the Bank of America on July 27. They were probably responsible for some of the thousands of other political bombings that took place over this period. Their most dramatic action was to spring Dr Timothy Leary, the apologist for LSD and the drug culture, from the prison at San Luis Obispo in California where he was being held in loose confinement on a drugs charge. Bernadine Dohrn had already claimed that 'guns and grass are united in the underground'. The Weatherman's attempt to make out that Leary was a 'political prisoner' was an even clearer illustration of the link they were trying to establish between hippie-dom and political radicalism.

According to their 'Communiqué No. 4', drugs like LSD, 'like the herbs and cactus and mushrooms of the American Indians and countless civilisations that have existed on this planet, will help us to make a future world where it will be possible to live in peace.'[20] The Weathermen at least managed to find sanctuary among the hippies and the drop-out communes. By the middle of 1971, the FBI were still hunting for Dohrn, Rudd and other leaders, although they had arrested two other leading members, Linda Evans and Diana Donghi, in April, 1970.

But by the end of 1970, after a year of hiding and running, some of the Weathermen were ready to admit defeat. In October, one Weatherman statement of self-criticism spoke of the criminal irre-sponsibility that was symbolised by the leaflet circulated by the movement that contained instructions for making simple explosives over the slogan 'Be Creative—Experiment'.[21] And in December, Bernadine Dohrn herself was ready to concede that a political sys-tem does not crumble because someone throws a few bombs at police stations: 'Most of our actions have hurt the enemy on about the same military level as a bee-sting.'[22]

The Weathermen are significant not as urban guerrillas (they lacked the political understanding, the popular base, and the technical expertise that involves) but because in their nihilism and their lust for self-immolation they represented an attitude to society that may lead other white western radicals to participate in sporadic acts of terror. One ex-Weatherwoman has discussed the 'structural incentives which induce psychological violence' that were embodied in the Weathermen communes—for example, the 'status system' that graded members according to their readiness to go out and blow things up and distorted system of values that glorified violence for its own sake.[23] Alienation is taking increasingly violent forms in America. In 1965, according to figures compiled by the radical *Scanlan's Magazine*, there were 16 'guerrilla acts of sabotage and terrorism' in the United States. By 1968, the figure had risen to 236. By 1970, it stood at 546.

In addition to the Weathermen, dozens of tiny groups of radical 'bombers' and unstable individuals have set out to attack the capitalist system through attacks on property. According to official estimates, there were 4,330 incendiary bombings in the United States in the fifteen months up to April 1970, and the targets included banks, universities, high school buildings, company offices and military installations.[24] The sabotage has not always been simply a matter of primitive dynamite-bombs: in California in 1968, bulldozers were used to knock down transmission towers belonging to the Pacific Gas and Electricity Company and in a singularly bizarre incident in the same state, a single-engine plane dropped a fire bomb over the Van Nuys air force base.

Attempts to rationalise the bombings were hardly designed to win over public opinion. A group calling itself 'Revolutionary Force 9' claimed responsibility for synchronised explosions at the New York offices of Mobil Oil, IBM and the General Telephone and Electric Company in March 1970. In a letter to the UPI press agency, the group 'explained' that their target companies were 'the enemies of all life', responsible not only for prolonging the Vietnam war, but also for such obscurer crimes as 'encouraging sexism' and 'the degradation of employees'. Another group, styling itself the 'Volunteers of America', sent a letter to the *San Francisco Chronicle* after bombing the Bank of America's Santa Barbara branch in June 1970, in which they claimed that the bank was responsible for 'the starvation of farmworkers' and likened its role to that of 'the German financiers during the rise of Hitler'. An alarming feature of the bombings has been the mounting number of attacks on secondary schools and individual teachers. Embittered high school students have been able to buy simple explosives through the mails.

The bomb attacks have forced both the administration and individual companies and school boards to spend more on security. After a bombing at the University of Wisconsin in 1969, for example, the state legislature voted an extra $1 million for campus security: which was used to finance electronic surveillance equipment and to provide overtime pay for 170 Madison City policemen who agreed to guard the campus in their off-duty hours. But random acts of sabotage have not impeded the workings of the American economy, although such forms of indiscriminate terror have sometimes built up a climate of fear and anticipation in which a further escalation of violence is possible.

The Weathermen and the radical 'bombers' are part of the lunatic fringe of American society. They cannot be regarded as a political force or as urban guerrillas in any meaningful sense. Their record also suggests that it will be extremely difficult for New Left radicals to win any significant support for a programme of political violence in other western societies. Terrorism without popular backing is not a strategy for anything, and people will support political violence only if they have no choice or believe that the government lacks legitimacy. In the United States, as in all western societies, the overwhelming majority of the population is on the side of the existing order. But there is a difference between the attitudes of the white community and those of the negro population that must be taken into account.

Public opinion polls conducted over the past decade have shown that the overwhelming majority of the white community has been willing to support tough measures in defence of domestic order. One poll conducted during the 1968 ghetto riots—to take a random example—showed that at least two-thirds of white Americans thought that looters and fire-bombers should be simply shot down in the streets.[25] In a similar poll, some 56 per cent of white Americans agreed that 'any man who insults a policeman has no complaint if he gets roughed up in return'.[26] In contrast, negro attitudes have become more rather than less radical over the past decade, despite striking improvements in the socio-economic and legal position of the black community. A Harris poll published in March 1970, showed that 9 per cent of negroes across the United States considered themselves as 'revolutionaries' and thought that only 'a readiness to use violence will ever get them equality'. The same poll also revealed that the proportion of black Americans who believed that they would 'probably have to resort to violence to win rights' had gone up from 21 per cent in 1966 to 31 per cent in 1970. The difference between black and white attitudes was even more striking when the public opinion pollsters focused on individual institutions, like the police. A 1967 poll showed that, while 51 per cent of whites in the $6–10,000 income bracket thought that the police did a 'very good' job in protecting people in their neighbourhoods, only 17 per cent of non-whites in the same salary range shared the same opinion.[27]

What all these figures point to is a *legitimacy gap* of the kind that was discussed in an earlier chapter. The fact that, according to one opinion poll, nearly a third of the negro community do not have faith in peaceful change is not peculiar to American society. Similar answers would probably have been given by Catholics in Northern Ireland, and perhaps also by the French Canadians in Quebec. The social values of the majority groups in those three democracies are not shared by a sizeable proportion of the minority groups. That provides an opening for revolutionary organisations: some two-thirds of black Americans, according to an April 1970 poll, said that they approved of what the Black Panthers were doing.[28]

THE BLACK PANTHERS

The Panthers differ from 'black racist' groups like the Black Muslims because they believe in the need for a 'revolutionary alliance' between negro militants, white radicals, and third world rebel movements. They quarrelled with the black power militant Stokely Carmichael (who briefly figured as 'prime minister' of the Panthers) over this issue. The Black Panthers were by no means the first negro organisation to take up arms in the cause of 'self-defence'. During the civil rights campaigns of the 1950s and early 1960s, groups of armed negroes banded together in the South to defend themselves against the terror of the Ku Klux Klan and other white supremacist societies. In 1959, Robert F. Williams—later the chairman of the extremist Revolutionary Action Movement (RAM)—first came to national prominence when the Union County Superior Court in North Carolina acquitted two white men of brutal assaults on two black women, but sent a mentally retarded negro to jail for arguing with a white woman. Williams, then a district organiser of the National Association for the Advancement of Colored People (NAACP), told a reporter after the sentences had been passed that 'We cannot take these people who do us injustice to the court, and it becomes necessary to punish them outside. If it's necessary to stop lynching with lynching, then we must be ready to resort to that method.'[29] That logic carried Williams a long way. Charged with kidnapping a white couple in 1961, he fled the country and took refuge in China and Cuba. He espoused the idea of a 'minority revolution' in which black guerrillas would seize the big cities and set up a separate republic in the South. His Northern-based organisation, RAM, schemed to murder moderate negro leaders like Whitney Young and was rumoured to have received a $1 million donation from the Chinese.[30]

The Black Panther Party for Self-Defense was founded in Oakland, the ghetto suburb of San Francisco, at the end of 1966. The name, according to Huey P. Newton, one of the founders and the Panthers' 'minister of defence', was chosen because 'the panther never strikes first, but when it is backed into a corner, he will strike back viciously'.[31] The 'self-defence' tag was soon dropped, but the Panthers always claimed to be using the threat of violence to counter the 'violence of the system'. In fact, their initial ten-point programme went very far beyond the limited goal of communal defence, although it was moderate by comparison with later statements. The first part of this programme, entitled 'What We Want', ran as follows:

1 We want freedom. We want power to determine the destiny of our Black Community.
2 We want full employment for our people.
3 We want an end to the robbery by the white man of our Black Community.
4 We want decent housing, fit for the shelter of human beings.
5 We want education for our people that exposes the true nature of this decadent American society. We want education that teaches us our true history and our role in the present-day society.
6 We want all black men to be exempt from military service.
7 We want an immediate end to police brutality and murder of black people.
8 We want freedom for all black men held in federal, state, county and city prisons and jails.
9 We want all black people when brought to trial to be tried in court by a jury of their peer group or people from their black communities, as defined by the Constitution of the United States.
10 We want land, bread, housing, education, clothing, justice and peace. And as our major political objective, a United Nations-

supervised plebiscite to be held throughout the black colony in which only black colonial subjects will be allowed to participate, for the purpose of determining the will of the black people as to their national destiny.[32]

The Panthers had already defined the negro community as a 'colony' inside the 'mother country'. Their demand for communal self-determination led them to align themselves with separatists like Robert Williams, although they remained insistent that an American revolution could not be brought about without white allies. The white allies that the Panthers actually found represented various marginal political groups. There was a period (lampooned superbly by Tom Wolfe) when east coast liberals considered it fashionable to hold fund-raising parties for the Panthers. The Panthers had some communist links. William L. Patterson, a veteran black communist, praised them in 1967 as 'the first black-led organization to understand the menace of anti-Communism and unqualifiedly to express opposition to it'.[33] Eldridge Cleaver and his wife Kathleen leaned further towards the communists than the other Panther leaders. Cleaver himself was put forward as the presidential candidate of the Progress and Freedom Party (a radical movement based in California) in the 1968 elections.

Although their political goal was revolution, the Panthers originally decided not to begin terrorist operations. This was essentially a tactical decision. Kathleen Cleaver wrote in 1968, for example, that 'the only questions are tactical and practical; how to exercise what kind of violence with what kind of preparations and for what ends.'[34] The Panthers wanted to stay on the right side of the law until they believed the conditions were ripe for revolution. Their recruiting techniques struck a rather different tone from their ten-point programme. The Panthers' appeal for the young negro on the block was not essentially political. It was an appeal to *machismo*, to the desire to prove oneself a man. Eldridge Cleaver recalls the impact that the first glimpse of a Panther squad dressed in their black berets, shiny leather jackets and sky-blue turtle-neck sweaters made on him. Above all, there were the guns. In the months after the Panthers were founded, Newton and Bobby Seale (the party's chairman) would go down to the street-corner flourishing their guns and tell the youths hanging about of how they were going to organise commando squads that would murder policemen and drop Molotov cocktails into strategic industrial installations once the signal was given.[35] As Seale later admitted, this meant that they roped in a lot of young thugs that he called 'jackanapes', people purely concerned with flaunting their weapons, stealing from supermarkets, and provoking the police. Most of the Panthers' recruits came from the street-gangs and petty criminals of the ghettoes. On the other hand, the Panthers also stressed the importance of 'revolutionary' social work—serving free breakfasts to black school-children and arranging free medical services. This helped them to win popularity among the negro poor. The money for these projects was mostly collected or extorted from ghetto businessmen and shopkeepers.

In order simply to survive as a legal organisation, the Panthers took care to abide by the gun-laws and stressed their 'self-defence' functions. But in their party newspaper, the *Black Panther*, they practised the rhetoric of vilification. If constant police harrassment, the illegal invasion of Panther apartments, and the arrest of Panther leaders on what sometimes appeared to be trumped-up charges seemed to substantiate their claims that the authorities were out to wreck them as an organisation, the Panthers themselves were partly responsible. They were guilty of extreme provocation and incitement to violence. A description of 'revolutionary art' published in the party newspaper is a fair specimen:

> This is revolutionary art—pigs lying in alley ways of the colony with their eyes gouged out—autopsy showing cause of death: 'They fail to see that the majority rules.' Pictures we draw show them choking to death from their inhuman ways—these are the kinds of pictures revolutionary artists draw—
>
> The Viet Cong stabbing him in his brain—black people taking the hearts of the enemy and hanging the hearts on the wall (put one more notch on our knife) skin them alive and make rugs out of them—
>
> We must draw pictures of Southern cracker Wallace with cancer of the mouth that he got from his dead witch's uterus . . .[36]

This was not an isolated statement that somehow eluded the editor's eye. It was characteristic of the language regularly used by the Panthers. In court and on television, Panther spokesmen often argued that their vocabulary was 'the language of the ghettoes' and should not be taken as a guide to what they actually planned to do. It was certainly true that the Panthers' actions trailed far behind their threats. But (as was argued earlier) the rhetoric of vilification is a preliminary and an incitement both to violence and counter-violence, as a second item published in the *Black Panther* suggests:

> America, you will be cleansed with fire, by blood, by death. We who perform your ablution must step up our burning—bigger and better fires, one flame for all America, an all-American flame; we must step up our looting—loot, until we storm your last hoarding place, till we trample your last stolen jewel into your ashes beneath our naked black feet; we must step up our sniping—until the last pig is dead, shot to death with his own gun and the bullets in his guts that he had meant for the people . . .[37]

There are not many societies that would allow the publication of this hymn to murder, pillage and arson. The problem for white America was whether or not to take this kind of thing seriously. For example, there was a minor uproar among liberal sympathisers when David Hilliard, the Panthers' chief of staff, was arrested on charges of having advocated the assassination of President Nixon. America's tragic history of high-level assassinations makes this kind of charge particularly sensitive. When Hilliard was asked to give account of himself before a television audience, he refused to give a straight answer to the question: Had he been misquoted when he was alleged to have said 'We should kill President Nixon'? Hilliard said to begin with that this 'was a statement that I made in the frame-work of a lot of other words'. Then he flatly denied having used that specific phrase about killing Nixon. When contradicted by a journalist who had been present when he made the offending speech in San Francisco and quoted him as saying, 'We will kill Richard Nixon. We will kill anyone, any blankety-blank who stands in the way of our freedom,' Hilliard tried yet another line. What he had said in San Francisco, he now maintained, was 'political rhetoric. We can call it metaphor. It is the language of the ghetto.'[38] Maybe. But this particular incident showed very clearly the problem that American justice faced in dealing with the Panthers. When were

they to be taken at their word? When a political crime had actually
been committed? It was the familiar dilemma of democracy confronted with the threat of political violence.

The problem has to be faced squarely. The Panthers never posed
a serious *military* threat to American society, although the capacity
of a disciplined black militant force to wreak havoc in the cities
should not be underrated. The House Internal Security Committee
reported in August 1971, that the Panthers had contributed to the
steady escalation of violence in America but had never constituted
'a clear and present danger to the continued functioning of the US
government or any other institutions of our democratic society'. [39]
The Committee rightly concluded that the Panthers' rhetoric had
'always exceeded their performance' and calculated that the peak
strength of the party had only been between 1,500 and 2,000. It
might be added that, from the very beginning, the Panthers were
closely watched and thoroughly infiltrated by police agents. The
Panthers' own slap-happy recruiting methods made it a simple
matter to get informers inside the movement, and as many as six
police undercover agents testified at the trial of two Panthers
charged with conspiracy in 1970. [40]

But the Panthers did pose a major problem for American justice.
It was easy enough for the police to deal with them *effectively*.
But in order not to alienate negro opinion, it was necessary for the
police to show that they had dealt with them *fairly*. By 1969, all of
the Panthers' original leaders had been imprisoned or (like Cleaver)
had fled the country. A lawyer sympathetic to the Panthers told the
press that between New Year's Day and Christmas 1969, a total of
twenty-eight Panthers had been killed by the police, sometimes
under ambiguous circumstances. The most controversial case
involved the death of two Chicago Panthers, Fred Hampton and
Mark Clark, who were killed when police invaded their apartment
on 4 December 1969. A federal grand jury heard evidence that they
had been asleep at the time, and charges against another seven
Panthers who had been with them in the same apartment were
dropped. The attorney of Cook County State, Edward Hanrahan (a
protégé of the mayor of Chicago, Richard Daley) was later indicted
by a special grand jury on charges of having conspired to prevent

the prosecution of the eight policemen responsible for the killings.[41]

The Chicago killings were among many cases of 'police harass-ment' alleged by the Panthers.[42] Many of the charges pressed against the Panthers in court failed to stick. Apart from the seven Chicago Panthers mentioned above, there was by mid-1971 a long list of militants who had been released from jail after the prosecution failed to obtain convictions. These included the 'New York 13', whose trial had dragged on for eight noisy, riotous months; Bobby Seale and Erica Huggins, charged with ordering the murder of a fellow-Panther in Connecticut; and twelve New York Panthers acquitted by a black-majority jury on a charge of having attempted to murder a police squad.[43] The trial, retrial and mistrial of Huey Newton on a charge of having murdered an Oakland policeman early in 1968 provided the Panthers with a durable *cause célèbre*. If the conditions under which some Panthers were arrested or killed or kept in jail for long periods without trial cast doubt on the actions of the state police in Chicago and Oakland, the fact that so many were acquitted showed that Kingman Brewster, the President of Yale University, was (happily) wrong when he publicly doubted whether a leading Panther could get a fair trial in America. But not everyone saw things that way. The response of Panther sympathisers to the death of 'Soledad brother' George Jackson on 21 August 1971, showed the depths of their alienation and their distrust of the American judicial system. According to the official account, Jackson was killed by guards while trying to escape from San Quentin prison. But many of those who had read the descriptions of jail brutality in his prison letters were ready to jump to the conclusion that he had been 'murdered', ignoring the fact that five whites in San Quentin—three guards and two trustees—had also been killed.

By mid-1971, the Panthers had fallen apart as an organisation. They were divided between the Newton and the Cleaver factions. The rift stemmed both from a personal squabble and a policy debate. It first developed after two New York Panthers, Richard Moore and Paul Tabor, jumped bail of $150,000 and fled to Algiers to join Cleaver in exile. Newton, outraged by their actions (which pre-judiced the case of ten Panthers who were still awaiting trial on the same conspiracy charge) expelled them from the party. Cleaver

demanded that they should be re-admitted. A bitter slanging-match
ensued, and the dirt fell thick and fast. Newton accused Cleaver, for
example, of keeping his wife locked up and of persecuting her 'lover'
(allegedly a fellow-Panther) while he enjoyed his own extensive
personal harem. Meanwhile, their supporters waged a gangland
battle for supremacy in Harlem. On 9 March 1971, one of Cleaver's
followers, Robert Webb, was gunned down in broad daylight in
Harlem, and the following month, Samuel Napier—one of Newton's
supporters—was found strangled, supposedly in retaliation. By the
beginning of May, Newton claimed to have won control of 38 of
the Panthers' 40 branches. But he inherited only the wreckage of the
organisation. Temporarily at liberty after the court declared a mistrial of his murder case, Newton indulged in self-criticism before a
university audience at the end of May. He admitted that the policy
of confrontation with the police had been ill-conceived: 'All we got
was war and bloodshed.' He declared that the Panthers were now
ready 'to operate within the system to see whether we can change it.
It is wrong to say the system cannot give you anything because it
just is not true.' He even said he would give his support to church
charity work. Eldridge Cleaver, on the other hand, still clings to the
idea that the moment is ripe for guerrilla operations in the United
States.[44]

GHETTO REVOLT

Whether or not the Panthers re-emerge as a potential guerrilla
force or are replaced by another militant group, it is important to
consider the broader prospects for ghetto revolt in the United
States. The experience of the Panthers suggests that while the
spectacle of an armed revolutionary group may appeal to ghetto
machismo and the basic craving for dignity and power, only a small
proportion of black Americans are ready to assist a militant organisation at this stage. The ghetto riots of the 1960s showed the depths
of black frustration but were an essentially pre-political phenomenon.
The Kerner Report on Civil Disorders generalised that 'while there
have been elements calling for a revolutionary overthrow of the
American social system or for a complete withdrawal of Negroes

from American society . . . these solutions have had little popular support. Negro protest, for the most part, has been firmly rooted in the basic values of American society, seeking not their destruction but their fulfilment.'[45] The future stability of America's cities is bound up with whether the system can satisfy those demands. The Kerner Report also claimed that by 1985, the Negro population of the major cities would have risen to just under 21 million. 'Coupled with the continued mass exodus of white families to the suburbs, this growth will produce majority Negro populations in many of the nation's largest cities.' But the future of these inner urban areas is grim. New industry and new employment opportunities are moving out to the white suburbs, so that the cities of America are assuming the pattern of a bull's-eye target: in the centre, the old hub of commerce, surrounded by the black ghettoes, with an outer ring of affluent white suburbs.

But the flight of white Americans to the suburbs is not a one-way process. First, there are the poorer whites who find it hardest to move and hang on at the fringes of the black ghettoes. It may be exaggerated to talk of a 'white ghetto' but the resentments and frustrations of the low-income white Americans have been too long ignored and are already taking explosive form. The problem of white poverty is probably greatest in the depressed farming zones of the South.[46] Second, as a recent study of the Cleveland riots of 1967 showed, negroes with steady incomes are tending to move out of the ghettoes, leaving behind those at the very bottom of the social scale. Increasingly, the black ghettoes of Cleveland or Chicago are not simply racial enclaves, but islands of deepening poverty.[47] A negro left behind in the 'riot zones' of a major city while a more enterprising neighbour moves out to a new factory job in the suburbs will feel an acuter sense of frustration and is more likely to join a rioting mob on a hot summer night. The fact that the black ghettoes are often located close to traditional centres of commerce or command vital services and communications like railway-lines, power-stations and gasworks makes racial unrest an immediate threat to the normal functioning of the economy.

An Australian writer, Alan Seymour, tried to sketch out the scenario for a second American civil war in his recent novel, *The*

Coming Self-Destruction of the United States of America.[48] Seymour pictured a disciplined 'Black Communist' movement sparking off a race war by the systematic assassination of white policemen and Wall Street businessmen. The Black Communists seize control of the ghettoes in major northern cities and set fire to whole blocks of tenements in order to drive the negroes into neighbouring white residential areas as an occupying force. By this means, they manage to take over several important cities and hold the white suburbs 'hostage'. Where black moderate leaders oppose their plans, they are simply murdered. They are aided and abetted by New Left elements and nihilist hippies who are uncharitably called the 'White Dropouts'. The conclusion? After an initial period of vacillation in which the army cordons off the 'occupied areas' and white vigilante groups are allowed to run amok, the government decides to pull the stops out and retaliate in force—regardless of the fate of the white hostages. The story ends, implausibly, with a military junta ensconced in Washington, holding the threat of nuclear weapons over the heads of the Black Communists who have pulled back to two Southern cities.

Seymour's novel is of course only political science fiction. It is highly unlikely, to begin with, that a black guerilla movement would be able to achieve the nationwide network his scenario presupposes without being broken up by the authorities somewhere along the line. And the scenario minimises the role of the moderate black leadership, which will almost certainly manage to contain the extremists. The Whitney Youngs of America are likely to prove more durable figures than the Eldridge Cleavers. But Seymour's scenario is close enough to the ideas of black militants like Robert Williams to be worth thinking about.

Williams has mapped out a plan for a black revolutionary move-ment that would be divided into three groups: armed self-defence squads operating openly on the model of the Black Panthers under the protection of the gun-laws; underground cells that would be used to 'stiffen' the riots and turn them into mass assaults on the police; and a chain of terrorist commandos and 'fire teams' who would be responsible for systematic sabotage and assassination. The terrorists would pose as 'patriots' and 'moderates' in order to infiltrate high-security organisations, including the police and the army. Their prime targets during an insurrection would be transport and communications in the big cities, followed up by random attacks on corporation buildings and military barracks. The 'fire teams' would try to excite a panic response among whites and throw the cities into chaos. Williams took a crazed arsonist's delight in the idea of lighting 'strategic fires' all across the United States. Fires in public parks and tenement buildings would be used to divert the security forces, to cut inter-city communications, and 'to elicit panic and a feeling of impending doom'. The final target would be the creation of 'liberated zones' in the Deep South. Williams' broader political aims can be shrugged off as apocalyptic nonsense. But he does prove that a sufficiently fanatical terrorist group could pose the threat of economic blackmail.

Racial tension has also affected the fighting capacity of the American armed forces. One of the most serious immediate effects of radical dissent in the United States has been to divide and demoralise a largely conscript army. Dissent in the ranks is clearly bound up with the fact that America has been fighting a prolonged, inconclusive and controversial war in Vietnam with conscripts. Eldridge Cleaver has declared in his quasi-apocalyptic way that 'the stockades in Babylon are full of soldiers who refuse to fight. These men are going to become some of the most valuable guerrilla fighters.' There was some basis for this statement. An opinion poll conducted among Black soldiers serving in Vietnam at the end of 1969 produced some alarming evidence of the strength of radical feeling in the ranks. Some 36 per cent of black combat troops answered 'yes' to the question: 'Do you plan to join a militant group like the Black Panthers or Students for a Democratic Society when you return home.' 6 per cent of black officers responded in the same way, and the average for all black soldiers interviewed was 31 per cent.[49]

No doubt many of the men who were interviewed would behave differently once they actually got home; but it does appear that disaffected conscripts have provided the American underground with arms, instruction and trained recruits. Many of the units in Vietnam had become mutinous and drug-ridden by the end of 1970, and officers who tried to restore discipline were threatened or physically attacked. There is an example in the treatment of Colonel Weldon Honeycutt, the man who led the costly attack on 'Hamburger Hill', when he returned to the United States to have his medals pinned on. An underground newspaper called *GI Says* published a 'wanted poster' describing Colonel Honeycutt as 'GI Enemy Number 1' and offering a $10,000 reward to whoever got rid of him. This appears to have been something more than black humour, since the notice was followed up by several attempts on his life.

The race factor has added to the dissension in the ranks of the army. Fighting between black and white soldiers not only became commonplace in Vietnam, but spread to some of the American bases on the Rhine, and there was also black rioting in 1970 at Ford Hood and the riot control training centre in Kansas. Characteristically, radical activists tried to pit conscripted men against officers and professional soldiers. A group of radical 'bombers' who attacked a military police post in San Francisco in 1970 declared, for example, that 'We consider the GI to be a civilian, whereas we consider the lifers and the military structure to be a structure which is evolving to a more Gestapo-type experience.' Muddy and wrong-headed thinking; but the situation in the lower ranks of the armed forces is likely to hasten a programme of reversion to a purely professional force. That would mean a smaller, if more reliable, army and would diminish America's capacity to maintain its present troop levels in Europe and to send expeditionary forces abroad. It may be that, for the outside world, the most important effect of continuing civil violence and radical dissent in the United States is that it will further inhibit the nation's capacity to act as a great power outside its own shores.

4
Ulster: The Guns Speak

The position of the Catholic community in Northern Ireland differs from that of ethnic and religious minorities in other independent states. In the view of Irish republicans and some Marxist analysts, Northern Ireland is in a 'colonial' situation: the Protestant majority are seen as 'settlers' and the British government as the 'metropolitan power'.[1] These people believe that the future of the province will not be settled until it is united with the Republic of Ireland. There are many reasons why, for the moment, that view of things is unrealistic. The most forceful is that basic changes in the constitution of Northern Ireland would only be viable if they won the approval of a majority of the Protestant community—it would be a violation of the basic principles of democracy to attempt to impose a solution from outside. The majority of the Protestants are determined to remain part of the United Kingdom, and there is every indication that they would fight to the hilt to resist being ruled from Dublin. While it is arguable that over a long period of economic exchange and political dialogue, the two parts of Ireland might come closer together, the effect of the campaign of terrorism waged by the IRA in the North has been to drive them farther apart. A unilateral declaration of independence by the Protestant right is more likely than peaceful unification of Ireland. What must be hoped is that a settlement can be found within the British framework.

All the same, it may be useful to define Northern Ireland as a *quasi*-colonial situation in order to understand the tactics of the IRA. Their political hopes are based on the idea that they can provoke a failure of the will at Westminster that would lead a British government to hand the province over to Dublin. They achieved a limited success in the terrorist campaign that followed the arrival of the British army in Ulster in August 1969. By late 1971, their actions had triggered off a bitter political debate in which the British

89

government, the British Labour Party, the Dublin government and
the Stormont opposition were all offering different solutions for the
security crisis and the future of the province was in doubt. The IRA
campaign helped to polarise the Protestant and Catholic communities and undermined the effect of the comprehensive reform programme that a series of moderate Unionist governments at Stormont
had promoted in the teeth of the resistance of the Protestant right.
To understand how this situation arose, it is necessary to take
account of the violent history of Ireland and the social and political
context into which the IRA terrorists inserted themselves.

Ireland is a kind of quicksand that sucks the observer down into
the morasses of its past. The Irish themselves sometimes seem to
be engaged in a macabre competition to raise the dead. In one
corner, there are the Orangemen decked out in their bowler hats,
orange sashes and furled umbrellas who turn out every July and
August in Belfast and Londonderry to the beat of the Lambeg drums
to relive seventeenth-century victories over a Catholic dynasty. On
the other side, there are Republicans suckled on Fenian history and
the words of Padraig Pearse (who said that patriotism 'is in large
part a memory of heroic dead men and a striving to accomplish some
task left unfinished by them')[2] who seem to cherish their bloody
tradition of insurrection, martyrdom and betrayal as Englishmen
cleave to their own heritage of bloodless reform and social integration.

It is impossible to comprehend the communal violence and urban
terrorism that is going on in Northern Ireland today without taking
account of popular attitudes that are completely alien to the rest of
the United Kingdom. Even the patterns of violence are turned into
ritual. There were plenty of precedents for the communal rioting in
Belfast and Londonderry that was triggered off by the civil rights
demonstrations of 1968 and 1969.[3] Between 1857 and 1912, there
were seven bloody mob-battles between Protestants and Catholics
in Belfast, and some of them had to be brought under control by
British troops equipped with artillery. There was more communal
violence after the partition of Ireland in 1921, when gangs of
Protestant roughnecks terrified of being eventually absorbed by the
Catholic majority in the South descended on the Catholic quarters
of Belfast and drove families from their homes. The city of Belfast

was placed under a curfew for more than four years in the early 1920s. Of course, the roots of communal violence in the North go back to Elizabethan and Cromwellian times, when Scots and English settlers hounded Catholics from their lands and the Protestant ascendancy was first established.

Over several centuries, the Protestant hegemony was upheld by the use or threat of terror by private groups ranging from the 'Peep O'Day Boys' to the Orange Lodges or the Ulster Volunteer Force. During much of this period, the relationship between Protestant and Catholic in Ireland as a whole could be described as 'colonial' or 'racial'. It was not the difference in religion that really counted; it was the difference in wealth and power. But in the North, religion did serve to mask the social divide between the Protestant middle-class and Protestant working-men whose living standards were sometimes comparable with those of the Catholic slums. It is a curious psychological fact that in Ulster, as in overtly 'racial' situations like Algeria or the southern states of America, it is this class of 'poor whites' that has been most easily led into sectarian violence in response to imagined threats to its interests or social identity.[4]

Political terrorism also has hoary antecedents in Ireland as a whole. Under various names and in successive incarnations, the Irish Republican Army has been active since the mid-nineteenth century. The cyclical ebb and wane of its fortunes opposed it to the British, the government in Dublin and the government in the North—and sometimes to all three at once. The IRA was the spearhead of the Anglo–Irish war that began with the Easter Uprising in Dublin in 1916. The casualties of that war were not great in comparison with later independence struggles: 600 killed and 1,200 wounded on the British side; 750-odd IRA men killed and 866 wounded. Nor did it lead to any kind of military victory. But 3,000 IRA men managed to tie up some 43,000 British troops, together with police and auxiliaries. Ireland became an increasing burden to the exchequer, while news of atrocities committed by the 'Black and Tans' and the police Auxiliaries heightened feelings of disgust with the war in London and won sympathy for the rebels in the outside world. This led to a political victory for the IRA—the

British decision to pull out—although the rebel leaders believed that true victory was snatched from them at the last moment when the Government of Ireland Act and the Treaty of 1921 sanctioned the partition of Ireland and set up an elected parliament in place of the 'revolutionary congress', the Dáil Eireann. Memories are long in Ireland. Today, the IRA in the North are hoping that their terrorist campaign will end with a similar kind of political victory.

The immediate aftermath of the establishment of the Irish Free State was a civil war triggered off in June 1922, when the IRA murdered Field Marshal Sir Henry Wilson (a top-ranking soldier who was also a keen Protestant sympathiser) in London and arranged for the simultaneous kidnapping of the chief of staff of the Free State army, General O'Connell, in Dublin. The civil war claimed 700 lives, but the IRA were crushed by April 1923. Historically, its leaders have swung back and forth between a policy of confrontation with 'the traitors in Dublin' and a direct attack on the North.

In 1938, the IRA tried to take their war to England. In the fifteen months from January 1939, bombs were exploded in station buildings, electricity plants, cinemas, post offices, public lavatories, shops and telephone boxes in London and other cities. The campaign may not have originally been intended to cause loss of life, but the choice of targets and the remarkable technical incompetence of the people who manufactured and delivered the bombs made casualties inevitable. The worst incident came on 25 August 1939, when five people were killed in a bomb explosion in Broadgate in Coventry. But the bombing campaign was wholly counterproductive. It took place at a moment when the British government was largely preoccupied with Nazi expansion in Europe, it generated violent feelings of hostility and revulsion both in England and Ireland, and resulted only in effective police measures to curb the terrorists. But again, new generations of IRA leaders seem to remember brute facts from the past more clearly than the lessons to be drawn from them. In August 1971, the IRA 'Provisionals' were again discussing a bombing campaign in British cities.

Political violence may be as Irish as Guinness, but the IRA campaign in Ulster differs significantly from earlier terrorist offensives. There have been a series of IRA campaigns against the North since the Second World War. In 1950, the Army Council defined Britain as its 'single enemy' and outlawed military actions inside the Republic of Ireland in favour of an offensive against Ulster. In the early 1950s, gunmen crossed the border from the South to carry out raids on military barracks and training posts in Ulster. The most important of these were the raids on Ebrington Barracks in Derry in June 1951; the raid on Gough Barracks in Armagh in June 1954; and a flying assault on the Felstead Officers' Training School in Essex that led to the arrest of a number of IRA men, including Cathal Goulding. Some of these raids produced sizeable arms hauls: the men who broke into Gough Barracks with the help of an inside agent got away with 340 rifles and 50 sten-guns.

The arms raids paved the way for 'Operation Harvest'—the Border Campaign that began in December 1956 and was formally terminated in February 1962. During these years, the IRA attacked customs posts, barracks and communications in the North, but failed to rally popular support on either side of the border. In the 1957 elections in the South, their political arm, Sinn Fein, polled a trifling 66,000 votes. In the North, the IRA were frequently forced to use intimidation to obtain shelter from the Catholic population. The campaign began with a series of hopeless blunders—an attack on a police barracks where the land mines that were used failed to go off, and a thwarted sabotage attempt at Endetubber where another land mine blew up in the faces of four terrorists who were trying to set it. The IRA were quickly seen as what they had become: military adventurers estranged from the Irish people on the border, without even the rudimentary technical competence required to carry out their attacks. Above all, their efforts to 'liberate' the North failed to strike any answering chord among the Catholics of Belfast and Derry. The gunmen from the South were fish out of water, and they quickly expired.

But the IRA offensive in 1970 and 1971 was different in kind. The terrorists in Ulster no longer appear as an isolated military force imported from Dublin. They have managed to exploit genuine political sympathy among the Catholics of Northern Ireland. This, rather than their developing military proficiency, was their source of strength. By August 1971, British army spokesmen were ready to concede that as many as a quarter of the Catholics of Belfast and Derry were helping the IRA, and that as many as a half were broadly in sympathy. For the first time in the history of the IRA, Belfast had become the true hub of a terrorist campaign, and a terrorist organisation had emerged, in the shape of the IRA Provisionals, that was basically composed of *Northern* Catholics and not merely another vehicle for Southern gunmen.

It was ironic that the IRA should have gained this new lease of life, and been able to pose a more serious threat to the political system of Ulster than at any previous stage in its career, precisely at the moment when the pace of reform in the North was accelerating. It was a moment when the Unionist party, by tradition the instrument of the Protestant hegemony, had shown itself capable of bringing about peaceful change. The governments of Captain Terence (later Lord) O'Neill, Major Chichester-Clark and Brian Faulkner all seemed willing to offer the Catholics a greater stake in the system. Yet the IRA managed to create a situation in which the Catholic and Protestant communities were polarised, a moderate in Stormont was threatened with being toppled by the hard men inside the ruling party, and the British army, originally called in to act as the referee between two hostile communities, had been cast in the role of a party to the quarrel. It was a situation calculated to arouse a bitter debate in London and Dublin over the future of Northern Ireland.

Social unrest in Northern Ireland partly stemmed from its economic problems and political structures. Ulster is one of the most economically backward areas in the United Kingdom. By mid-1971, unemployment had risen to over 8 per cent and the problem was aggravated by the fact that the region had proportionately more school leavers (and more old people) to accommodate than any other part of the United Kingdom. Massive economic subsidies are poured into Northern Ireland each year by the British government and they helped to lessen the steady drop in the number of jobs provided by two of Ulster's three traditional industries (linen and agriculture) and to arrest the process in the third, shipbuilding. But by the end of 1970 it had become clear that the riots, shootings

and bombings, on top of Ulster's geographical isolation, had initi-
ated a vicious circle of violence and industrial stagnation. To root
out the causes of social unrest, the province needed more jobs in
industry; to create more jobs, it needed to put a stop to social unrest.
Although 6,500 jobs were created in Ulster in 1970 (compared with
6,000 in 1969) more than two-thirds of these were created by old
firms that expanded their capacity. New firms were not coming in
fast enough, despite the system of financial incentives. And tourism
suffered most visibly from the security crisis: tourist revenue
dropped by £4½ million between 1969 and 1970.

If the sorry state of the economy meant more restless young men
on the streets, Ulster's long-standing political structures and social
institutions had inspired a more diffuse sense of alienation among
Northern Catholics. Northern Ireland was ruled since partition by
the Unionist party. In twelve elections since 1921, it never failed
to gain fewer than 30 of the 52 seats at Stormont, and in times of
crisis the number usually rose to 40. The politics of the Unionist
party has been likened to Disraeli's ideal of Tory democracy: an
alliance between all classes of the (Protestant) community from the
landed gentry to the man on the factory floor, united in defence of
the status quo. For practical purposes, the fact that there are roughly
a million Protestants in Ulster compared with half that number of
Catholics (although Catholic birth-rates are higher) and that the
Unionists managed to keep a tight grip over the Protestant community meant that a single party had a built-in majority so long as
it chose to hold on to it.

So far as the government of Ulster is concerned, the politicking
inside the Unionist camp has counted for more than the jostling
between government and opposition, and this has recently taken
form as a battle between a moderate leadership and hardliners (like
Mr Bill Craig) backed up by many of the powerful party branches
and associations. The Unionist party rests very squarely on its grass-
roots supporters, and the fifty-one party associations have considerable influence over politics at the top. By tradition, they have
tended to limit the room for manoeuvre in a liberal or leftward
direction. The most important opposition forces are the Labour
party (a non-sectarian movement loosely linked to the British

Labour party), the Social Democratic and Labour party (SDLP) founded by Mr Gerry Fitt in 1970 (non-sectarian but Catholic-based) and a cluster of left-wing ginger groups like People's Democracy. None of these groups stood any chance of presenting an alternative to Unionist rule, and they failed to present a strong opposition voice at Stormont. When the crisis of 1971 erupted, the SDLP and other opposition deputies simply walked out of Stormont and left the government to fight a duel with the IRA. That action suggested that the only two genuine political forces in Ulster were the Orangemen and the terrorists.

In fact, the failure of Catholic moderate leadership contributed greatly to that polarisation of forces. It is easy enough to blame their failure on their visible political impotence, the lack of choice that confronts the voters at the polls. It also had something to do with the fact that there is a paucity of Catholic professional men, intellectuals and businessmen in the province. But—another touch of irony—it was also a question of the tactics adopted by the opposition leaders themselves. At a moment when they were offered the chance of a greater measure of participation in the political system, they chose to turn it down. There are so many moments when one goes back to de Tocqueville: when men are given more, the revolution of expectations takes place and they are suddenly demanding twice as much.

The communal violence of 1969 had very little to do with the IRA. It stemmed from the hysterical response of Ulster Protestants to the civil rights marches that began in Derry in October 1968, and from the partisan bias and inefficiency of the Royal Ulster Constabulary. It has been reported that Cathal Goulding, the chief of the 'Official' wing of the IRA, was brought into a conference held by the civil rights organisers in 1967; if this is true, the IRA leaders certainly kept their heads down during the later demonstrations. The civil rights movement degenerated after 1969 and drifted into the hands of radical groups like People's Democracy whose extremist politics had nothing to do with the original programme of protest espoused by moderate leaders like John Hume and J. A. Currie. The civil rights movement had a great deal to protest about, including the blatant gerrymandering that enabled the Protestants to keep control of local government even in a town with a majority of Catholics like Londonderry, and a sectionally biased housing programme. Police brutality and Protestant rioting, as much as the civil rights marches themselves, showed the urgent need for basic reforms.

The result was the Downing Street Declaration of August 1969— a joint statement by the British and Stormont governments that laid down a framework for reform. In August 1971, Brian Faulkner, then prime minister of Northern Ireland, issued a facts sheet dealing with the steps taken over the past two years to implement the Downing Street principle that 'every citizen of Northern Ireland is entitled to the same equality of treatment and freedom of discrimination as obtains in the rest of the United Kingdom, irrespective of political views or religion'. He pointed to the disarming of the police and the disbanding of the 'B Specials'; the introduction of the franchise in local elections for all persons over eighteen (as distinct from ratepayers only); the neutral control of housing; and the setting-up of a ministry of community relations.[6]

The other immediate effect of the breakdown of law and order in Ulster in 1969 was to bring in the British army. It arrived at a moment when the British public generally saw the Catholics of Ulster as the injured parties. The army's role was conceived as a peace-keeping mission in which it would function as an impartial arbiter. In two years, the IRA changed the situation completely. By August 1971, the IRA had emerged as the chief menace to security and social integration in Ulster, and the army had embarked on an offensive designed to root it out.

COMMUNAL VIOLENCE AND URBAN TERRORISM

The army had to deal with two kinds of violence in Ulster. The first was the mob violence that grew out of the original civil rights demonstrations. The pattern of communal strife between Protestants and Catholics is almost a part of the yearly calendar. It is bound up with the annual cycle of sectarian parades, when members of one community turn out to flaunt their banners and their historical memories in the faces of the other group. The most serious rioting in Belfast took place during the two parade 'seasons'—at Easter, when Catholics commemorate the Easter Uprising, and from late June until mid-August, when the Protestants stage some 700 parades (and rehearsals for parades). There are other equally predictable, if somewhat less serious, occasions for communal strife. The police know that there will be trouble, for example, if they fail to keep a close watch on Protestant football fans trooping home from a match past the Catholic Unity Flats in Belfast on a Saturday afternoon. They also know that the fighting is likely to start when a crowd of hotheads who have been drinking hard are bundled out into the street at 10 o'clock on a Friday or Saturday night.

The British army was generally able to contain the mass riots, and often to avert them—at a certain price. For instance, about 18,000 police and soldiers were deployed during the Protestant march in commemoration of the Battle of the Boyne, which was staged on 13 July in 1970. The parade went smoothly, without fisticuffs, because the security forces were there in sufficient numbers to keep Protestant marchers and Catholic spectators from each others' throats. There were so many troops on the ground, in fact, that one security man quipped that 'A sparrow could not have coughed without being arrested'.

Crowd control on this scale ate up manpower and resources, but it proved difficult politically for Unionist governments to adopt the obvious solution of banning the parades. However, it was the second kind of violence—organised terrorism—that came to present the greatest threat to the security of Ulster. After the Border Campaign, the IRA had entered one of the periods of internal schism and decay that followed each of its defeats. As a military organisation, it was dormant when the civil rights marches got under way. Cathal Goulding, the new leader of the organisation, had announced a basic shift in strategy in a speech delivered over Wolfe Tone's grave at Bodestown in the South in June 1967, in which he declared that it had been a mistake to concentrate on ending partition and that the IRA should now lay greater stress on social and economic goals. The IRA, like most clandestine organisations, has had a labyrinthine history of internal feuds and betrayals and policy reversals. The leadership has swung back and forth between a 'military' and a 'political' orientation, between nationalist and socialist doctrines, and between tactics aimed primarily at the North and tactics designed to topple the 'Green Tories' in Dublin.

These ideological and tactical oscillations stemmed from the fact that the IRA lacked formal ideology and a coherent guerrilla strategy. In place of original pamphlets, the IRA reprints the thoughts of Padraig Pearse or (for the socialist-minded) James Connolly; in place of tactical innovation, it rehearses the techniques tried out in the Easter Uprising, the Irish Civil War, or the Border Campaign. It is true that the IRA's organ in the South, the *United Irishman*, started discussing such 'up-to-date' topics as the EEC and nationalisation of basic industries from the late 1960s, but in the last analysis the real appeal of the organisation to successive generations of brash young Catholics has been its tradition of trench-coated, pistol-swinging force and its appeal to the ideal of an elusive and quasi-mystical Republic. 'The great purity of the Republic' according to Joe Christie, a Republican active in the IRA in the early 1950s, 'the sublimity even of its object—the guarantee of equal rights and equal opportunities—is precisely that which makes our force and our weakness . . . The Republic is not a formula to be dispensed at Ballot boxes every five years. It is the way of life.'[7]

The IRA formally split into Official and Provisional wings after two resolutions were passed by the Army Council at the end of 1969, calling for the creation of a 'united socialist workers' republic' and 'the opening of electoral options'. The rebel wing, or Provisionals, rejected both those resolutions. The Provisionals are deeply traditional in a double sense: they want a united, but not a socialist (or communist) Ireland, and they rely wholly on the use of force to achieve their ends. A Belfast spokesman for the Provisionals said that 'We are traditional republicans fighting to free our people. When they are free, they will decide what kind of government they want. But the Communists in Dublin want to ram a ready-made workers' republic down the people's throats.'

The IRA Officials, and their political arm, Sinn Fein, subscribe to a revolutionary socialist ideology and view the government in Dublin with as much hostility as the Unionists in Belfast. Tomas MacGiolla, the president of Sinn Fein, has defined as one of the goals of his movement 'the reconquest of Ireland from the ground landlords, the river barons, the speculators, the cartels and monopolies'. From 1969, the Officials worked to infiltrate civil rights groups and to form a broad-based left-wing alliance. But there were signs from late 1970 that the Officials had decided to play a more vigorous part in the terrorist campaign in Ulster. In July 1971, Cathal Goulding made a ferocious speech in County Cork in which he declared that 'the bullet and the bomb' would provide the final solution both for Ulster and the Republic. And a spokesman for the Belfast wing of the Officials told an Irish journalist about the same time that his movement had never renounced armed struggle and prophesied intensified urban guerrilla warfare: 'You can defeat any army no matter how big by guerrilla warfare with the support of the people.'[8]

The rise of the Provisionals not only mirrored rank-and-file dissatisfaction with the left-wing policies promoted by Cathal Goulding, but also a transfer of power from Dublin to Belfast. The IRA campaign since 1969 has been a predominantly Northern phenomenon. The IRA Provisionals claimed in 1970 to control some 90 per cent of the members of the movement in Belfast, although the Officials were stronger in some smaller towns. The terrorists were clearly weakened by their internal rifts. Although the Provisionals and the Officials joined forces for some individual operations in Ulster, they waged a bloody gang-war for supremacy in the province from early in 1970 that may have cost them as many casualties as those that died in skirmishes with the security forces. Early in March 1971, to take a dramatic example, the Provisionals raided the Officials' headquarters in the Falls Road in Belfast. This was intended to avenge an earlier incident in which a Provisional had had his knuckles ground into fragments of bone by a group of Officials using their revolver-butts. The Provisionals staged other raids later the same night, although they lost one of their leaders, a roof-slater called Charles Hughes, when an Official sniper opened fire from an upstairs window. The Officials, in turn, decided to pursue the vendetta and planned the assassination of eleven Provisional leaders. Although a truce between the two terrorist groups was patched up at the last moment, another Provisional leader, a milkman called Thomas Cahill, was badly wounded by a gunman who was not called off in time.

That vendetta was symptomatic of the gangland atmosphere in which the IRA operates, and of the endemic violence of Northern Ireland as a whole. British army officers rightly talk of Ulster as a 'frontier society', and the level of violence accepted as normal startles those who live in the tamer parts of the United Kingdom. It is illustrated by the number of guns in circulation among private citizens. Recent figures show that more than 100,000 guns are held under some 70,000 individual licenses in Ulster; these include some 4,500 pistols and revolvers and more than 1,000 rifles. Of course, these are very modest figures by American standards, but they are high by British standards. And they do not take account of the numbers of lethal weapons that are held illegally by groups like the IRA or the Ulster Volunteer Force (UVF). Both those organisations are suspected of having received arms from communist countries. New arms are undoubtedly being smuggled in regularly across the border. It has been estimated that there are some 100,000 border crossings daily, and it is an impossible task to police effectively a twisting frontier 300 miles long with more than 200 crossing-points. The evidence produced at the Dublin Arms Trial in 1970 (though not held conclusive by the court) suggested that the IRA may also have been supplied by individual officials in Dublin. The increasing use of automatic weapons (including heavy machine-guns) and sophisticated explosives by the IRA in the North suggests that they solved their logistic problem.

What is the strategy of the IRA in Ulster? In 1959, Cristoir O'Neill declared that the border would be abolished in the course of 'a successful military campaign against the British forces of occupation in the Six Counties'. But no rational IRA leader today believes in the possibility of a military victory against the British army. The IRA hopes for a political victory, as in 1921. To the extent that it has a long-range strategy at all, it is to spark off a political crisis in Ulster in order to provoke direct intervention from Westminster or a Protestant backlash so violent that it would lead to outright civil war between the Catholic and Protestant communities and possibly compel the Dublin government to intervene. Provisional spokesmen have sometimes talked about these possibilities in ludicrously unrealistic terms. In March 1971, for example, the Provisionals claimed that they had formed an urban guerrilla force in the North capable of a protracted campaign that would lead to the collapse of the Stormont government and direct rule from Westminster. They prophesied that world opinion would then force the British to hand the province over to the United Nations, which would proceed to divide it into Catholic and Protestant zones. The IRA would follow this up by a programme of selective assassination designed to kill off the leaders of the Protestant community and clear the way for the unresisting absorption of Ulster into a united Irish republic. The last stages in this IRA scenario are pure fantasy; but it is important to note that the first stage is a very real possibility, and the crisis that followed the introduction of internment without trial in the North in August 1971 created a climate of opinion in which much wilder suggestions were being seriously considered.

During the early stages of the campaign (up till early 1971) the technical performance of the terrorists was almost as amateurish as their political pronouncements. This was partly due to the fact that many young Provisionals had to learn by experience. The bomb attacks in 1970 often consisted of a man nervously lobbing a Molotov cocktail so badly made that the wick fell out before it reached the target. In the first year of the campaign, the Provisionals failed to make a systematic assault on strategic targets like basic services (telephone exchanges, power stations and so on) or to extend their snipings and selective assassinations to senior officers and politicians. The strength of the IRA over this period was rooted in its growing popular support. The terrorists could count on otherwise peaceable men to open their doors to them in the night, and on the occasional priest to stow their stockpiles of arms away in a country church. From mid-1971 they set out to bring about the total alienation of the Catholic community from the Ulster system by forcing the authorities to adopt tougher measures and by playing upon the fears and prejudices of Protestant extremists.

It would be mistaken to credit either branch of the IRA with a closely-knit organisation or a coherent policy over this period. The terrorists often spoke of their military chain of command, with a 'chief of staff' and 'division' and 'battalion' commanders at the top. In fact, it is doubtful whether this guerrilla hierarchy really functioned except in fond imaginings and Protestant nightmares. The IRA's blunders, as well as its capacity for survival in the face of the army offensive that got under way in mid-1971, depended in large measure on the looseness of its cell structure. Individual cells often seem to have been left with no more precise instructions than to 'smash the British' as the opportunity arose. After internment was brought in on 9 August 1971, many IRA men seem to have simply buckled on their guns and gone out to bag a British soldier. The result was a wasteful series of gun-battles in which the terrorists lost heavily.

It is also easy, in the attempt to define the evolution of the conflict in Ulster and its effects on British politics, to credit the IRA leaders with a rationality and a capacity to adjust to changing circumstances that they simply lacked. These were men rooted in the past, falling back on old devices, repeating themselves over and over again. In military terms, they were swimming against the stream. But the political tide changed in 1970 and bore them along, at least temporarily. The muddle-headedness of the terrorist leadership and the autonomy of the IRA cells explain why their campaign in the North often looked like a sputtering string of fireworks, exploding at unpredictable intervals, rather than a military offensive evolving through planned phases. With these major qualifications, it is possible to define four phases in the Ulster conflict over the two-year period from the time the army assumed responsibility for security in August 1969.

The first phase consisted of largely spontaneous mob violence in the streets. The role of the army in this communal strife was to try to shepherd angry and distraught Catholics and Protestants out of each others' reach. In geographical terms, this meant camping along the 'peace' lines that divide Protestant and Catholic zones in Belfast and Derry: the barbed wire was rolled out and the familiar system of sentry-posts and armoured patrols was set up.

In the second phase (from June to October, 1970) the rioting assumed a new character. The British troops suddenly became the prime targets for hostile mobs—and above all for petrol-bombers, snipers and *agents provocateurs* in the crowds who hoped to break down army discipline. The rioting was no longer essentially spontaneous; the mobs were orchestrated and incited by the IRA. Street violence was drawn out in Belfast and Derry for five or six nights on end. And it assumed a more sinister character as IRA snipers in nearby buildings used the crowds as cover for their attacks on British troops. The riots became associated with methodical arson and the destruction of property. Casualty figures rose dramatically. For example, after two nights of rioting in Belfast in the last week of June, 1970, five people had been killed and 248 injured—including 38 British soldiers. Along the Crumlin Road, where Catholic and Protestant areas met, IRA gunmen hidden in the side-streets sniped at soldiers. In the early hours of Sunday, June 28, the mobs embarked on an orgy of destruction. More than a hundred fires were started, and shops, cars and filling stations were set ablaze. A few hours later, soldiers in Balymacarett on the eastern side of the city were fired on by snipers using machine-guns. The events of that violent weekend forced the government of Major Chichester-Clark to impose tough new anti-riot laws. They also showed the extent to which the riots had been converted into a military weapon by the terrorists. Early in July, a riot in the Falls Road area was triggered off by a successful army hunt for a cache of arms. Ten British soldiers were wounded by snipers firing from first-floor windows. IRA snipers continue to use crowds as a human shield, but the tactic has proved costly. It is impossible to draw up a reliable balance-sheet of casualties in these encounters, but some British officers believe that the terrorists have lost several times as many men as the army in the course of sniping incidents. The army has better marksmen, and also the benefit of technical equipment like night-sights and telescopic lenses.

In the third phase of the conflict (October 1970–August 1971) the IRA relied increasingly on systematic bombing and selective terrorism. The assassinations were sometimes timed to have instant political repercussions. The wave of attacks on British troops at the end of October (fourteen soldiers were wounded on the night of October 30) was widely believed to have been designed to embarrass Mr Jack Lynch, the prime minister of Eire, on the eve of a vote of confidence. The most notorious terrorist attack over this period was the murder of three soldiers of the Royal Highland Fusiliers outside the Squire's Hill Tavern in Belfast on the night of 10 March 1971. Although both wings of the IRA immediately denied responsibility for the murders, the method of assassination—a bullet in the back of the neck—was a traditional form of IRA 'execution'. The March killings stirred up a furious uproar in Stormont, and the Protestant right-wing rose on its haunches to denounce both Major Chichester-Clark and the British army for being too 'soft'. Chichester-Clark's resignation a week later, after stormy sessions with his constituency association, was regarded by the IRA as a political victory of the first order. It seemed to convince the IRA that selective terrorism could bring down another Unionist government. The bombing campaign continued, and IRA saboteurs concentrated on targets similar to those that were chosen during the Border Campaign: police stations, customs posts, railway lines, and so on. Sporadic rioting also continued—the precipitating incident was often an army search operation—and from June 1971, there was a resurgence of mob violence in Derry, where Catholics erected barricades and troops were attacked by men throwing gelignite nail-bombs.

The fourth phase in the fighting began with the introduction of internment without trial on Monday, August 9. For reasons that are studied more closely below, the effect of internment was to change the whole political context of the conflict in Ulster. In purely military terms, it formalised a basic shift in the army's role from the time it was first brought in in the guise of a neutral peace-keeping force. It was now used in an offensive role in the attempt to root out the IRA as an organisation. In the early hours of Monday morning (the operation was conducted at 4.30 a.m. instead of 4 a.m., the time originally planned, so as to give gunmen who had been out late time to get back to their beds) the army arrested some 300 suspects. 70 of them were immediately released. Of the remainder, some 80—according to Brigadier Marston Tickell, the army chief of staff in Ulster—were known officers of the two wings of the IRA. It was hard to determine the effectiveness of the swoop. Many IRA leaders, including the Provisionals' battalion commanders in

Belfast, had anticipated the arrests and had made their escape across the border. Others got away among the crowd of Catholic refugees who streamed South in the following days. The holes in the army net were shown up dramatically when Joe Cahill, the Provisionals' leader in Belfast, appeared at a press conference in Belfast attended by some fifty reporters and cameramen a few days later.

The IRA's initial military response to the arrests was clumsy and uncoordinated. Army spokesmen claimed that between fifteen and thirty terrorists died in the gun-battles that took place in the week following internment. The stand-up street-battle is nearly always counterproductive for the urban terrorist, since he is bound to be outgunned by the security forces. Over this week, the IRA seemed to forget the most elementary principle of urban guerrilla warfare: to hit and run, to stay on the move. On Wednesday, August 11, for example, one group of IRA gunmen occupied a bakery in the Markets area of Belfast and were promptly besieged by some 300 soldiers. After a few hours' fighting, one gunman was dead and several were taken prisoner. In the Whiterock Road on the same day, in contrast, the gunmen resorted to their old tactic of using a rioting crowd as a human shield. Some twenty snipers armed with automatic weapons fired on troops from behind a crowd during a search for hidden radio transmitters.

After a week of open confrontation, the IRA returned to more selective tactics: the bomber and the assassin took over from the gunman in the street. Terrorist murder squads adopted a policy of 'an eye for an eye', picking off a British soldier each time an IRA man fell in battle. And on Wednesday, August 25, IRA sabotage assumed a new and inhuman face when the terrorists followed up a series of indiscriminate bombings of shops and factories in central Belfast with an attack on the central office of the electricity board in Malone Road. One man was killed and thirty-five people, mostly young girls were injured in the blast. Many of the girls were disfigured for life. The IRA did give a few seconds' warning, but their warning seemed designed to provoke general panic and to trap a maximum number of casualties in the crowd streaming down the central stairs to get out of the building.

THE BRITISH PRESENCE

Before considering the political impact of the IRA campaign in Ulster, it is necessary to examine the methods applied by the security forces in the province. The British army was brought into Ulster at a moment when the local police had come close to total exhaustion. The Royal Ulster Constabulary (RUC) was discredited in the eyes of many Catholics from the moment when three armoured cars manned by policemen cruised down Divis Street before daybreak on 15 August 1969, and sprayed the Catholic Unity Flats with machine-gun fire. As a result, the police were disarmed and efforts were made to step up Catholic recruitment in order to give the force a less partisan image. In theory, a third of its members should be Catholics, but by the end of 1970 the real proportion was still only 11 per cent. A heightened recruiting drive showed some results: at the start of 1971, some 18 per cent of new recruits were Catholics. But mounting civil violence and IRA intimidation deterred many potential Catholic recruits. Catholic reluctance to join the force, or the Ulster Defence Force (a militia responsible for static defence) was analogous to negro attitudes in America, and mirrored the traditional hostility of the ghettoes towards the security forces.

The division of labour between the police and the army in Northern Ireland was fairly strict—although the army was assigned some functions that would be regarded as police prerogatives in most other countries. The army relied on Police Special Branch for much of its local intelligence. The army, in turn, assumed complete responsibility for riot control. Although the police included mobile Special Patrol Groups (equipped with riot equipment including motorcycle helmets and shields) these were instructed to withdraw once serious trouble started. The army and the RUC conducted joint patrols in Catholic zones, but it was generally agreed that it would be suicidal for Ulster policemen to patrol alone on the model of the British 'bobby on the beat'.

Compared with some 4,000 men in the RUC, the British army deployed 14,000 troops in Ulster by December 1971. This was a serious drain on Britain's limited military resources. Of the nineteen regiments engaged in Ulster in mid-1971, five had been detached from the British Army of the Rhine on four months' tours of duty, and there was a growing fear that, if the army were called upon to cope with a state of open civil war between the Protestant and Catholic communities, it would be stretched beyond endurance.

In dealing with civil disorder, the British army has traditionally been guided by two basic principles:

1 *The minimum use of force* This means that the use of all army weapons is closely controlled. When a riot breaks out, for example, the army practises 'controlled escalation'. The crowd is initially ordered to disperse and then, if the oral warnings are ignored, the army may respond by hosing them with plain water. If the riot continues, the range of anti-riot weapons may be extended to include dyed water, CS gas and baton rounds (5-inch rubber bullets that are capable of knocking a man down at up to 300 yards). From late in 1970, baton rounds were generally preferred to CS gas in Belfast, because experience showed that gas was frequently both indiscriminate and ineffective. The resourceful Catholic housewives of Belfast, wise to the ways of street-fighting, found a simple way of minimising the effects of CS gas by simply placing basins of vinegar on their doorsteps. (A rag soaked in vinegar makes a tolerable gas-mask.)

In principle, the army proceeds to the use of firearms only as a last resort, when threatened by snipers or bomb-throwers planted in the crowd. Even at this stage, many precautions are taken to make sure that no more bullets are fired than are absolutely necessary. Automatic weapons used by the army in Ulster were altered to fire only one round at a time, and trained marksmen were used to shoot down snipers in the crowd. Every British soldier also carried a 'yellow card' which listed the conditions under which it was considered permissible to fire, and was required to account for each round that was actually fired. How this worked out in practice can be illustrated by a skirmish that took place in Belfast on the night of 3 February 1971. In the course of rioting in Clonard and the Ardoyne, the IRA fired a total of 97 shots at the soldiers, and 138 bombs were thrown. In retaliation, the army fired only 11 shots and some 400 rubber bullets. Of course, in the mounting tension of Belfast as IRA assassins took their toll, soldiers were bound to get jumpy and accidents were bound to happen. There were several incidents in mid-1971 that stirred up a bitter Catholic reaction, including the shooting of a deaf-mute in Londonderry. Allegations of army 'brutality' played a major part in the propaganda war that began in August that year, but the rhetoric far exceeded the reality.

2 *Respect for the legal process*   The central problem for the army in coping with the IRA in the period up to August 1971, was to get enough evidence to have terrorists convicted in court. Before internment was introduced, it was necessary to capture IRA men red-handed in order to take legal action against them. This created a number of difficulties, since IRA leaders rarely exposed themselves by using guns or petrol-bombs during a riot, while snipers regularly got rid of their guns as soon as they fired in order to remove the evidence against them. In order to attack the IRA *as an organisation* (and to shore up the position of Mr Faulkner's cabinet in Stormont in the face of Protestant critics) the British government equipped the army with greater legal powers by bringing in internment.

But the introduction of internment had far-reaching political repercussions. The slanging-match that was sparked off in Belfast, Dublin and London illustrated the complexity of the Ulster problem as well as the success of the terrorists in helping to create a political climate in which the future constitution of the province began to appear as an open question. Mr Jack Lynch, the Irish prime minister, went so far as to call for the abolition of the Stormont parliament and to lend his support to a campaign of civil disobedience in the North. He was sternly rebuked both by Mr Heath and by Mr Faulkner. On the other side of the border, the killings and bombings that continued after internment inspired calls for tougher measures and the reactivation of the B-Specials (the Protestant special constabulary) from the Protestant right—although Mr Faulkner shrewdly guarded his flank by announcing plans for the enlargement of the Ulster Defence Regiment.

In military terms, the most pressing danger after the introduction of internment, apart from the terrorist campaign itself, was the possibility of a revival of communal violence in the streets. There were signs that, through a series of vicious and indiscriminate bomb attacks (one bomb was planted in a car-park under the Ministry of

Community Relations) the IRA was hoping to trigger off an out-right civil war that would severely strain the army's resources. In political terms, the immediate need was to find a way of isolating the IRA from the Catholic community by patching up a compromise with moderate Catholic leaders and to persuade the Irish government to take steps to limit IRA activities on their side of the border. Both things were easier thought than done.

At the end of 1971, the outlook for Ulster remained very grim. The casualty figures for the four months that followed the introduction of internment made depressing reading. In November alone, 7 soldiers, 4 policemen and 11 civilians were killed, and 134 bomb explosions were logged. Early in December, IRA terrorists visited a policeman's home and shot him dead at his door in the eyes of his family. Besides the death-toll, there was the burden of widespread social disruption, as Protestants and Catholics fled the 'mixed' areas of Belfast, and 7,000 refugees streamed south across the border. In the first week of December, a Northern Ireland minister disclosed that there were still some 22,000 Catholics participating in a rents and rates strike. Commerce in Belfast slowed to a standstill as the IRA staged random bombings among the shops and office-blocks.

Some observers were inclined, on the basis of these figures, to blame the decision to use internment for the subsequent increase in violence. The real question, perhaps, is whether the British army was not held in check for too long at the outset. Of course, there were powerful political and psychological reasons why it would have been difficult to have brought in emergency measures at an earlier stage. These involved the popular image of the Catholics of Northern Ireland as 'underdogs'—a notion relevant to the situation late in 1969, but not to the vastly changed situation in 1971, when the IRA had clearly emerged as the prime threat to security and development in the province. This is why the army (whose methods were likened by otherwise moderate Catholic leaders to those of Genghis Khan) found itself in the nerve-wracking position of having to confront mobs of rioting youths organised in shifts night after night who would never have turned out had they felt that they stood much chance of getting seriously hurt.

One comes back to one of the central questions for all counter-guerrilla operations: whether or not it makes sense to 'overreact' when the terrorist threat first becomes visible. The government of Mr Trudeau in Canada chose to do that at the time of the Montreal kidnappings in 1970. He aroused a predictable storm of objections; but by the time his parliamentary critics were shouting 'No, no,' the FLQ had already been crushed. For better or worse, in Northern Ireland the British army was initially committed to a policy of 'graduated response' that failed to contain IRA terrorism. That does not mean that the army lost the battle. As the British expanded their intelligence network late in 1971, for example, there was a notable increase in the quantity of arms and ammunition unearthed in secret caches. In September, the army picked up 30 assorted weapons and 1,000 rounds of ammunition. In November, 89 weapons were discovered, together with more than 15,000 ammunition rounds. The army also claimed to have captured many of the IRA's unit commanders—although there seemed to be plenty of men ready to step into their shoes.

On the political front, the hope of a meaningful compromise seemed remote: for the simple reason that few Catholic politicians were willing to accept the idea of a compromise *within the British framework*. The real battle for Ulster continued to be waged in the minds of the British public. The key to the future of Northern Ireland is whether the British people (and their political leaders) will be prepared to shoulder the considerable human and economic burden of maintaining order in the province over an indefinite period. What must be constantly borne in mind it that there is no immediate workable alternative. Under present circumstances, the peaceful reunification of Ireland is impossible. The role of the British army must be to establish the conditions under which a lasting political settlement can be patched together. But it is arid rhetoric to talk of a political settlement until the IRA has been defeated.

5

Quebec: The Fireworks of Hate

Terrorism in Quebec springs from the same sources as the violence in Northern Ireland. Like the IRA, the Front de Libération du Québec (FLQ) set out to exploit the frustrations and sense of deprivation of a cultural minority: the French Canadians. Like Cathal Goulding's Official wing of the IRA, the Montreal terrorists have harnessed their Marxist ideology to a traditional, atavistic cause: separatism. But the FLQ does not share the advantages of the IRA. While the Belfast terrorists have always been able to look southward across the border to the Republic of Ireland as a safe refuge and a source of fresh recruits, the FLQ regard Canada's southern neighbour, the United States, as an even greater enemy than the federal government in Ottawa. Political terrorism in Ireland has its roots in the distant past; in Quebec, it is a recent phenomenon that has inspired widespread revulsion.

The FLQ has had a chequered career since a small commando group first signalled its existence by lobbing a Molotov cocktail into an army barracks in March 1963.[1] Between 1963 and 1970, there were successive waves of bombings, bank-robberies, and attempts to set up guerrilla camps in the Laurentian mountains. On several occasions, the Canadian police announced that they were confident that they had finally rooted out the terrorists. But after each announcement that the FLQ was 'finished', the name of the organisation was resurrected by a new 'generation' of would-be revolutionaries drawn from the same social circles: the university, the urban unemployed, and the lunatic fringe of separatist politics. Even so, the FLQ seemed close to extinction after the murder of a Quebec cabinet minister, Pierre Laporte, late in 1970. The wave of public revulsion that followed that killing showed just how hard it is for terrorists to win acceptance of their methods in a democratic society. On the other hand, by forcing the government to take emergency measures and place the administration of Quebec on a wartime footing, the FLQ succeeded in one of their tactical goals: to bring the army into the streets and place in doubt the norms of democratic society. Pierre Trudeau, the federal prime minister, told parliament just before the Laporte killing that 'It only took a handful of fanatics to show us how terribly fragile a democratic society can turn out to be when the democracy is not ready to defend itself.'[2]

THE ROOTS OF FRENCH SEPARATISM

The FLQ was born in the slums and *hangars* (or gang-territories) of Montreal, and in the restaurants and *boîtes* of St Denis Street and Sherbrooke where university students and café philosophers get together to talk about Parisian literary trends and to exchange pipe-dreams of revolution. There are upwards of 6 million Canadians who speak French as their mother-tongue; 83 per cent of them live in the province of Quebec. They have a strong sense of separate identity and of economic inferiority to the English Canadians. Under the long rule of the authoritarian premier Maurice Duplessis, Quebec was run very much as a separate enclave within Canada, under the tight grip of the Roman Catholic church and the Union Nationale party machine. Since Duplessis' death in 1959, there has been widespread French resistance to the idea that Quebec should be administered simply as one state among ten, and every candidate who has stood for election as state premier has promised to bring greater autonomy.

The findings of the Royal Commission on Bilingualism and Biculturalism partly explain why French Quebeckers have developed an acute sense of relative deprivation. According to the 'B and B' report, English-speaking Quebeckers are earning nearly twice as much as people who only speak French. On the average, English-speakers were found to be earning $5,502 a year; but the average annual wage for bilingual French Quebeckers was $4,772, and for French-speakers it was only $3,099. Only Italian immigrants and Red Indians earn less than the average French-speaker in Quebec. But the disparity between the standards of living of the English and French communities in Quebec is not simply a matter of wages. The difference in the general level of education is quite as central. The average English Quebecker spends two-and-a-half years longer in school than the average French-speaker.

But the most emotional single issue is the language problem. The FLQ has claimed in its manifestoes that English has taken over as the working language in all the big corporations (80 per cent of which are controlled, directly or indirectly, by the Americans). There are genuine problems of assimilation for a French Canadian who wants to move upwards in business or professional life. The men at the summit of the job pyramid are mostly 'English', and since most of the big firms are subject to head offices in Ottawa or the United States, it is natural enough that English should have become the standard medium of communication.

For this reason, the 'B and B' Commission concluded that the French Canadian who wanted to get ahead in industry would have to make what amounted to a cultural sacrifice: he would have to acquire a flawless knowledge of English and even 'to modify his value system', besides being ready to move outside Quebec to secure promotion. 'The young French speaking person who plans a career in industry,' the report adds, 'finds himself in a dilemma: he recognises that he must choose between his personal advancement and the partial loss of his personal and cultural identity.' This fear that a man will be compelled to become 'English' in order to get to the top is part of the psychology of French Canadian chauvinism. Some separatist propagandists have even argued that it is 'treasonable' for a French-speaking family to send their children to an English-speaking school—an attempt to dig in their heels in the face of a process that is gathering momentum for obvious material reasons. The talk about the loss of separate identity that goes on in Montreal among separatist politicians may seem exaggerated, especially in the light of the fact that a good two-thirds of the population of Quebec speak only French. But it is that concern with group identity that is behind the rise of separatism in state politics over the decade of the 1960s.

The appeal of separatism is also linked to the structural problems of the Quebec economy. It has become traditional for Quebec separatists to complain that local industry is in the hands of foreigners, and it is true that French Canadian companies only operate about 15 per cent of the local industrial plants. The most striking thing is that Quebec is more closely linked economically to America than to Ottawa. The dominance of the Americans in local manufacturing has been used both by 'conservative' separatists who would like to achieve political independence within the economic framework of a North American common market and by left-wing extremists with a theory of global revolution and a compulsive desire to drive out the Anglo-Saxons.

Despite the enormous stake of American private enterprise in Quebec, new investment in the province has been lagging in recent years, and the upsurge in terrorist violence hardly helped to reverse the process. 1969 was a record year for foreign investment in the state of Toronto, but in the same year investment in Quebec slumped by almost 15 per cent. This contributed to rising unemployment, which was nudging 10 per cent in the following year. But heavy unemployment and urban overcrowding have been familiar problems in Quebec for more than a century. A significant proportion of the young men who made their way into the ranks of the FLQ were from the slums and shanty-towns of Montreal. The social effects of economic recession drove some young Quebeckers towards the pursuit of irrational or extreme solutions. The FLQ and its revolutionary goals form only one strand in the more complex web of French separatism.

The ideal of an independent Quebec has been held out as a political panacea at various stages of Canadian history. Historically, successive régimes have tried to contain the separatists in various ways. The British granted special religious and political rights to the French Canadians under the Quebec Act of 1774; then opted for a programme of 'progressive assimilation' in 1840; and finally for a centralised kind of federation that left some scope for provincial autonomy in 1867. Today, there are basically two variants of French Canadian separatism: the moderates and the revolutionaries. The moderates are most notably represented by René Levesque, the leader of the Parti Québecois. Levesque was a minister in the Liberal government until October 1967, when he presented a motion urging the Quebec section of the party to back the idea of political independence for the state. His motion was thrown out by an overwhelming majority. But Levesque went on to prove that he can command considerable grassroots support. Two years after it had been founded, his Parti Québecois pulled in some 23 per cent of the votes in the Quebec state elections held in April 1970. That was quite a jump away from the 8·7 per cent of the votes that were polled by separatist groups in the previous state election.

But a chasm divides men like Levesque from those who joined the FLQ. Like the FLQ, the Parti Québecois is seeking political independence for Quebec. The difference is that Levesque wants to get state control of finance, not to overturn the capitalist system. And he is committed to parliamentary democracy. The contempt and bewilderment of moderate separatists in the face of terrorist violence was given voice as early as 1963 by Marcel Chaput of the Parti Républicain, who speculated that the FLQ had been founded by English Canadian *agents provocateurs* in order to discredit the separatist movement, and had then been taken over by Communists. Levesque said in an interview that (in contrast with the FLQ) he represented a movement 'of the head, not the stomach'. He added that 'Trudeau is trying to identify the Parti Québecois with terrorism. In the long run, that's alright. It will become clear that the people who want change can only get it by our way. Not through a revolutionary romanticism that battens on to a social malaise. We are not living in Paraguay.'[3]

The intellectual premises of both 'moderate' and revolutionary French separatists are very shaky. Trudeau himself has challenged them cogently in a series of essays. Mr Trudeau has described Quebec separatism as a 'reactionary' and 'counter-revolutionary' force (language designed to steal the thunder of agitators out to recruit student radicals)—not just because it is a cause close to the hearts of right-wing chauvinists, but because it defines the common good as a 'function of an ethnic group' and is therefore discriminatory and, in the long run, totalitarian. He caricatures French separatism as an attempt to 'make the tribe go back to the wigwams'.[4]

But Trudeau is at his best when he digs into the roots of political violence in Quebec. The degree of popular support that a revolutionary movement is able to enlist is always closely connected to the question of whether the government is generally recognised as legitimate and to the level of violence that is accepted as 'normal' in a given society. Trudeau argues that Quebec differs from the rest of Canada in that it has always had a higher level of criminal and political violence, while lacking a genuine tradition of democracy.[5] The democratic system was originally imposed from on high by the British government as a substitute for the autocratic rule of the French colonial governors. In the time of Duplessis (1944–59) French Quebeckers had little reason to place their trust in the electoral process, and they were instructed by the church that authority was conferred on political leaders from above rather than below. A religious broadcast dating from the Duplessis era is a startling example of one clerical view of politics in that period:

> Sovereign authority, by whatever government it is exercised, is derived solely from God, the supreme and eternal principle of all power. It is therefore an absolute error to believe that authority comes from the people, to pretend that authority does not properly rest with those who exercise it but that they only have a simple mandate revocable at any time by the people.[6]

Of course, Quebec has changed radically in the years since those words were intoned. But the absolutism of the Duplessis era bred a kind of counter-absolutism among the early leaders of the FLQ and those, like Pierre Vallières, who were to become their political mentors.

Who joined the FLQ? What was their motivation? There was probably no continuity of leadership between 1963 and 1970. The terrorist sallies were brief, and after each campaign the organisation was smashed by the police. One is dealing, as a Montreal journalist has pointed out, with at least three revolutionary 'generations'. (L-B Robitaille in *Le Monde* 27 October 1970). But they had certain things in common. They were mostly students or unemployed labourers, and they were usually under twenty-five years old. Those who joined in 1963 used to meet in the little bohemian cafés of Montreal's east end and talk with alarming abandon about Marxism and revolution; but few had any real grounding in revolutionary theory. Some were merely from the aimless gang warfare of French

slums like the Parc Frontenac; others, like the girl student who told
the court that 'Je faisais ça pour les kicks',[7] were merely chasing the
kind of thrills that others might pursue on the back of a motorbike.

A Montreal psychologist who interviewed a fair cross-section of
FLQ members in prison has argued that it is possible to define a
kind of stereotype image of the Quebec terrorist. He found in most
of the people he talked with an above-average intelligence combined
with emotional immaturity; the rejection of the father and the
values he represents; impatience with the constitutional process and
accepted morality; a simplistic view of world politics; and the
substitution of a 'Maoist new religion' for a Catholic upbringing.
'When you speak with these youths,' Dr Morf observed, 'you are
always struck by the imbalance between an overdeveloped intellect
and an underdeveloped heart. The affective qualities, necessary to
round out the human personality, seem to have been replaced by the
instincts—sexual lust, craving for notoriety, and a thirst for power.'[8]
This interpretation may be oversimplified, but it has a wider
application.

Two of the early leaders of the FLQ who diverge in some ways
from the pattern that Dr Morf described were Georges Schoeters
and François Schirm. Both were roughly the same age when they
migrated to Montreal from Europe in 1957, and both had experience
of irregular warfare that was invaluable to the FLQ at a stage when
it still lacked foreign contacts. Schoeters was born in Belgium in
1930 and had fought with the Belgian resistance as a courier while he
was still a schoolboy. He married a French Canadian girl soon after
he migrated to Quebec, and later drifted into the heady atmosphere
of separatist politics at the University of Montreal. He made trips
to Cuba and Algeria to study techniques of guerrilla warfare, and
took part in training the FLQ's first recruits. It was a remarkable
coincidence (and may have been rather more than a coincidence)
that François Schirm arrived in Quebec at about the same time as
Schoeters. He was about the same age, and had seen action in
Indochina and Algeria as a paratrooper with the French Foreign
Legion. After he arrived in Montreal, he drifted through a series of
odd jobs, rarely earning as much as his wife (another native French
Quebecker). He finally drifted into separatist groups, and helped to

set up one of the groups that took over from the FLQ after the collapse of its 1963 campaign. Perhaps it was no accident that these two men with strange pasts arrived in Montreal at almost the same moment. But the wild-eyed students and raw recruits who were being introduced to the FLQ in 1963 may have been able to learn something about weaponry and primitive sabotage techniques in other quarters— for example, among the flood of immigrants from Algeria who streamed in around the time that General de Gaulle gave the country its independence in 1962. Some of these former *colons* had served their apprenticeship as terrorists with the OAS.

The man who emerged as the chief theorist of the FLQ was Pierre Vallières, a radical journalist who achieved international notoriety after he was extradited from the United States and put on trial for manslaughter. Vallières was a child of the Montreal slums, the son of a railway workman whose communist sympathies were kept in check by a conservative and strong-willed wife. Vallières speaks of the world of his infancy as 'a universe of violence, where the children dreamed of gigantic fires, or rape, of terrible murders . . .'[9] Later his family moved out to a shanty-town where he came under the influence of a radical physician who later became a prominent separatist politician.

Vallières was educated by Franciscans, and it was in church schools that he developed his obsessional hatred of the Catholicism —an obsession that colours almost every page of his remarkable autobiography-cum-political-credo. He attacks the church for encouraging 'the traditional aptitude of the Quebeckers for resignation' and castigates the church foundations as 'the fattest French-Canadian financial institutions'.[10] The revolt against the faith is central to Vallières' political ideology—as to that of many others who joined the FLQ—and yet he admits that he became a political rebel through the same psychological process that nearly led him to become a priest at the age of twenty. He writes of 'le pari révolutionnaire' (the gamble on revolution) as the French philosopher Pascal talked of the wager about God: the need to place a bet that he exists and leave reason aside.

Vallières led a marginal existence as a part-time scribbler and *habitué* of cafés until he made a trip to France in 1962. It was his disillusionment with what he saw of the role of the French Communist Party in the Côte d'Or region that made him turn away from the brand of politics that attracted his father. He decided that the French Communists were sheepishly servile to Moscow, and later recalled that 'the French left possessed the stupidest leaders in the world'. [11] On his return to Quebec in 1963, he built up a reputation as an outspoken left-wing journalist (and tangled with Pierre Trudeau, then the editor of the liberal periodical *Cité Libre*) before he was recruited by the FLQ in 1965.

Vallières' attempt to justify political terrorism is recorded in his book *Nègres blancs d'Amérique* (White Negroes of America). There he expresses his rabid anti-clericalism, his black-and-white image of the class struggle, and his hopes for a global revolution aimed primarily at the United States. He argues that the French community in Quebec is in the position of a deprived racial minority, and tries to reconcile his dream of an international upheaval with his backward-looking separatism. 'The revolution,' he writes, 'must take account not only of the proletarian character of the worker, but also his culture, his ethnic origins, his customs and traditions; otherwise, the revolution will not be total, human and liberating.' [12] Unlike most contemporary urban guerrillas, Vallières has a vision of his ideal future society. It is founded on a curiously naïve view of human nature and the role of government in society. He refuses to accept that men work best for incentives or that competition plays a useful role in social development. He maintains that the reason some people are richer than others has nothing to do with native capacity or technical competence but is merely the result of the unfair distribution of privileges. He has no conception of the complexity of modern industrial societies. And he turns an anarchist's eye upon the state. 'Mankind,' he insists, 'is capable of finding the means of auto-regularisation within itself.'

Much of this can be passed aside as self-indulgent utopianism. But the most alarming feature of Vallières' book is his impassioned rationale for political violence, which owes a great deal to Fanon. He rejects the democratic process in a single ill-tempered sentence as 'the absurd freedom to choose between two, three, five and eight thieves'. He regards revolutionary violence not only as the counter to what he calls 'the violence of the system' but as a kind of medicine that cures and heals the people who practise it. 'A victorious people's revolution is an act of collective psychoanalysis which has succeeded.' This kind of apologia for violence has become depressingly familiar; in Vallières' case the argument reflects the deep-seated personal frustrations of a man who made his way up from a poverty-stricken background without ever quite managing to fit into the intellectual circles to which he aspired. It also has the quality of an act of conversion. In turning away from Catholicism, Vallières never managed to shed the character of the 'true believer'. A renegade from one faith, he tried to commune at the altar of another.

THE BOMB AND THE BALLOT-BOX

The FLQ first emerged in 1963, from the wreckage of a terrorist group called the Réseau de Résistance that modelled itself on the French *maquis* but failed to get beyond arid café intrigue and a bit of illicit gun-running. The FLQ began its first series of bomb attacks with an assault on three army installations in Montreal early in March 1963. The first communiqué from the group, broadcast on March 9, promised that 'suicide commandos' would be sent out to sabotage government buildings, barracks, English-language newspaper offices, and businesses that practised 'cultural discrimination'. The bombings continued in April with assaults on railway lines, government offices and a police station, and an attempt to blow up a television transmitter. An attack on an army recruiting station in the same month triggered off the FLQ's first internal crisis. An elderly night watchman, Wilfred O'Neil, was killed when a bomb that had been hidden in a rubbish-bin at the back of the building exploded.

Up to this point, the FLQ had chosen buildings, not individuals, as their targets, and some of its members were shaken by the fact that sabotage had led to murder. But the hard men in the organisation won. On May 9, a manifesto from the FLQ not only accepted responsibility for O'Neil's death, but stated as a principle that 'A revolution cannot be achieved without the spilling of blood. The guilty ones are not The Patriots. They are the collaborators, the low exploiters who have forced Quebec Patriots to take up arms.'[13] But the fact that the FLQ also warned that a tribunal had been set up to pass summary judgment on 'criminals and traitors' suggested that the group was still having trouble silencing dissent within the ranks.

The murder of O'Neil drove most of the moderate separatists to publicly dissociate themselves from the FLQ. The operations that followed were even more spectacular, but hardly better designed to enlist popular support. On the night of May 17, FLQ squads dropped dynamite bombs into fifteen street-corner pillar-boxes in the comfortable English suburb of Westmount in Montreal—an exercise in indiscriminate terror against an alien community that might have been modelled on the FLN bombings in Algiers. It was probably designed to provoke an English Canadian backlash that would have deepened the feelings of suspicion and mutual distrust between the two communities. As it happened, only five of the bombs exploded, and no one was hurt. And by this time the police were hot on the trail. In June, the police moved in on a terrorist training camp at St Faustin in the Laurentian hills and made a series of arrests. The original FLQ was broken, and none of its most important members were involved in the later series of bombings.

The ideology of the FLQ in the early 1960s was reflected by the manifesto that was issued on 17 May 1963. It declared that the people of Quebec were 'a colonised people, politically, socially and economically' and that the federal government had always 'without exception' favoured Anglo-Saxon interests at the expense of those of French Canadians. The manifesto abounded in fine phrases: 'A revolution is not a parlour game . . . There is only one way of overcoming colonialism: to be stronger than it is.'[14] But there was no sign at this stage of a coherent strategy or even of a reasonably competent knowledge of primitive military techniques. And the two terrorist groups (the Armée de Libération du Québec and the Armée Révolutionnaire du Québec) that were formed in 1964 to succeed the original FLQ survived only for a few months before they, too, were broken up.

The second FLQ campaign began in May 1966, with a bombing attack on a shoe factory, La Grenade, at a time when it was having labour troubles. Pierre Vallières and his friend, the radical sociologist

Charles Gagnon, were both involved in this attack, which led to the
death of a 65-year-old woman and their later trial and imprisonment
for manslaughter. The La Grenade bombing was followed by a
second attempt to take advantage of industrial unrest: a bombing at
the Dominion textile plant during a strike. But the death of a boy
courier while he was trying to lay a second charge at the same
factory and a passionate public attack by his father on 'those who
try to make boys do men's work' blackened the image of the FLQ
still further, and the police captured ten of its members, including
Vallières and Gagnon, in July. The second campaign was over, after
less than two months, and it seemed doubtful whether anyone would
be able to conjure new fire from the ashes of the organisation.

The following years were marked by mounting popular discontent,
by strikes and student rallies, and an upsurge in separatist feeling
that was given an additional boost by General de Gaulle's flying
visit to Montreal in July 1967. It took a great deal of careful diplomacy, and de Gaulle's death, to restore friendly relations between
Paris and Ottawa after that extraordinary day when the General
stood up before a cheering crowd in Montreal and cried out, 'Vive
le Québec! Vive le Québec libre!' Student rioting and violent strikes
were encouraged by the Front de Libération Populaire (FLP),
formed in 1968 and generally regarded as a political front for the
third FLQ. By the end of 1969, after militant Montreal taxi-drivers
had overrun the garages of a private limousine service during a
police strike, the government imposed a ban on all demonstrations.

The third FLQ bombing campaign got under way early in 1969.
The targets included banks, the home of the mayor of Montreal, the
Liberal Club, and the visitors' gallery of the Montreal Stock
Exchange. But by early in 1970, the FLQ leaders were already
considering trying out a new technique that had become popular in
Latin America: political kidnapping. The police discovered a plan
to kidnap the United States consul in Montreal in a raid on a cottage
in the Laurentians in June. The phrasing of the draft kidnap note,
and the conditions that were to have been imposed for the consul's
release, bore a striking similarity to the terms that were later laid
down in the FLQ communiqué that was issued after the abduction
of the British consul later in the year. The note ended with an

'internationalist' flourish: 'Long live the Cuban people. Long live Fidel. Long live the Cuban revolution.'

By this stage, the FLQ had started to cultivate extremist organisations in other countries. There was an old connection with black power groups in the United States; in 1964, a Montreal television actress and some black militants had concocted a zany scheme to blow up the Statue of Liberty. Intellectuals connected with the FLQ formed a committee to translate and distribute Black Panther publications early in 1970, and a Panther spokesman called Zaydmalic Shakur turned up at the first meeting and announced that 'We understand that Quebec is colonised by the same system that colonises us'. There was also an important link with the Palestine commandos. A Montreal journalist claimed to have interviewed two FLQ terrorists at a guerrilla camp in Jordan in August 1970. Their host appears to have been the Popular Democratic Front, a Communist group led by Naif Hawatmeh. The FLQ members said that they were learning 'how to kill rather than how to mobilise popular movements'. They criticised the bombing campaigns on the grounds that this technique had proved ineffective, and spoke of the necessity for a campaign of selective assassination. They doubted whether they would be able to murder the premier of Quebec, Robert Bourassa, but thought that 'the head of a syndicate who is really nothing but a stooge for the bosses' might do as a substitute.

While increasing its range of contacts abroad, the FLQ was also working to extend its influence over other left-wing political groups in Quebec. One of the documents captured by the police in 1970, entitled 'The Revolutionary Strategy and the Role of the Avant-Garde', projected a common front of 'all the progressive forces in Quebec'. It stressed the need for political agitation and the systematic infiltration of trade unions and left-wing parties. It even set out a scenario for revolution, starting with a process of 'generalised agitation' that would lead to a political and economic crisis in Quebec and, finally, to an armed insurrection characterised by the occupation of factories, schools, government buildings, 'and the national territory'. The scenario was wildly unrealistic; but there is evidence to suggest that the FLQ did manage to establish a working relationship in 1970 with a wide spectrum of political groups, including the National Confederation of Trade Unions, student associations, and the Front d'Action Politique (FRAP)—formed early in 1970 to contest the municipal elections. The FRAP did not resemble a conventional political party. It was formed out of various radical *groupuscules* and the movement of 'social animators' (intellectuals who set out to organise and politicise the poor). Its stated objectives included a system of workers' control in industry and local politics and 'the abolition of capitalism'.[15] Its original leader, Paul Cliche, resigned at the end of 1970 after the movement failed to take an unambiguous stand against the use of political violence.

The FLQ moved from random bombings to selective terrorism in October 1970. On Monday, October 5, four gunmen abducted James Cross, the senior British trade commissioner in Montreal. The kidnap note imposed seven conditions for his release, including a 'voluntary tax' of $500,000 in gold bullion, the liberation of twenty-three political prisoners and their transportation to Cuba or Algeria, the reinstatement of postal workers who had been fired, the broadcasting of a political manifesto and 'the name and picture of the informer who led police to the last FLQ cell'. The communiqué contained some rhapsodic praise for revolutionaries in other continents, and offered the Cubans and the Algerians the sincerest sort of flattery: imitation. 'During and after our fight,' the FLQ promised, 'we shall offer much more than the traditional sympathy of intellectuals-shocked-at-seeing-aggression-pictures-projected-in-the-midst-of-a-scenery-of-bliss-and-peace.'

The Cross kidnapping triggered off an immediate crisis inside the Quebec state cabinet. Robert Bourassa, the young prime minister who had only taken office a few months earlier, was in New York on October 5, trying to coax new investments from the Americans. In the days that followed, Bourassa's cabinet was beset by doubts and irresolution and deeply divided over strategy, while Mr Trudeau and the federal government in Ottawa were determined from the start to dig in their heels and refuse to bargain with kidnappers. The Quebec government at first refused to accept the kidnappers' demands, although on Thursday, October 8, it agreed to broadcast the FLQ manifesto.

The 'October Manifesto' was designed to appeal to union militants.[16] It contained a chronicle of strikes and lay-offs and a whole lexicon of abuse for the Canadian leaders: 'We live in a society of terrorised slaves, terrorised by large owners . . . Beside them Remi Popol, the gasket (Mayor) Drapeau, the dog, Bourassa, the sidekick of the Simards, and Trudeau, the queer, are peanuts.' The document contained also the mad vision of '100,000 revolutionary workers, armed and organised' flooding into the streets of Montreal, reinforced by the down-and-outs of the back alleys. The violent language of the manifesto, which uncoils like a Ginsberg poem, made it the more alarming that it met with a favourable response in several quarters: it was fully endorsed, for example, by the FRAP and the Montreal executive committee of the National Confederation of Trade Unions as well as by rallies of students shaking their fists on university campuses and junior colleges.

Meanwhile, the police disregarded the kidnappers' threats and carried on rounding up suspects. They had arrested forty-four people by the time that a second FLQ cell (the Chênier cell) kidnapped Pierre Laporte, the Quebec minister of labour, on October 10. By this stage, the FLQ itself was divided over how to play the cards it was holding. Successive ultimata had been issued and ignored; now the group holding James Cross announced that it was ready to reduce its original demands to two—the cessation of all police operations and the release of all 'consenting' political prisoners. The Chenier cell (which now develops into the villain of the piece) refused any offer of compromise and insisted on the original conditions.

Mr Bourassa was torn between the appeals of members of his government and community leaders and the pressure for more vigorous action that was coming from Ottawa. On October 14, sixteen prominent French Canadians, including René Levesque and Claude Ryan, the editor of *La Presse*, urged Bourassa to give in. But on the same day, the premier of Toronto insisted that Quebec had entered 'a state of total war', and on the previous night Pierre Trudeau had made a tough television broadcast in which he declared that

There are a lot of bleeding hearts around who just don't like to see people with helmets and guns. All I can say is, go on and bleed, but it is more important to keep law and order in the society than to be worried about weak-kneed people . . . I think society must take every means at its disposal to defend itself against the emergence of a parallel power which defies the elected power in this country.

It was Trudeau's policy that won out, but not before Mr Bourassa had made an offer to release five political prisoners that was turned down by the FLQ. The outcome was the introduction of the War Measures Act in the early hours of October 16. For the first time in its history, Canada was put on a wartime footing to face an internal emergency. The War Act raised the terrorists to the status of belligerents against the realm. By 10.30 a.m. on the day the Act was announced, another 238 people had been arrested. But the sight of federal troops in the streets of Montreal (they had been first called in several days earlier) and the adoption of emergency powers provoked a vigorous political debate. The only party to oppose the introduction of the Act was the marginal left-wing New Democratic Party, but the parliamentary Conservatives expressed their doubts about the need for such drastic measures.

All the same, the cold-blooded killing of Pierre Laporte on October 18 silenced many of the critics, temporarily at least. He was found in the boot of a car. He had evidently been strangled with the chain of the small crucifix he wore round his neck, and the state of his wrists suggested that he may have been tortured as well. The sadistic killing of a French Canadian politician who was generally regarded, even by his political enemies, as a man of real stature and integrity, destroyed much of the popular support that the FLQ had managed to build up. René Levesque commented that the crime resembled the Sharon Tate killing rather than a political act, and promised the government his backing for the duration of the 'postwar situation'.

James Cross was finally freed through a tactical compromise: his kidnappers were allowed safe passage to Cuba. Throughout the period of his imprisonment, the police came under fire for inefficiency. They were handicapped at the outset by lack of coordination between the three separate intelligence services involved in the manhunt; for example, it took the Quebec state police three days to inform the Royal Canadian Mounted Police of the capture of an important suspect. There were also some extraordinary blunders. Three men involved in the Laporte killing hid in a closet in a room occupied by police for twenty-four hours before making their escape. While searching for a 21-year-old student called Gerard Pelletier, one police squad mistakenly invaded the Montreal apartment of the federal minister of the same name.[17] The FLQ may also have been helped by contacts inside the Quebec administration. For example, Jocelyne Despatie, a girl suspect arrested in November, had been working as a telephonist in Mr Bourassa's Montreal office.[18]

The government was later charged with spreading its net too wide, with making the counter-terrorist campaign an excuse to clamp down on legal separatists, and with 'using a mortar to kill a mosquito'. It is arguable that the government did over-react, although Mr Trudeau and Mr Bourassa both had solid political reasons for doing so. Trudeau was determined to show that the federal government would not tolerate political violence in Quebec, to root out the FLQ as an organisation and to show that, in the last instance, he was ready to preserve the territorial integrity of Canada by force. Some fairly wild things were said at the time about the strength of the FLQ and its hold over political groups like FRAP. Mr Jean Marchand, the federal minister of regional development, claimed in mid-October that the FLQ had about 3,000 members, a huge stockpile of arms and ammunition, and some 2,000 pounds of dynamite ('enough to blow up the centre of Montreal') in its possession.[19] The figure for membership was almost certainly exaggerated. The FLQ was organised in small cells of between 3 or 5 men, and it is perfectly conceivable that its total membership never exceeded 150.

On balance, the Cross–Laporte kidnappings were wholly counterproductive as a terrorist operation. In the first place, the FLQ excesses mobilised the 'law and order majority' in Quebec. A public opinion poll organised by the Montreal paper *La Presse* showed that 72 per cent of those interviewed believed that the government had been perfectly justified in the action it had taken under the War

Measures Act (later replaced by the Public Order Act). It was the same drift of opinion that led to the overwhelming victory of Jean Drapeau, the Mayor of Montreal, in the municipal elections. He was re-elected with a huge majority, and the fact that his party won all fifty-two seats on the city council was related to the general feeling that a vote for the FRAP, the main opposition force, would amount to a vote for the FLQ. Finally, the kidnappings forced the government to mount an offensive that broke the back of the third FLQ as a revolutionary organisation. Although Mr Bourassa expressed his alarm when the emergency legislation expired at the end of April 1971, it was clear that it would take some time before a new terrorist group would be able to unleash a new programme of violence in Montreal.

At the time that he introduced the War Measures Act, Pierre Trudeau commented that 'The only thing that methods like those employed by groups like the FLQ can produce is an aggravation, not a diminution, of the injustices from which we suffer; an accentuation, and not a reduction, of the social ills, like unemployment and poverty, that afflict our people.'[20] The FLQ, like most of the other urban guerrilla groups discussed in this book, dealt in the politics of catastrophe. They set out to provoke an economic crisis, not to avert it, because they believed that their popularity would grow as the norms of social life broke down under the stress of changing circumstances. The ultimate weakness of the FLQ, as of most minority groups in western societies, was that even if they had managed to rally significant French Canadian support, no federal government would have been ready to parley with separatism: neither a political nor a military victory was possible.

The City and the Countryside

THE URBAN REVOLUTION

The cities of the third world are like saturated sponges, mopping up the people that the land can no longer provide for faster than they can absorb them. The visible results of this process are the slums, shanty-towns and squatter camps that have cropped up like fungi on building sites, vacant lots and along the 'misery belts' that encircle most third world cities. Every Latin American country has its own name for these encampments of the poor. The Chileans talk of *callampas* ('mushrooms'), the Venezuelans of *ranchos* ('camps'), the Argentinians of *villas miseria* ('misery towns') and the Mexicans, more prosaically, of *colonias proletarias* ('proletarian colonies').

They are the first image of the Latin American city for the traveller who staggers out of the torrid inferno of Rio de Janeiro's Galeão airport, or the cooler confusion of Mexico City's international air terminal. Row upon row of shacks pieced together from scraps of tin and timber, old packing cases, mud and rubble straggle across the dusty plain that surrounds Mexico City; a kind of human garbage-dump where the stench of rotting food and human ordure clings to the nostrils. The diary of a woman from São Paulo's *favelas* (one of those rare social documents that immediately carries the reader inside what Oscar Lewis has called the culture of poverty) puts it thus: 'I classify São Paulo as follows. The Governor's Palace is the living room. The mayor's office is the dining room and the city is the garden. And the *favela* is the back yard where they throw the garbage.'[1]

But there is a hierarchy in poverty, as in most things. The Mexicans, who call the thousand or so rural immigrants who drift into the capital every week[2] 'parachutists', as if they had dropped out of the sky, have a saying that a man is only really poor if he has no roof over his head. Along the goat-tracks and cat-walks of Rio's *favelas*, that climb higgledy-piggledy over each other up the steep hillsides,

you can find proud family men who have built themselves solid little
two-room bungalows, equipped with a television-set and an ice-box.
I sat and drank with one satisfied squatter who patted the concrete
wall of his hut and pointed out that it had not been swept away
down the hillside, like his neighbours' wooden shacks, during the
last thunderstorm. Some of the men who put up their shacks on
public lands hold steady jobs and earn a decent living by local
standards. It is just that the government gave up trying to cope with
the chronic housing shortage long ago. But the real problem for
most people is not shelter but jobs.

Third world cities are growing at a rate of between 3 and 8 per
cent a year. That means that most of them are doubling in size every
ten or fifteen years. The process has taken place most rapidly in
Latin America. About half of the population of Latin America are
townsmen, compared with 14 per cent in southern Asia, and about
13 per cent in black Africa.[3] Countries like Venezuela, Uruguay and
Argentina—where the proportion of city-dwellers is 67 per cent,
74 per cent and 72 per cent respectively—are as highly urbanised as
Britain or the United States. The change in employment patterns is
almost as dramatic as the rate of urban growth. In 1930, 63 per cent
of the total Latin American work-force was engaged in agriculture.
By 1969, the proportion had dropped to under 42 per cent. The
migration from the land took place almost as quickly as in the
United States, where the proportion of workers engaged in agriculture also dropped from 63 per cent to 42 per cent over a 35-year
period between 1855 and 1890, and three times as fast as in Italy and
France, where a similar process took place over a period of 90 and
94 years respectively.[4]

There are many reasons why peasants are packing up and leaving
the land. Overpopulation and land-hunger are the most important.
The developing world as a whole is faced with the terrifying prospect
of increasing its population fivefold over the next seventy years
unless governments begin to comprehend that the contraceptive is as
crucial to social stability as agrarian reform or a disciplined army.
Ironically, the introduction of farm machinery and modern farming
techniques has sometimes caused extra redundancies on the land.
It is also easier for peasants to get to the cities now that better roads

and communications have been constructed. But one of the most important factors is simply that people's hopes and expectations have changed. The schools that have brought increased literacy have also brought teachers whose values are *urban* values and who often encourage bright boys to try their luck in the towns. The radio and the newspapers have helped to create a glamorous image of city life that has very little to do with what actually goes on in the shanty-towns.

It must be added that political disturbances and natural disasters have triggered off the most dramatic population shifts. The Brazilian painter Portinari has left scalding images of the *retirantes*, the starving hordes who take flight from the arid *sertão* in the north-east of the country every two years or so as the drought sets in. In Guatemala, peasant unrest and a prolonged campaign of political terrorism over the past decade drove wealthy *hacenderos* (landowners) and better-off peasant farmers as well as the landless poor to take the road to the major towns.[5] In South-east Asia, the Indochina war has led to a kind of artificial urbanisation in Cambodia and South Vietnam as refugees flee from the fighting: Saigon is reckoned to have doubled in size between 1963 and 1968.[6]

The growth of third world cities is often compared to the process of urbanisation in Europe and North America in the nineteenth century, but there are some striking differences. The first is simply that third world cities are growing faster. The average rate of urban growth in Europe in the second half of the nineteenth century was only 2.1 per cent. Second, the rise of the European cities was bound up with industrialisation. In most third world countries, the Urban Revolution is taking place without an Industrial Revolution. British factories were crying out for manpower at the start of the industrial revolution, but in the third world industrialisation has lagged behind urban growth. Failing to find jobs in industry, most of the rural migrants who have streamed hopefully into the third world's cities without chimneys have been reduced to scraping a living in the service sector—a polite phrase that often means nothing more than a daily round of peddling scrap or souvenirs, begging for odd jobs, or sweeping the streets. It must be added that most third world economies are *dependent* economies, sources of raw materials and local processing plants for the great industrial powers.

In Latin America as a whole, only about 31 per cent of the non-agricultural work-force are employed in industry (in contrast with a figure of 48 per cent for the United States at a comparable stage of urban development in 1890, or 57 per cent for France in 1921).[7] In Brazil, a country with an exceptionally dynamic economy, more than three-quarters of the non-agricultural work-force are employed in jobs that do not produce goods.

These dry statistics point to something of crucial importance. The gap between the number of rural migrants looking for work and the number of new jobs being created by local industry is not likely to narrow. The overblown service industries, the slums and shanty-towns cannot be shrugged off as a 'transitional phase' along the road to industrialisation. They are there to stay. Government plans to develop medium-size towns to absorb some of the influx of rural migrants (as is happening in Brazil), to curb birth-rates or to sponsor local industry may alleviate the basic problem, but they cannot erase it over a few years: third world cities have become the reservoirs for an enormous floating population that may be the source of violent social and political upheavals.

This makes it doubtful whether any meaningful analogy can be drawn between urban disturbances in nineteenth-century Europe and the third world situation. We have inherited a conventional view of the life-cycle or urban protest in western societies that has recently come under the pruning-knife of a new school of social historians. According to that view, there was an early phase 'consisting of chaotic responses to the displacements and disruptions caused by the initial development of urban industry, a middle stage consisting of the growth of a militant and often violent working class, and a late stage consisting of the peaceful integration of that working class into economic and social life.'[8] That view of the past is inaccurate and simplistic even for western societies; it simply does not fit the very different circumstances of the third world, where the flight of peasants to the towns has created a whole new social class that the Brazilians call *marginais* (or 'marginal people') and that Marx, who had a notoriously low opinion of their revolutionary potential, called the *lumpenproletariat*. Soaring birth rates and crawling industrialisation (often associated with a capital-intensive technology borrowed from the west that whittles down the number of jobs provided by a new factory) makes it rather doubtful whether these people will be 'peacefully integrated' into the system.

Veering over the hills and valleys of Rio in a helicopter, one is irresistibly drawn to compare the lean clean sweep of the beaches at Leme and Copacobana, walled in by the glass-and-concrete façade of modern apartments, with the filthy warrens set high on the bushy slopes. Is this the setting for class-war? Are the people of the slums a potentially revolutionary force? Friedrich Engels agreed with Marx that the members of this 'underclass' were 'absolutely venal and absolutely brazen', wholly concerned with the arid routine of eking a living.[9] Frantz Fanon, on the other hand, saw them as the armies of future revolutions. He thought that this 'horde of starving men, uprooted from their tribe and from their clan, constitutes one of the most spontaneous and most radically revolutionary forces.' He added melodramatically that 'This *lumpenproletariat* is like a horde of rats; you may kick them, throw stones at them, but despite your efforts, they will go on boring at the roots of the tree.'[10] Who was right? It has been argued that men who have just moved to a new town are too preoccupied with the business of surviving from day to day to lend their support to a political movement. The diary of Caroline Maria de Jésus, mentioned earlier, shows how living from hand to mouth is a totally time-consuming business. She spent her days rummaging around for bits of paper and scrap metal to trade for food; except on lucky days, she would not know until late afternoon whether she would be able to afford the ingredients for a simple *virado* (a Brazilian dish made from black beans, manioc flour, eggs and pork). 'We are slaves to the cost of living,' she complained. When they were not engaged in scraping a living, most of her male neighbours were sunk in self-pity, aimless violence, or *pinga* (a white, powerful liquor made from sugar cane that is the cheapest way of getting drunk in Brazil).

Oscar Lewis traced the physiognomy of deprivation in a series of books. He found that both Mexican and Puerto Rican slum-dwellers lived in a world of broken families, crime and sudden violence, and very little social organisation beyond the family. He also argued that despite their hatred of the police and their general mistrust of

officialdom, the slum-dwellers are just as likely to vote for conservative politicians as for liberals or radicals (for example, about
half of his sample group in the La Esmeralda slum in San Juan
backed the conservative Republican Statehood Party) and that
they tended to feel status-conscious rather than class-conscious,
to envy the rich rather than to dream of overthrowing the
system.

Quite apart from psychology, one obvious constraint on the
political activity of slum-dwellers is that men who are on the move
from job to job and from shack to shack are not easily organised. In
Guatemala, for example, less than 5 per cent of the working population is unionised and most slum-dwellers have very little contact
with the administration (even the nominal tax of $1 on heads of
families is rarely collected). There are no political associations
indigenous to the 'marginal people' of Guatemala City—although
there have been attempts to form residents' associations to get
improved local services. On the contrary, the slum-dwellers are
dominated by political committees organised by the major middle-
class parties that are only really active at election-time.[12]

The general experience has been that the slum-dwellers do not
produce their own leaders or their own causes. On the other hand,
they have provided willing political cannon-fodder for populist
leaders. In Latin America, the 'marginal people' have been notoriously susceptible to the non-ideological appeal of demagogues like
Rojas Pinilla in Colombia or Juan Perón (who was carried to power
by the *cabecitas negras* who had migrated to Buenos Aires from
upcountry) in Argentina. They have tended to vote for the man, not
the party or the slogan, and to be strongly influenced by promises of
local improvements. A public opinion poll conducted among one
slum community in Manila in the Philippines on the eve of the 1963
municipal elections showed, for example, that most of those interviewed wanted to re-elect their current mayor because they remembered that he had made a promise to them (as a candidate in the
previous elections) to build cat-walks to link up their stilt-shanties.[13]

This general tendency to trail along behind a father-figure or a
charismatic leader can be explained in various ways. It partly reflects
the rudimentary political consciousness of those who have exchanged

the relatively integrated society of the village community for the fragmented, 'atomised' life at the fringes of the towns.

But there are other reasons for the generally apolitical or conservative attitudes of slum-dwellers. The rural migrants have neither entirely shaken off traditional peasant attitudes nor been absorbed into urban forms of social organisation. As Douglas Bravo, the Venezuelan guerrilla leader, observed, they are in an ambiguous half-way house:

> The floating population of Caracas (he wrote) cannot be described as urban, since the 300,000 men who live in *ranchos* in the city have brought with them typically peasant customs and habits. It has proved impossible to rid them of their peasant, rustic mentality. Apart from this, these people are unemployed, they do not work, they have not yet entered industry and cannot be described as working-class. They are neither peasants nor workers; they have never worked in a factory and in some cases they are not classified as unemployed.[14]

Like the peasants, the slum dwellers look at the world through very parochial eyes and dread any threat to their daily routine as a threat to their very subsistence. What Eric Wolf has observed about peasant political behaviour in Latin America also applies to the *marginais*: they 'are often merely spectators of political struggles or long for the sudden advent of the millennium, without specifying for themselves and their neighbours the many rungs on the ladder to rebellion.'[15]

In Asia in particular, the ties of the extended community that have helped to absorb individual crises and cancel out the class divide have also provided a form of insulation for rural migrants—although the pattern does not really apply to Latin America. The so-called 'bazaar system' that operates in third world cities provides a safety valve: a means of containing the constant stream of rural migrants. After all, underemployment is a bit better than no job at all, and the profusion of uneconomic service industries and petty retailing in the pre-industrial cities at least makes it possible for people to eat. Although the foreigner finds the most dramatic contrasts between riches and poverty in the third world cities, the greatest starvation and misery (in Latin America at least) is generally found in the countryside.[16]

Assuming that rural migrants have only modest expectations, the service industries are capable of absorbing new arrivals into what has been described as 'a system of shared poverty':[17] a buffer-zone between the traditional and the modern economies. Alongside the modern factories, there are the boys with old men's eyes who jostle each other to sell you chewing-gum; the women who squat at street-corners with half a dozen oranges or three little pyramids of nuts carefully arranged on a handkerchief for sale; the endless middle-men who share out one man's job into enough parts to feed several families.

The question is how long this temporary equilibrium can last. There is a limit to how many extra clerks or street-sweepers a government can hire for the sake of charity or social stability. And people's expectations change. The *favelados* of Rio may be poor, but many of them have access to radio or television and they see fine clothes and big cars in the streets every day. It has been argued that the slum-dwellers are 'basically conservative so long as life is barely livable' but catapult to revolution 'the moment that life is no longer seen as livable for whatever reason'.[18] That has not happened so far, although the slum-dwellers showed something of their political potential when they poured into the streets to show their sympathy for Jorge Eliecer Gaitán (the Colombian Liberal Party leader whose murder in 1948 was the signal for civil war) and again in 1965 in Santo Domingo. In Latin America, illegal squatters have shown increasing assertiveness in defence of their tiny plots. Second-generation squatters living in more permanent settlements have shown greater interest in local self-defence groups.

But the basic element of organisation and political direction is lacking, and the short-term effect of rural migration has been to lessen the importance of existing trade union bodies (employers rarely have trouble finding blacklegs).[19] The slum fringes of the third world cities contain a volatile mass that may explode during periods of rapid social transition or economic recession. But the way in which that will actually take place has still to be mapped out.

In South-East Asia in particular, the urbanisation process has had more immediate side-effects by heightening racial tensions—often at the expense of the Chinese, who dominate the commercial life of many South-East Asian countries. There have been anti-Chinese riots in several cities in the region, and the frustrations of young Malays who had migrated to Kuala Lumpur from the east coast (egged on by Malay political leaders disappointed by the results of the recent elections) was at the root of the bloody race riots in Malaysia in May 1969.[20] I talked with a leader of the Pan-Malayan Islamic Party (PMIP) in Kelantan some time afterwards. He complained that Kuala Lumpur was 'a Chinese city' where young Malays sometimes had to suffer the indignity of performing menial tasks for Chinese businessmen.

THE NAXALITE EXAMPLE

The increasing concentration of wealth and power in third world cities has affected revolutionary strategy. Although the capital city has a quasi-mystical significance in many Asian countries, where the ruler has traditionally been regarded as the man who held the capital, postwar insurgencies in Asia have been based in the countryside. It is rather surprising that there have been so few attempts by Asian rebel movements to launch a campaign of urban terrorism. The Vietcong are one exception, and the Tet offensive of 1968 might be viewed as an attempt to stage an urban insurrection.

More recently, the Maoist groups in India have experimented with urban guerrilla techniques. The level of urban violence in India is highest in the state of West Bengal, where it was reported that on the average, one political murder a day was being committed early in 1971. The Naxalites of West Bengal are Maoists who take their name from a peasant uprising in Naxalbari in May, 1967. Their main political organ is the Communist Party of India (Marxist-Leninist) or CPI (M-L), that broke away from the more pro-Chinese Communist Party of India (Marxist) in 1969. The new party was praised by the Chinese for 'having unswervingly taken the correct road of seizing political power by armed force'.[21] Its leaders included Kanu Sanyal, who had headed the Naxalbari revolt, and Charu Mazumdar. Initially, the CPI (M-L) clung to the Chinese

line on armed struggle, the primacy of the countryside in revolutionary strategy, and the border dispute with India with a doctrinaire
rigidity. The party planned to construct small, scattered political
cells that would form the core of a People's Liberation Army and
promote a nationwide guerrilla campaign.

Charu Mazumdar maintained that 'the path of India's liberation
is the path of people's war' and that the first step down that road was
to establish 'small bases of armed struggle' all over India.[22] He also
believed that rural guerrilla operations and agitation among the
village poor was an essential apprenticeship for the students and
urban unemployed who formed the backbone of the commando
groups. He called on university students to form Red Guard squads
to go among the peasants and disseminate 'revolutionary propaganda with a view to frustrating imperialist war plots'.[23]

But Mazumdar, like the other Naxalite leaders, tended to be a
little confused on purely military questions. In the Naxalite newspaper, *Liberation*, for example, he issued an extraordinary piece of
advice on the finer points of guerrilla warfare: 'We should not use
any kind of firearms at this stage—they will only fall into the hands
of the police. The guerrilla unit must rely wholly on choppers,
spears, javelins and sickles.'[24]

The central reason why the Indian Maoists turned towards an
urban campaign in 1970 was that they suffered a series of military
setbacks in the countryside that persuaded their leaders that it
might not be as simple to implement the Chinese strategy as they
had at first imagined. The Naxalites, for example, were active for
several years among the Girijan tribesmen, who are settled on an
area of some 500 square miles of rugged upland in Srikakulum. It is
the right kind of terrain for rural guerrillas, and, more important,
the Naxalites latched on to a popular grievance that they were able
to exploit. Since the early 1960s, there had been widespread unrest
among the Girijans, a backward people who had fallen victim to the
processes of economic modernisation. Merchants and moneylenders
from the towns had been extending their control over tribal lands
through usury. But when the government adopted legislation to
check the transfer of tribal land, peasant support for the Naxalites
melted away. On top of that, the Naxalites were divided by personal

rivalry and political dissension, and by mid-1970 the police were confident that they had eliminated all of the six original rebel leaders in Srikakulum.

As in Latin America, the tactic of urban terrorism was adopted by the Indian Maoists both as an attempt to recoup their losses in the rural campaign and in the hope of diverting the security forces and adding to West Bengal's chronic political confusion. In May 1970, the CPI (M-L) declared that 'While the main task of armed struggle would be in the villages, the party would not allow towns and cities to become strongholds of bourgeois terror.'[25] About the same time, the Naxalites appeared for the first time in New Delhi, and their spokesmen promised that 'red terror activities in cities and towns have come to stay'. In the capital, their recruiting drive was primarily aimed at university students. In West Bengal, the number of political assassinations rose sharply. In mid-November, 1970, the Indian minister of home affairs commented on the campaign of selective terror that had been aimed against the police; he announced that since March that year, there had been 526 attacks on individual policemen, and that 25 members of the force had been killed. The number of political murders continued to rise as the Maoists set out to disrupt the 1971 elections.

The Naxalites' urban terrorist campaign remains fairly exceptional in Asia—partly because Asian societies are still predominantly rural in character, partly because local guerrilla leaders tend to cling with a doctrinaire rigour to the principles of revolutionary warfare that were formulated by Mao Tse-tung and General Giap. It is also worth noting that the immediate postwar strength of Asian guerrilla movements was based on two things that have generally been lacking in Latin America: communist support (which also implied a consistent ideology) and popular backing for the cause of national liberation from colonial rule or the Japanese invaders. The Asian models do not really apply to Latin America, and even the Cuban model was largely irrelevant to the possibilities for the continent as a whole. In the major Latin American countries, no less than in Europe or North America, a successful revolution would have to be city-based. It took a series of reverses in the countryside to drive that lesson home.

7
Che Guevara and his Heirs

A successful revolution at once arouses and stunts the imagination. If it is often true that generals prepare to fight the last war, it is no less true that rebels try to repeat the last revolution. The Bolsheviks probed the history of the Paris Commune; the Chinese Communists saw Shanghai and Canton as their Moscow and Petrograd in the failed uprisings of the 1920s. In Latin America, Fidel Castro's victory in 1959 provided a new model of revolution that dominated insurrectionary strategies over most of the following decade. The Cuban revolution, in the simplified and distorted version handed down by Che Guevara, Régis Debray, and Castro himself, appeared to show that a Latin American uprising could be led to triumph by a small band of guerrillas in the hills, acting without the support of the traditional left-wing parties. Dr Castro's would-be imitators in Venezuela, Guatemala, Peru, Bolivia and other places discovered in the course of the 1960s that the reality was much more complex.

Broadly speaking, there have been two waves of guerrilla movements in Latin America since 1959. The first wave, incited by Cuban propaganda and sometimes assisted by more concrete forms of Cuban aid, consisted of the *plagiarists*. They failed, partly because they tended to believe uncritically that any Latin American régime would prove as brittle as Batista's and that any range of hills would provide the safe harbour and the springboard for rebellion that Castro found in the Sierra Maestra. Guevara's ill-fated expedition in Bolivia in 1967 was almost a parody of this approach.

After the plagiarists came the *improvisers*. Since 1967, the middle-class rebels who took to the hills with copies of Guevara's *Reminiscences of the Cuban Revolutionary War* or Debray's *Revolution in the Revolution?* in their rucksacks have crept back to the cities they came from to wage the war of the urban guerrilla. The heirs of Che Guevara share his élitist faith that a small band of armed rebels can serve as

the 'little motor that can start the big motor of the revolution' and
also his contempt for the traditional forms of political agitation and
for party allegiances. But they have shifted their ground. They have
made the city their target.

THE CUBAN MODEL

To understand the failure of the rural guerrillas in Latin America in
the 1960s, one must begin with the fact that they often set out to
reproduce a mistaken image of the Cuban revolution. Castro's
victory has often been represented as the work of a dozen men
washed up on the beach after the *Granma* landing in November
1956, who became the nucleus of a guerrilla army in the Sierra
Maestra. In fact, Castro's victory was the work of a much broader
coalition of political forces opposed to the brutal and unpopular
dictatorship of Fulgencio Batista, who had seized power with the
support of the army after meeting defeat in the elections of 1952.

Since the guerrilla faction of the rebel alliance (the *barbudos*, or
'bearded ones') managed to establish its supremacy over the rival
opposition groups, it was able to dictate its own version of Cuban
history. It was clearly in Castro's interest to downplay the role of the
urban support groups and of bourgeois supporters like the exile,
Prío Socarrás, who kept him supplied with money during the rebellion.[1] Che Guevara's memoirs helped to consecrate the *barbudo* view
of the past. Guevara discussed the success of the Cuban revolution
in a highly technical and narrowly military way. He paid little
attention to the revolutionary situation that existed in Cuba before
Castro made his appearance (as Hugh Thomas has observed, Castro's
victory was 'the culmination of a long series of thwarted revolutions').[2] Guevara underrated the role of the resistance movement in
the towns. He shrugged off the urban terrorist campaign, in which
other movements such as the student organisation, the *Directorio
Estudantil*, participated, in the following terms: 'There were acts of
sabotage, ranging from those which were well-planned and carried
out on a high technical level to trivial terrorist acts arising from
individual initiative, leaving a tragic toll of innocent deaths and
sacrifices among the best fighters, without their signifying any real
advantage to the people's cause.'[3]

In fact, the urban struggle was of vital importance to the revolutionary cause. Quite apart from individual incidents (like the attempt on Batista's life in 1957) the urban front succeeded in pinning down about half the government forces—15,000 troops. It was true that the Havana terrorists proved vulnerable to government attack and that the general strike scheduled for April 1958 was a miserable failure. On the other hand, the Cuban terrorists managed to provoke an intensified use of counter-terrorism that lost Batista his last shreds of popular support and shattered the morale of the armed forces, who became aware that they were upholding a totally immoral dictatorship: some 20,000 people were later alleged by Castro to have been tortured by Batista's forces between 1956 and 1958.

Guevara's memoirs also minimised the effect of political agitation. In fact, the carefully cultivated 'democratic nationalist' image of himself that Castro promoted until some time after he came to power played a leading role in securing broad-based popular support and above all, perhaps, the neutrality of the Americans. Castro used a newspaper and a radio station which were set up in the Sierra Maestra to conduct a skilful political campaign. In order to capture his peasant audience, he even modified his original Moncada programme (published after the attack on the Moncada barracks on 26 July 1953). This programme had mentioned the idea of rural cooperatives, as well as the redistribution of surplus land to landless peasants, the nationalisation of public services, and a return to the liberal constitution of 1940. Castro explained in his Sierra Maestra manifesto that these cooperatives would not involve the confiscation of land by the state, and in his draft agrarian reform of October 1958, he stopped talking about them altogether. And Castro also had a wary eye for reactions over the other side of the Mexican Gulf: in interviews with journalists that began with the famous encounter with Herbert Matthews of the *New York Times* in 1957, he projected himself to the Americans as a patriot opposed to the 'monstrum horrendum', Batista. At the height of the guerrilla campaign, his supporters were able to collect money for the cause of 'human liberties' in Cuba from passers-by in the streets of New York.

Finally, Guevara's memoirs lacked any element of serious class

analysis. The peasants of the Sierra Maestra, unlike the agricultural
labourers on the sugar estates who made up the bulk of Cuba's rural
population, were independent-minded smallholders fighting a battle
for survival against large proprietors eager to swallow up their tiny
coffee-plots.[4] The arrival of the guerrillas coincided with one of the
classic forms of peasant unrest: defence of threatened property
rights. As Guevara himself observed,

> the Sierra Maestra, locale of the first revolutionary beehive, is a
> place where peasants struggling barehanded against latifundism
> took refuge . . . Concretely, the soldiers who belonged to our first
> peasant-type guerrilla armies came from the section of this social
> class which shows most strongly love for the land and the posses-
> sion of it; that is to say, which shows most perfectly what we can
> define as the petty-bourgeois spirit.[5]

Thus the social context into which the guerrillas inserted themselves
differed significantly from rural society in general in one of the most
highly-capitalised countries in Latin America. Here, the guerrillas'
promises of land struck a responsive chord; later guerrilla movements that chose their bases less carefully ran up against a blank
wall of apathy, distrust and incomprehension.

In short, the 'received' version of the Cuban revolution emphasised the subjective factors, and the rural character, of the anti-
Batista movement at the expense of the broader processes of social
change in Cuba, Castro's remarkable capacity to present himself as
all things to all men, and the urban corollary to the Sierra Maestra
campaign. Those who accepted this version uncritically and set out
to reproduce it suffered as a result. The Cuban revolution did
provide some useful lessons about the conditions under which guerrilla movements can enlist peasant support: the need, first of all, for
the rebels to carry off successful armed operations in order to
present themselves to the traditionally cautious peasantry as a
credible military force, *a possibility*; and, secondly, to survive long
enough to counteract the adverse effects of the first government
offensive through a psychological warfare campaign. As a Peruvian
guerrilla leader later observed, 'the peasant thinks in harvests'.[6]

Guevara claimed in his manual of guerrilla warfare that the Cuban revolution contributed 'three fundamental lessons to the conduct of revolutionary movements in Latin America':

1 Popular forces can win a war against the army.
2 It is not necessary to wait until all conditions for making revolution exist; the insurrection can create them.
3 In underdeveloped America the countryside is the basic area for armed fighting.[7]

That statement summed up both Guevara's voluntarism and his view of the guerrilla as an agrarian rebel. The guerrilla, he wrote, 'interprets the desires of the great peasant mass to be owners of land, owners of their own means of production, of their animals, of all that which they have long yearned to be their own.'[8] He saw the rebellion progressing from an initial nomadic phase, in which the guerrilla band would be preoccupied with keeping out of the way of the government forces and with constructing logistic support bases and lines of communications, to the creation of 'liberated zones' and finally to a war of movement in which the government forces would be defeated in battle.

This was more or less the pattern of the Cuban revolution—with the important qualifications noted above. Guevara also observed, on the basis of the Cuban experience, that it is not necessary to take on the *whole* of the government army: the destruction of its élite forces will paralyse and demoralise the rest. He laid great stress on the subjective factors: the importance of rebel motivation and of disciplined conduct towards the civil population. 'The guerrilla fighter, as a person conscious of a role in the vanguard of the people,' he observed, 'must have a moral conduct that shows him to be a true priest of the reform to which he aspires.'[9] He stressed the importance of *hatred* in sustaining guerrillas over a long campaign: the need to burn all emotional boats.

Guevara, despite his rural bias, did not discount the possibility of an effective urban campaign altogether. He observed in his guerrilla manual that a terrorist network could disrupt industry and commerce, tie up troops, and place the population 'in a situation of unrest, of anguish, almost of impatience for the development of violent events that will relieve the period of suspense'.[10] But he refused to accept the idea that the urban front could enjoy any measure of autonomy. He insisted that it would play a secondary role, and that the terrorist network would remain under the orders of chiefs located in the rural zone. Again, he was distorting the Cuban experience, which showed the difficulty of maintaining close communications between rebels in the city and the countryside, and the need for tactical autonomy among urban terrorist groups.

The 'Cuban line' as presented by Guevara was criticised as 'Blanquist' by most of the leaders of the traditional left in Latin America, and their attitude was summarised by the Uruguayan Communist leader Rodney Arismendi (more sympathetic towards Castro than most) in the following terms:

> Today Chinese garb is being donned by petty bourgeois radicals, who in the matter of methods of revolutionary struggle adhere to moth-eaten ideas about 'the inspiring effect of direct action', ideas imported into the Rio de la Plata area half a century ago by anarchistic sects. Contrary to the marxist orientation towards mass action, these groups maintain that direct action carried out by a handful of bold men can rouse the people and hasten the social revolution. These concepts are akin to Blanquism or to the antiquated Socialist-Revolutionary and populist idea (borrowed today by the APRA youth and certain nationalistic petty bourgeois trends in Latin America) that the leading role belongs to the peasant and not to the proletarian masses.[11]

Both the conspiratorial and the 'peasant' aspects of Guevara's theories were exaggerated to an absurd degree by the French Marxist, Régis Debray, whose most important work—*Revolution in the Revolution?*—first appeared in print in 1967, at a moment when it appeared that events had already disproved its central thesis. All the same, there was something apposite about the appearance of this scion of French radical intelligentsia in the role of exegist of the Cuban model. In Latin America no less than in the west, the New Left has outflanked the traditional communist parties: a fact that was appropriately dramatised by the tardy enlistment of the Cuban Communist Party on the side of Castro's revolution. The Cuban Communists originally denounced Castro as an adventurist, and sided with him only in July 1958, when he seemed to be on the way to winning.[12]

Debray expressed contempt for all the normal forms of political agitation, and scepticism even about 'armed propaganda': group indoctrination by armed rebels. He expanded the familiar argument that a guerrilla group can help to create the conditions for revolution by disrupting the existing social order and proving the vulnerability of the régime. He also developed the élitist thesis that revolution can be built *from the apex down, rather than from the base upwards*. He was right to observe that few Latin American guerrilla movements have been able to profit from the conditions that favoured communist rebels in Asia—the existence of a popular cause in national resistance to an invader or a colonial régime, and the presence of sanctuary zones in neighbouring countries.

But he jumped to the conclusion that because of this, the political and psychological indoctrination practised by the Chinese and Vietnamese Communists could be dispensed with in Latin America. He swung over to the coldly mechanistic view that a guerrilla force without a political base, neither explaining its motives nor protecting its peasant sympathisers, could develop the *military* power to topple a government. He not only lost sight of the Leninist principle that revolution is impossible without a 'vanguard party' which must retain control over the combat organisation; he forgot the basic rule of all guerrilla warfare, which is that the guerrilla fighter is a political partisan as much as a soldier and that his real battle is for minds.

Debray's view of guerrilla warfare mirrored an unreasoning lust for action and a bourgeois radical's romantic view of the *sierra*. He described the cities as 'luke-warm incubators' where no important political struggle could take place. 'The mountain,' he wrote, 'proletarianises the bourgeois and peasant elements, and the city can bourgeoisify the proletarians.'[13] The extent of Debray's élitist distrust for the people the revolution was supposed to help can be gauged by his remark that the peasants should not be organised in cells or committees because they would be bound to give the game away to the police.[14] In fact (as Guevara discovered in Bolivia) Latin American guerrillas have probably had more to fear from the dubious elements who have been attracted to a programme of violence whose political motives have often remained obscure. It had already become obvious by 1967 that those who adhered most closely to Debray's 'revolution in the revolution' had been beaten, not merely by the forces arrayed against them, but by the tremendous flaws in their own strategy.

THE DEFEAT OF THE RURAL GUERRILLAS

The rise of urban guerrilla movements in Latin America was the direct consequence of the failure of the Guevara–Debray strategy. In the decade that followed the Cuban revolution, there were a series of peasant revolts and attempts to establish guerrilla *focos*, starting with Castro's own efforts to promote rebellions in Guatemala and the Caribbean region. The most important of these rural insurgencies (in chronological order according to the year in which they began) were in Guatemala (1962), Venezuela (1962), Peru (1962; 1964; 1965), Colombia (1964) and Bolivia (1966).[15] They ranged from attempts to found a separate enclave or to set up a system of armed self-defence (like the short-lived 'Republic of Marquetalia' in Colombia or Hugo Blanco's peasant collectives in the valley of La Convención in Peru) to isolated guerrilla *focos* like Guevara's tiny expedition in Bolivia. Some of the rebels managed to establish a working alliance with broader political movements like the Moscow-line communist parties: this was a major source of strength for guerrillas in Guatemala and Venezuela. Others remained estranged from the traditional left. The death of Che Guevara in the hills around Vallegrande in Bolivia on 8 October 1967, symbolised the failure of the rural guerrilla movement as a whole. At the expense of some simplification, it is possible to make some generalisations about the reasons for the defeat of the rural guerrillas:

1 *Lack of external support*   Between 1959 and 1962, there was close collusion between Castro's government and guerrilla movements throughout Latin America. Castro's call to the rebels on 26 July 1960 to turn the Andes into the Sierra Maestra of Latin America belonged to the 'universalist' phase that has followed most successful revolutions. The Cubans actually made armed raids on Haiti, the Dominican Republic, Nicaragua and Panama in 1959, in the hope that these would trigger off revolts. A supply of arms and propaganda leaflets was scattered far afield: in mid-1960, for example, the

customs men in Buenos Aires found propaganda material and instructions for a campaign of political agitation in a Cuban diplomatic bag. The Cubans used their scholarship scheme for 'poor students' from other countries to provide military training and political indoctrination. A deserter from the Cuban army claimed that at the end of 1961, there were students from Chile, Ecuador, Argentina, Brazil and Guatemala being trained in Cuba in guerrilla techniques. Direct Cuban support counted for most in Guatemala and Venezuela. The Cubans sent instructors as well as arms to both the Movement of November 13 (MR-13) in the hills of Guatemala and the FALN (Armed Forces of National Liberation) in Venezuela. A cache of Cuban arms was unearthed in Falcón state in the north-west of Venezuela in December 1963.

But Cuban support was never of central importance for any of the guerrilla movements in southern countries—with the obvious exception of Guevara's own enterprise in Bolivia—and it proved to be a diminishing force. Castro's support for armed struggle brought him into conflict both with the traditional left in Latin America and with his Russian patrons. He managed to patch up a temporary compromise with the Moscow-line communist parties at a conference held in Havana in November 1964, but little came of it. The conflict centred as much on the question of the class nature of the struggle (whether the proletariat or the peasantry was 'the revolutionary class') and on the issue of political control (the communists wanted to direct the guerrilla movements) as on the broader debate about whether or not violence was the appropriate strategy.

The quarrel came to a head at the Latin American Solidarity Conference (OLAS) held in Havana between 31 July and 10 August 1967. Several months earlier, Castro had made a speech highly critical of the Moscow-line parties in which he declared that 'If in any nation those who call themselves Communists do not know how to fulfil their duty, we will support those who—even though they do not call themselves Communists—behave like real Communists in the struggle.'[16] In retaliation, a number of Communist parties boycotted the OLAS conference, where the rhetoric of armed struggle crashed like a thunderclap. It was only a passing storm. Although Castro declared that the word 'ceasefire' would be henceforth abolished from the revolutionary lexicon, while the convention issued the famous watchword 'The duty of every revolutionary is to make the revolution', the Cubans were on the way out.[17]

The Russians, leaning towards a policy of coexistence with the west, had been increasingly sceptical of Castro's plans for continental revolution. The death of Guevara two months after the OLAS meeting inspired a spate of articles in the East European press attacking the Cuban strategy as 'left-wing adventurism'. On his side, Castro had been increasingly dissatisfied with the Russian connection. He attacked the Russians early in 1968 for using their aid programme as a political lever. And relations were hardly smoothed over when Castro purged a 'microfaction' headed by the Moscow-line Cuban Communist leader, Aníbal Escalante.

But in the course of 1968, he made an extraordinary about-face. Ten days after he had made a bitter speech attacking Russian economic 'imperialism', Castro signed new trade protocols with the Soviet Union. By the middle of the year (after a new economic agreement had been signed with the Rumanians, on terms highly favourable to Cuba) Castro had come to terms with the Russians.

If the testimony of an important defector from the Cuban secret service, Orlando Castro Hidalgo, can be trusted, Castro had actually been brought to heel. Castro Hidalgo told the Americans early in 1969 that the Russians had threatened to suspend economic aid and cut off oil supplies to Cuba unless Castro agreed to stop criticising the Soviet Union and ceased to support guerrilla groups that did not enjoy Moscow's approval. In return for obedience, the Russians were ready to continue their aid programme, to provide 5,000 more technicians, and to send increased shipments of oil.[18]

Castro could not hold out against the threat of economic sanctions. According to the same witness, he even agreed to merge the Cuban secret service with the Russian KGB. The most dramatic proof of loyalty came in August 1968, when Castro expressed his full approval for the Russian invasion of Czechoslovakia. From this time onwards, there was a mounting sense of mutual disenchantment between Castro and the guerrillas. The Cubans clung to the theory of armed revolution throughout Latin America, (Carlos Rafael

Rodriguez, a leading member of the Cuban party secretariat, declared on a visit to Santiago that 'the fundamental path for the
development of the revolution' in Latin America was still armed
struggle) but most concrete forms of aid for Latin American guerrilla
movements seem to have been suspended in 1968.

This left bitter feelings on both sides. The Venezuela guerrilla
leader Douglas Bravo let out a cry of protest in January 1970. 'What
is happening in Cuba?' he demanded. 'Why don't Radio Havana
and Fidel Castro talk the way they used to? Have the Cubans given
up the struggle for the continent?' Castro's reply was swift and sour.
In the following month he derided Bravo and other guerrilla leaders
as 'pseudo-revolutionaries' and lost hopes. Cuba, he made it clear,
was not going to subsidise failures. At least temporarily, the guerrillas
had lost their only significant source of outside support.

Although the Russians have been careful to keep their options
open, their efforts to secure better relations with Latin American
governments in order to step up trade and exercise non-violent
forms of leverage have led them to endorse 'united front' tactics in
the continent. But there has also been evidence of Russian involvement in the training and upkeep of Mexican guerrillas, and this may
not be an isolated phenomenon. Chinese involvement since the
Brazilian coup in 1964 has been limited to propaganda broadcasts
and translations of the thoughts of Chairman Mao. The North
Koreans have provided training for Latin American guerrillas.
There have also been some contacts with the Palestinians, who
were given permission to set up an office in Santiago early in
1971.[19] But none of this was sufficient to keep the struggling rural
guerrilla movements alive.

2 *The lack of a political base*   The rural guerrillas were also
weakened by their quarrel with the orthodox communist parties.
The Latin American Communist Parties have traditionally been so
subservient to the Russians that the Argentine Trotskyists derided
them as 'the Sepoy left'. Their changes in tactics have mirrored the
erratic course of Soviet foreign policy.[20] Between 1935 and 1939,
for example (after the failure of a communist-inspired insurrection
in Brazil) the Latin American Communists were instructed to
follow 'united front' tactics and participate in 'anti-fascist' coalitions

with other leftist parties. This policy was briefly dropped between
1939 and 1941, when Stalin was allied with Hitler. After war broke
out between Germany and Russia, the communists returned to
popular front tactics, and communist ministers were included in the
cabinets of President Velasco Ibarra in Ecuador, President Fulgencio Batista in Cuba (during his first term in 1938–44) and President Gonzalez Videla in Chile.

During the 1950s, as the cold war intensified, the communists
adopted a posture of violent and uncompromising opposition to
Latin American régimes—except in Guatemala, where the Communist Party rapidly gained influence under President Jacobo
Arbenz (1951–54). Over this period, the communists declined in
political importance. They were by-passed by new reformist movements like the Christian Democrats, and outflanked on the left by
revolutionary movements like the MNR in Bolivia, which lampooned the local communists as 'the post-revolutionary vanguard of
the non-revolutionary rearguard'.

After the Cuban revolution, the attitude of the Moscow-line
communists towards the new guerrilla groups was partly dictated by
the Russians, who were moving towards a policy of 'peaceful
coexistence', and partly by their own judgments of the chances for
revolution in individual countries. There was a general enthusiasm
for armed struggle, and the communists had no desire to be left out
of a second Cuban revolution. On the other hand, they were equally
concerned to recover the leadership of the far left and their theoretical role as the revolutionary vanguard. In general, the communists
were opportunistic in their attitude towards the rural guerrillas up
till 1967, and openly hostile from that time on—when it had become
clear that the movement had been defeated.

The three countries where communist backing for the guerrillas
counted for most were Venezuela and Guatemala (discussed in
detail below) and Colombia. After 1965, the communists abandoned
the Venezuelan guerrillas as a lost cause. In Guaetmala, the rift
came later—in 1968—and communist urban guerrillas still play a
secondary role in the terrorist campaign that is being waged in the
capital. In Colombia, the Moscow-line communists formed a guerrilla organisation, the Revolutionary Forces of Colombia (FARC)

under the leadership of a notorious rural bandit, Manuel Maru-
landa, as late as 1966. Their continuing support for the guerrilla
campaign was partly influenced by their shattering defeat in the
1968 elections, when a communist-backed popular front only
managed to pull in 1·9 per cent of the votes.

In other countries, communist support for the guerrillas has been
transient and insubstantial. The Bolivian Communists were informed of Che Guevara's plans for a campaign when the party's
secretary-general, Mario Monje Molina, visited Havana in 1966.
The Bolivian Communist Party, chronically short of funds and influenced by a Cuban subsidy, agreed to help the East German girl
guerrilla, Tamara Bunke ('Tania') to set up an urban support group
for Guevara in La Paz. But the urban network melted away after
Monje visited Guevara at his base at Ñacanhuaza in December 1966,
and quarrelled with him over tactics and political control. Monje
later recalled that Guevara refused to accept the communist view
that 'The military as part of politics and not politics as part of the
military is the right approach to revolution.' He also put his finger
on the greatest flaw in the Guevarist strategy. 'Revolutions,' according to Monje, 'cannot be planned and predetermined by decree, by
simple act of will. They come about, grow and mature with a combination of factors, not all of which depend on man's will. Men can
contribute to its ripening, and make it happen faster, but they can't
set time periods for it.'[21] This was the orthodox Leninist position.
Once the Bolivian Communists had abandoned him, Guevara—who
had failed to establish contact with the other important radical
opposition groups in Bolivia, the National Liberation Movement
(MLN) and the Revolutionary Party of the Nationalist Left (PRIN)
—was condemned to political isolation. This reduced his guerrilla
campaign to a period of nomadic wandering in the hills that was
more like a high school adventure course than an insurgency.

After the OLAS conference of 1967 and the failure of Guevara's
expedition, Communist Party theorists throughout Latin America
began a systematic assault on the central tenets of the Guevara–
Debray strategy. Symptomatic of this critical furore was a pamphlet
by the Argentine communist, Rodolfo Ghioldi, who listed four basic
errors in the guerrilla strategy: (i) the un-Marxist downgrading of

the role of the urban proletariat in revolution; (ii) the cult of personality and the glorification of the guerrilla leader; (iii) incomprehension of individual situations (for example, that a rural campaign was less relevant to Argentina, where 30 per cent of the population were peasants, than to Bolivia, where the proportion living in the countryside was almost 85 per cent); and (iv) subjectivism and a mechanistic view of how people are persuaded to join rebellions.[22]

The victory of a Marxist, Salvador Allende, in the Chilean presidential elections in September 1970, looked like a clear vindication of Moscow's preference for 'popular fronts' rather than armed uprisings. It is worth noting that in general, both the Russians and the local communist parties have been even more critical of the urban guerrillas in Latin America than they were towards their rural counterparts. Even the Cubans have expressed doubts about their methods—particularly the technique of 'self-funding' through bank-raids and armed robberies.

Support from other extreme left-wing parties for armed struggle in Latin America has been equally erratic. The Trotskyist Fourth International set out to make Guatemala, Peru and Brazil the bases for continental revolution in the early 1960s. The Trotskyist Hugo Blanco had some success in setting up peasant collectives in southern Peru, and Trotskyist agents succeeded for a brief period in gaining control of Yon Sosa's movement in Guatemala. But the Trotskyists have been discredited among the far left by their ceaseless intrigues, and their support for guerrillas was a diminishing force. The Maoist parties, despite much sabre-rattling, have not played a direct role in guerrilla movements. The potential support for urban guerrilla movements lies in other sources: in the radical wings of populist movements like the Peronists in Argentina, among the extreme left-wing elements in the lower ranks of the clergy,[23] and among disaffected students and junior officers.

3 *Lack of popular support* This was obviously connected with the lack of a political base, but the failure of the rural guerrillas to enlist large-scale peasant backing in most areas also showed up their distorted view of the political potential of the peasantry and their failure to study the human terrain. Again, Che Guevara's ill-conceived Bolivian campaign was the supreme example of these deficiencies.

The area north of the fairly prosperous oil-town of Camiri that was chosen as a base for operations was entirely unsuitable. It was an area of sparsely-settled peasants who mostly owned their own land and sold their surplus produce to the townsmen of Camiri on fairly satisfactory terms. The agrarian reform platform that had been used by Castro in the Sierra Maestra was irrelevant here; and Guevara left for Bolivia without comprehending the extent of peasant xenophobia (they even regarded miners from the north-west of the country as foreigners) or the success of the Barrientos government in cultivating *campesino* support.[24] Halfway through Guevara's campaign, in June 1967, President Barrientos held a peasant congress which adopted a resolution branding the guerrillas as an anti-national force.

Guevara's diary chronicles his persistent failure to enlist peasant support. At the end of August, he observed that 'We continue without incorporating the peasants, a logical thing indeed, if the little contact we have had with them lately is considered.'[25] Certainly, the fact that the guerrilla front was detected four months after it had been set up, in March 1967, left little time for 'armed propaganda' and drove Guevara further and further away from the settled areas in search of hiding-places.

But he was wrong to describe that as the only reason, or even a major reason, for his failure to find friends in the villages. The tin-miners of the north, as the revolution of 1952 had shown, were the radical force in Bolivia, and they remained bitterly opposed to the military government that had seized power in 1964. Of the twenty-nine Bolivians who joined Guevara, a majority were unemployed miners. The others were mostly students, taxi drivers recruited by 'Coco' Peredo, and low-level dissidents from the Bolivian Communist Party. The calibre of these recruits can be gauged by the fact that about a third of them deserted or went over to the other side.

Of course, Guevara's Bolivian campaign was unusual in that it represented the attempt by an outside force to insert a guerrilla *foco* into another country. But its uniqueness can be exaggerated. The bourgeois radicals who formed the backbone of guerrilla movements in Latin America were often just as alien to the peasants they tried to recruit. As Héctor Béjar, the leader of a fighting unit of the Peruvian National Liberation Army (ELN) observed, in areas with a predominantly Indian population there is a formidable language barrier: 'peasants identify Spanish with the boss'.[26] And there are a number of psychological and practical obstacles to peasant revolt. Poor peasants are bound to the soil by an endless cycle of work; to miss a harvest or a seeding-time may be to lose a livelihood. Isolation and distrust of outsiders make organisation difficult. The landless labourer, in addition, is often completely at the mercy of his employer, without sufficient resources of his own to move over to revolt unless a major outside force appears to challenge the power that constrains him.

The Latin American experience has shown that it is the middle sectors of the peasantry (those with land of their own and a modest agricultural surplus) and the traditional communities in marginal areas outside the bounds of landlord control who are at once most vulnerable to the economic changes brought by commercialisation and the encroachment of the big landlords and most susceptible to revolutionary appeals when their interests are threatened. These elements have been described by Eric Wolf as the 'tactically mobile peasantry'—the people who already have enough to challenge the power structure. 'It is the very attempt of the middle and free peasant to remain traditional,' he observes, 'which makes him revolutionary.'[27] That exactly describes what happened in Peru, where Hugo Blanco was able to build upon the ambitions of the relatively prosperous 'middle peasantry' of La Convención, while Luís de la Puente and Héctor Béjar had more limited success in appealing to the Indian communities of the Sierra that had a tradition of resistance to the encroachments of the big landowners.

All the same, the character of the 1965 guerrillas themselves limited their appeal to the Indians, who realised that the rebels were doomed as soon as the counter-insurgency campaign began. As Béjar admitted, 'Discipline, warm affection for the peasants, and modesty are not always characteristics of young students or of politicians filled with an intellectual self-sufficiency that offends simple people and which originates in daily habits that are often just the opposite of the way of life of the country people.' The

Sierra Indians may have been dissatisfied; but they certainly did not regard the students who turned up, talking of foreign theories in a language not their own, as a liberating force.

4 *Improved counter-insurgency techniques* The vastly improved capacity of Latin American armies to cope with rural insurgencies was one of the decisive reasons for the defeats inflicted on the rural guerrillas in the course of the 1960s. This was largely due to American training and support. Latin American officers were sent to the United States or the Panama Canal Zone to study counter-insurgency techniques. According to official figures, more than 50,000 Latin Americans were trained by the Americans under the military assistance programme between 1950 and 1969.[28] The comprehensiveness of the programme is also illustrated by the estimate that more than half of the officers in the Brazilian army have received American training. On the ground, American agents (sometimes working under AID or diplomatic cover) and military advisers provided intelligence and tactical guidance. Cuban exiles in the service of the CIA managed to penetrate several guerrilla organisations.

American involvement sometimes extended to direct intervention. One of the four American Special Forces training bases is located at Southern Command in the Panama Canal Zone, and it was reported that the Special Forces conducted fifty-two anti-subversive missions in Latin America, including parachute drops into guerrilla areas, in the single year of 1965. In 1967, American bombing missions (sometimes using napalm and other defoliants) were co-ordinated with Colonel Arana Osorio's ruthless pacification programme in the north-east of Guatemala. In the same year, American training camps were established in Bolivia and Nicaragua. Under American guidance, counter-insurgency programmes were broadened to include 'civic action' projects designed to improve the living conditions of the peasants. This approach was also tried out in Guatemala and—with rather more success—in Colombia.

The guerrillas' choice of terrain also made victory easier for an airborne enemy. The Peruvian guerrillas who went into the mountains in 1965 were not counting on the fact that the armed forces would fly bombing missions or use napalm. Caught on broken, difficult terrain, the Peruvian guerrillas were cut off from the towns by an army pincer movement and forced to rely on their local resources. The guerrillas were pushed back into the tangled, sparsely populated jungles of the eastern part of the country, and were crushed as a military force within six months from the start of the campaign. The isolation of the Peruvian guerrillas—forced, like Guevara, to wander like nomads in an unknown waste as the only hope of survival—pointed to a crucial fact: that provincial revolts rarely posed a serious threat to the government in countries where industry, wealth and power and concentrated in a few enormous cities. That was part of the reasoning behind the Latin American guerrillas' shift to the towns. So long as a government kept its grip over the industrial centres, it would be able to mobilise overwhelming numbers of troops for operations in the countryside.

One comes back to the conclusion that the central reason for the defeat of the rural guerrillas has to be sought in their own strategy: a strategy that was founded on an erroneous image of the Cuban revolution and the heady romanticism of middle-class intellectuals who hoped to find the certainty and conviction that was lacking in their city lives among an unknown peasantry. This was compounded with a kind of revolutionary *machismo*: the desire to prove oneself a man by running the gauntlet of hunger and armed combat. Instead, as Guevara's diary shows, many of the guerrillas got bogged down in petty bickering over a can of sardines or a point of theory. The fools' gold of a second Sierra Maestra glittered ever more distantly on far-off ranges; until suddenly someone caught the same glint in the back streets of the capital.

8
The Shift to the Cities

The shift to the cities was not simply the product of failure in the countryside. It was also an attempt to take advantage of Latin America's astonishing urban growth. Peasants and rural guerrillas in countries as highly urbanised as Venezuela or Argentina are no more likely to bring about revolution than Scots fishermen and Norfolk sheep-farmers in Britain. Urban terrorism, in various forms, has descended on most Latin American cities. The tactics are similar although the social context varies greatly. Like Che Guevara, the urban guerrillas dream of a continental, rather than a purely national, revolution. Because of the entrenched position of foreign corporations and the background threat of American intervention, most guerrilla leaders agree that 'Castroism in one country' would be impossible on the Latin American mainland. Brazil's urban guerrillas are not the only ones who have suggested that they would actually welcome American intervention because it would enable them to cast themselves in the role of a movement of national resistance to a foreign power.

The urban guerrillas are strongest—at least potentially—in the countries where they have been able to hitch their wagon to a broader popular movement. Argentina is a notable example. In Argentina, several guerrilla groups have aligned themselves to a vague and tarnished form of populist ideology, Peronism, that still commands the support of a third of the country's voters.[1] These groups include the Montoneros, the Peronist Armed Forces (FAP) and the People's Revolutionary Army (ERP), the combat wing of the outlawed Trotskyist Workers' Revolutionary Party (PRT) that also makes use of the popular appeal of Peronism. Sixteen years after the exile of the deposed dictator, Juan Perón, his name has lost none of its old magic in Argentina. The Montoneros are still waging a bloody vendetta against the army leaders who toppled Perón, and early in 1970 they were responsible for the bizarre abduction and murder of General Aramburu, one of the men behind the coup of 1955. They offered to produce his body so it could be given decent burial in exchange for the remains of Perón's first wife, Eva, whose body had been secretly interred after her death so as not to become an object of popular veneration.

The FAP first operated as rural guerrillas in the early 1950s, but moved their base to the capital after the army wiped out a base at Plumenillo in 1959. From 1969, they carried out a campaign of assaults on police posts, bank-robberies and sabotage of American company offices. But their level of expertise was minimal: when they occupied Radio Rivadivia in 1970, for example, they discovered that no one knew how to work the transmitter, and left without making a broadcast. The FAP are not anxious to secure the return of Perón from his exile in Madrid, since they realise that the old dictator might not approve of everyone who uses his name for political purposes. But, as one of their spokesmen told a Cuban reporter, 'the only way to make the revolution here is to be a Peronist.' That is why the 'revolutionary Peronists' may in the long run pose a more serious threat to Argentina's military government than rival urban guerrilla groups that show a greater proficiency in military operations— notably the Castroite Revolutionary Armed Forces (FAR) and the Argentine Liberation Forces (FAL).

Paradoxically, Latin America's urban guerrillas have come closest to success in the continent's few functioning democracies. There are eleven countries in Latin America that enjoy constitutional governments, but elections have rarely brought radical changes in the way the state is run. Some of these countries are really governed by a party machine. Mexico, for example, is a de facto one-party state where the ruling Institutional Revolutionary Party (whose name is an excellent indication of the way it combines revolutionary rhetoric with bureaucratic methods) has habitually polled between 80 and 90 per cent of the votes cast in each election over half a century. In Colombia, after a purposeless civil war known simply as *la violencia*, a seesaw system of government was devised that enabled the two traditional parties to pass the reins of power back and forth for so long that they came to be nicknamed Tweedledum and Tweedledee.

Guatemala's civilian governments have been completely over-shadowed by the armed forces.

Chile, Venezuela and Uruguay (with Costa Rica) were exceptions to this pattern of predictable democratic government. Yet each saw the rise of powerful urban guerrilla movements. In Venezuela in the early 1960s, a rebel movement supported by the Communist Party came closer to bringing about revolution than any similar group since the Cuban revolution. In Uruguay, the government has failed to contain the best organised urban guerrilla movement in Latin America, and it would be dangerous to discount the possibility of armed insurrection. In Chile, despite the election of a reformist Christian Democratic government in 1964, an urban guerrilla movement sprang up that later posed a Marxist president with the same problem that Mrs Bandaranaike, the prime minister of Ceylon, confronted during the 'Guevarist' insurgency early in 1971: the confrontation between the proponents of armed struggle and a left-wing government containing Communists and Trotskyists.

These three cases suggested that the ideal climate for armed rebellion in Latin America was not necessarily to be found in repressive dictatorships or among long-suffering peasants. Paraguay, for its sins, remained one of the more stable societies in the continent. There is mounting pressure for social change throughout Latin America. The combination of soaring birth-rates, misdirected foreign investment, and lopsided industrial development confronts every existing régime with urgent structural problems. The Americans have too often been willing to uphold repressive and unrepresentative régimes in order to safeguard their economic interests, although there has been a visible reluctance since the late 1960s to practice the old forms of 'gunboat diplomacy' or to apply legislation like the Hickenlooper Amendment (which decrees that the government should cut off aid to a country that confiscates American investments without compensation). There is a new wave of economic nationalism in Latin America, exemplified by the Andean Pact and the investment laws issued by Peru's 'radical generals', as well as by the nationalisation of foreign interests in Chile and of natural gas in Venezuela. The United States has collided with a united front of Latin American governments at recent regional conferences over the terms of trade and American import restrictions.

Dr Raúl Prebisch, the distinguished United Nations economist, has argued that 60 per cent of the population of the region have missed the benefits of economic growth. He also claims that foreign investment has often contributed to underdevelopment by promoting the export of natural resources at the expense of growth in manufacturing, and by securing too generous terms. Prebisch's figures show that Latin America has had to pay back about 19 per cent of the total value of foreign loans received from the public sector each year in the form of repayment, interest, and servicing charges. Foreign aid and investment has clearly often been a mixed blessing. But what also has to be borne in mind, as Dr Prebisch argued to the author in Santiago, is that the foreign corporations are no longer 'queuing up' to get into Latin America, while the need for outside capital and technology is more urgent than ever. Prebisch issued a warning to Latin American governments that they would have to contend with violent explosions of popular discontent if they failed to attain annual growth rates of 8 per cent by 1980.[2]

The economic imperative is there, and in the long term all Latin American governments will be judged by whether they succeed in promoting economic growth and a more equable distribution of goods. But there is no simple panacea. Brazilian economists tend to argue, for example, that there is not much point in cutting the national cake into smaller slices unless one can also increase the size of the cake; that economic growth must take precedence over the redistribution of wealth. That argument is hard on the 50 per cent of the population who have missed out on the benefits of the country's dramatic industrial growth. On the other hand, Brazil's economy is undoubtedly the most dynamic in Latin America. And on present experience, it seems that the agents of radical social change will not be the advocates of violent revolutions but reformist military juntas (as in Peru) or Chilean-style left-wing coalitions in some of the countries where the system can be altered via the ballot-box.[3]

The four case-studies that follow study the course of the most important Latin American urban guerrilla movements in the context of the social and political conditions in each country and the methods that were applied to contain the rebels. In Guatemala, the guerrilla movement was originally a response to the blunders committed by those who toppled the Arbenz régime in 1954. The urban terrorist phase followed the defeat of the guerrillas in the countryside. In Venezuela, in contrast, the urban guerrilla movement was an attempt by a varied alliance of left-wing groups to take advantage of the vulnerability of an infant democracy so as to repeat the Cuban revolution. In Brazil, urban terrorism was partly a response to the military coup of 1964, while in Uruguay the urban guerrillas have set out to erode popular faith in the democratic system and open the way for an armed uprising.

In each case, the government adopted different counter-guerrilla tactics. In Venezuela, the government of President Romulo Betancourt conducted what might be described as a model counter-insurgency operation. Betancourt combined the effective use of military force in graduated doses with respect for the law-book and political measures designed to win public opinion away from the rebels. In Brazil, a military government broke the back of the first urban insurgency (between 1968 and 1970) by tough and crudely unselective measures. The Brazilians' 'military solution', characterised by mass interrogation and the massive deployment of troops in built-up areas, was successful in containing the guerrillas, but deepened the rifts in society in general and created new political tensions. In Guatemala, the army's counter-guerrilla campaign included the use of private right-wing terrorist groups to provide intelligence and kill off opposition leaders. These 'white terrorists' came to pose a greater threat to a civilian, middle-of-the-road administration than the guerrillas they were used to suppress. In Uruguay, finally, a hopelessly divided government with pitifully weak and inexperienced security forces at its disposal failed to contain the urban guerrillas, although the presidential election held in November 1971 showed that more than two-thirds of the voters were still ready to back the traditional parties.

The experience of these four countries showed that it is vital for a government confronted with urban guerrillas to know when to coax and when to coerce. A purely military solution is unlikely to provide any lasting guarantee of stability. On the other hand (as Uruguay has shown) formal respect for a democratic constitution and the liberties of the individual citizen may not be enough to save a government incapable of applying force when it is required.

VENEZUELA: THE PROTOTYPE

Venezuela is the one country in Latin America where an urban insurrection nearly succeeded. Many observers, including Fidel Castro, believed that the country was ripe for revolution in 1962. Teodoro Petkoff, a leading theorist of the Venezuelan Communist Party (PCV) has commented in retrospect that

> The decisive battles—those that could have yielded victory, or in which we suffered defeat—were fought in the towns. In my opinion, we could have won in 1962 if we had properly combined the armed struggle in the towns with risings by army patriots and revolutionaries. In January 1962 we were close to victory: the transport strike in the state of Tachira grew in a matter of days into a national strike of transport workers and merged into a popular rising in Caracas. By that time we had an effective apparatus in the armed forces, which, if we had activated it, would have made a revolutionary victory very likely.[4]

The urban guerrillas of Caracas in the early 1960s, unlike their successors in other parts of Latin America, represented a powerful coalition of political forces, including the local Communist Party (with some 35,000 members), a rebel wing of the ruling Democratic Action Party (AD), students and dissident sections of the armed forces. The moment was opportune: a dictatorship had been overthrown, but the nation was not accustomed to the democratic system that President Romulo Betancourt was trying to shore up, and no constitutional government elected in the past 150 years had succeeded in completing its term. The Cuban revolution in 1959 had seized the imagination of young radicals, and Castro's support for his Venezuelan imitators extended beyond fine words and a glowing example. The Cubans sent instructors and shipments of arms. Somehow, Betancourt and the moderate forces he represented survived this many-headed attack. They managed to find a liberal solution for one of the most serious urban guerrilla assaults that a Latin American government has so far had to withstand.

Venezuela is one of the most highly urbanised countries in Latin America (over two-thirds of the population are townsmen) with the highest per capita national product. Its apparent riches are easily explained: more than 90 per cent of Venezuela's export income comes from oil. The age of the military *caudillos* ended in Venezuela when the repressive autocrat Marcos Pérez Jiménez was toppled by a broad alliance of opposition groups in 1958. After a short interregnum, Romulo Betancourt was elected president and organised a coalition government comprising his own Democratic Action Party (AD), the Democratic Republican Union (URD) and the Christian Democrat (Copei) Party. From the start, Betancourt was highly unpopular with the communists and other left-wing groups, including the AD's youth section, that had participated in the movement against Pérez. Although he had already committed himself to a programme of reform including redistribution of land and oil revenues, he made no bones about his distrust of the local communists. In his inaugural address, he insisted that 'The philosophy of communism is not compatible with the development of Venezuela.'

At first, the communists pursued 'united front' tactics, but as rifts widened inside the régime and it became clear that Betancourt was not prepared to be pushed too fast, they became increasingly aggressive, and at the Third Party Congress in January 1961, they announced a new party line: the 'non-peaceful' development of the Venezuelan revolution. This was the prelude to the war in the streets. The communists were merely keeping in step with a series of crises that placed Betancourt in a perilously shaky position. The men who had agreed that Pérez was a bad thing found it very difficult to agree on anything else once the dictator had gone. The radicals in the AD broke away to form the Movement of the Revolutionary Left (Mir)—a name that has been popular with guerrilla movements ever since—in April 1960. Later in the same year, there was a cabinet rift after Betancourt decided to support an anti-Castro resolution in the Organisation of American States.

Venezuela had already become a prime target for Cuban propaganda, and Betancourt had been alarmed by the acclamation Castro received during a flying visit to Caracas. He sacked his foreign minister (a member of the URD) who did not share his hostility towards Castro, and the upshot was a series of cabinet resignations. In November 1960, the URD left the governing coalition. Betancourt was increasingly isolated in the presidential palace. And he had to face trouble on other fronts as well. Pérez' monumental corruption and mismanagement of the economy had left a legacy of social discontent, and militant union leaders accused Betancourt of dragging his heels in implementing his programme of social reform. During a particularly violent strike at the Venezuelan Telephone Corporation in November 1960, a 'National Liberation Council' that included the communists, the Mir, and extreme elements of the URD called for a mass insurrection.[5] Jésus Faría, a communist leader, had promised the Third Congress that it would be the party's last conference before it seized the reins of power.

At this stage, it seemed that there was good reason for his optimism. Although Betancourt was able to suppress the 1960 uprisings (only a minority of workers supported the general strike) he was left confronting an explosive situation, uncertain even of his troops. There were plenty of young hotheads in the officer corps who resented the novelty of being ruled by civilians. But the series of comic-opera attempted putsches in the first years of Betancourt's régime were less menacing that the fact that the communists had managed to win over several units. In mid-1961, there was a revolt by two army garrisons, followed by two naval mutinies in 1962 at the Carupana and Puerto Cabello naval bases. The rebels who escaped joined the rural guerrilla bands that had been forming since early in 1961.

All the militant groups opposed to Betancourt finally came together to form a unified command on 20 February 1963. They set up a military organisation, the National Liberation Armed Forces (FALN) under the leadership of one of the Puerto Cabellos rebels, Captain Manuel Ponte Rodriguez. The FALN planned for a two-pronged campaign in the cities and the countryside, drawing its troops from the rural guerrillas and 'Tactical Combat Units' in Caracas that had already been formed. The style of the FALN's original manifestoes was soldierly and patriotic. Its documents talk of 'fulfilling the nationalist thought of Simon Bolivar' and of 'defending the national heritage' rather than of any precise political goals. There was even a 'Code of Honour' instructing recruits to respect property and lives, observe discipline and (something probably without parallel in guerrilla literature) to avoid killing servicemen whenever possible.[6]

If the FALN mirrored the values and methods of the ex-soldiers who organised it, the new political alliance—the National Liberation Front (FLN)—was largely in communist hands. There was some initial resistance to the setting-up of a political front (especially from members of the Mir, who argued, like later guerrilla leaders, that a party organisation would inhibit action and usurp the 'spontaneity' of the revolution). But the communist insistence on the 'primacy of politics' won out. The FLN manifestoes emphasised broad and suitably vague nationalist goals designed to attract the widest possible range of support. As it turned out, the FLN was to lead little more than a paper existence. Its activities were completely overshadowed by the guerrilla campaign, and it has significance chiefly as a gambit in the communists' attempt to take command of the insurrection. Nor could any written agreement guarantee tactical unity between the rebel forces. There was no love lost, for example, between the communists and the *miristas* (who were regarded by the PCV leadership as romantic adventurers without any sense of timing).

But the groups that joined the FALN added up to a formidable opposition. This was one of the few occasions to begin with, when a Latin American communist party threw its full weight behind a guerrilla campaign—so that the urban terrorists in Caracas had an initial advantage that few later urban guerrillas have enjoyed. From the end of 1961, a number of communist militants, including Douglas Bravo, had left Caracas to try to set up guerrilla *focos*. These early commandos lacked co-ordination and soon lost touch with the capital. They also found it very difficult to win support among the conservative peasantry who formed the backbone of Betancourt's electoral support. The army snuffed out most of the rural guerrilla groups early in 1962; Bravo's own 'Chirinois Front', operating in the rugged hills of Falcón state in the north-west of Venezuela, was one of the few that showed any capacity for survival.

The rural campaign was always secondary, for obvious reasons. Venezuela is an 'urban' society to the extent that Britain or the United States are urban societies. As Moises Moleiro, one of the leaders of the Mir, later conceded, 'It is not possible in Venezuela to start a rural campaign that will end with the countryside encircling the cities. This is out of the question, because the rural areas are marginal to the life of the country . . . A peasant war is impossible, in the last analysis, because we are not a peasant people.'[7] The importance of Venezuela in the development of urban guerrilla warfare in Latin America is that the Venezuelan rebels accepted the logic of the situation: although inspired and encouraged by the Cuban example, they did not blindly try to follow precepts irrelevant to the local situation.

The terrorist campaign in Caracas got under way in 1962. The terrorist tactics included sabotage of vital services and oil pipelines and installations (although they never succeeded in disrupting the petroleum industry); a programme of selective assassination that the terrorists themselves described as a policy of 'kill a cop a day'; and a series of spectacular exploits designed to gain easy publicity. These included the hijacking of the Venezuelan freighter *Anzoátegui* (February 1963), the kidnapping of an Argentine football star, Alfredo di Stefano, who was touring with the Spanish team Real Madrid, and the abduction of Colonel Chenault, a member of the American military mission (August and November 1963). They even stole (and promptly returned) a visiting collection of French impressionist paintings in January 1963. That was perhaps the supreme example of an operation engineered solely for fun and cheap headlines. None of these dramatic gestures were designed to extort a ransom.

At the height of the campaign, the FALN cadres in Caracas were organised in large units of 101 men, each with its 'rear-line base': a system of secret hiding-places, arms caches, and transport pools.[8] They profited from the communist network and their considerable support among students at the Central University of Caracas. At that stage, the university, like most Latin American universities, enjoyed considerable autonomy which was abused to enable radical students to provide sanctuary for terrorists. Students played a major part in the FALN campaign, and as recently as December 1966, troops who were ordered to comb the Central University found arms and ammunition, stolen cars, printing presses (used both for turning out pamphlets and for minting counterfeit money), radio transmitters and pilfered weapons permits, government seals and army uniforms.[9]

At the start of the campaign, the terrorists were able to make quick getaways and to rally substantial popular support. The FALN organised a series of mass confrontations between demonstrators and the police. But they overplayed their hand by calling for a general strike in November 1963. Despite communist backing, only a handful of unions were ready to support the strike. The final goal of the rebels, according to the 'Caracas Plan' that the government claimed to have captured at the end of 1963, was to time the general strike to coincide with an armed uprising and seize the capital on the eve of the presidential elections scheduled for December 1963.

The plan failed for both political and military reasons. The rebels overestimated their popular strength and underestimated the psychological effect of the impending elections. Although it was a key element in their strategy to force Betancourt to resort to increasingly repressive measures that would further divide his cabinet and alienate moderate opinion, the president showed a very astute sense of timing. Betancourt delayed using emergency measures until the public was thoroughly frightened and conscious of the danger that the terrorists represented. For example, the naval mutiny at Puerto Cabellos provided the pretext to suspend some constitutional liberties and to ban the Communist Party and the Mir. After a month, the constitutional guarantees were restored.

Similarly, Betancourt was very careful to secure the backing of moderate union leaders and the army before he again resorted to emergency measures on 7 October 1962. A vicious attack by the FALN on an excursion train in September 1963, mobilised the 'law and order' majority and enabled Betancourt to order the wholesale arrest of communists and *miristas* who had previously enjoyed parliamentary immunity. Throughout, the president took great pains to show his respect for the due legal process, and exceptional measures were applied only when moderate opinion was already convinced of the need for them. It is hardly necessary to point out the dangers that were involved in this 'fabian' tactic. Betancourt always ran the risk of responding too late, and his cautious behaviour angered some of his generals and might have provoked a right-wing military coup (a possibility that the rebels were counting on).

The election was the final political gesture that enabled Betancourt to get the situation under control. The very prospect of a free election destroyed the rebels' argument that change could only be brought about through violence and triggered off a bitter internal debate inside the FALN. The FALN finally decided to 'order' a boycott of the polls. But 90 per cent of the electorate turned out to vote in December—a massive vote *against* the terrorists. When Raúl Leoni, Betancourt's chosen successor (who had pulled in 32 per cent of the votes) finally took office in March 1964, he set a new precedent for Venezuela: this was the first time that an elected president had managed to hand over his power to an elected successor.

But Betancourt's victory has to be understood in military terms as well. In the early stages of the battle for Caracas, the police were forced to evacuate their stations in the slum fringes and some working-class suburbs. According to Petkoff, the FALN 'led full-scale battles between the people of an entire city quarter and the police and the army. The fearlessness and the tenacity shown by our comrades in the street fighting were little short of miraculous. The hills of Caracas became fortresses and were a nightmare for police and troops. After any large-scale operation, with the city quarter blocked off, the police searches usually yielded next to nothing (fighters and arms "vanishing" inexplicably) because the vanguard was closely linked with the people in the area.' In the early stages, it was easy to stage an ambush by setting a 'bait': exploding a bomb in an area that had been quiet up to that point, or issuing false alarms. But in the later stages, the Venezuelan urban guerrillas found themselves trapped by their lack of mobility. It was impossible to muster large bodies of men for an operation without being quickly detected, and surprise attacks usually had to be staged at night. The army found it easy to cordon off 'sympathetic' areas (or *ranchos*) and carry out mass searches. In the later stages of the campaign, the Venezuelan army and national guard controlled movement in the streets by the methods that have become familiar in Belfast: heavy machine-gun posts and watchtowers were placed at key points on roofs, hilltops, and at cross-roads.[10] This put an end to major urban engagements.

After the 1963 election, the insurgents were hopelessly divided, and the communists gradually returned to the policy of 'peaceful coexistence' and the 'united front' tactics that were formally reinstated as the party line in 1967. At the Eighth Plenum of the party's central committee, held in April–May 1967, shortly after three 'soft-line' leaders—Petkoff, García Ponce and Pompeyo Márquez—had escaped from prison, the communists engaged in a bout of self-criticism. The Plenum's report catalogued a series of 'errors' committed by the party in the early 1960s, including overestimating the prospects for armed insurrection; the boycott of the 1963 election; and 'adventurism' and mistaken trust in guerrilla tactics. The PCV had returned to the fold. Like the other Latin American Moscow-line communist parties, it had now taken its stand against armed struggle.

But some of its members refused to fall in with official policy. Douglas Bravo, with the backing of some *miristas* and of Dr Castro, broke away to form a new guerrilla front in 1966. Their new campaign of urban terrorism fizzled out by the end of the year, and the murder of the brother of the foreign minister early in 1967 was hotly denounced by the PCV leadership. Since 1967, the remnants of the guerrilla movements have operated in two rural areas: Bravo's group in the north-western states of Falcón, Lara and Yaracuy; and *mirista* guerrillas in the El Bachiller ranges in the eastern part of the country. Despite several attempts to form a new rebel alliance, the guerrillas have squandered their energies on personal squabbles and arid theoretical debates. One leader of the Mir, Eduardo Ortiz Bucarán, claimed in 1968 that Douglas Bravo and his men had inherited 'some of the sectarianism which characterised the Communist Party's relations with the Mir, to the detriment of the revolutionary movement'.[11] A second attempt to organise an election boycott, in December 1968, failed miserably. Rafael Caldera, the Christian Democrat candidate, was elected president and announced a 'pacification programme' that provided for the legalisation of the Communist Party, an amnesty for guerrillas who wanted to give themselves up, and a 'peace commission' headed by the Archbishop of Caracas. This encouraged a few defections. The termination of Cuban aid to the guerrillas in 1969 was followed by a bitter public exchange in which Douglas Bravo reproached Castro for abandoning the continental revolution.[12] The guerrillas had reached their nadir.

Although rural guerrillas were able to survive longer than urban terrorists in Venezuela, they operated at the fringes of the country's political life, often cut off from the cities for months at a time.[13] Once Caracas was won, the country was won. Betancourt's victory in the battle of Caracas in 1963 was a rare example of the successful application of a 'double strategy' for counter-insurgency in Latin America. He won against considerable odds. Other Latin American régimes, faced with rather different situations or defending different political interests, have tried other solutions.

GUATEMALA: ZONE OF TERROR

In Guatemala, as in other parts of Latin America, urban terrorism outlived the rural guerrilla campaign. The experience of the Guatemalan rebels who first pitched their tents in the rugged north-eastern provinces in 1962 is an object-lesson in the problems that confront a guerrilla movement in contemporary Latin America. On the face of it, the Rebel Armed Forces (FAR) and the Movement of the 13th November (MR-13) had a number of things in their favour. They went into action at a time of widespread social unrest. They had the backing of the local communist party—which called itself the Guatemalan Labour Party (PGT)—and of Fidel Castro. Their first leaders were radical young army officers who brought a fund of specialised knowledge of guerrilla tactics and counter-insurgency operations with them. And they faced an unpopular and unstable government.

But by 1967, the rural guerrillas had ceased to be a significant military force. The key to the government's victory lay in a 'pilot plan' for counter-insurgency that combined brutal military repression with civic action projects. The transfer of power from a military junta to an elected government in 1966 also helped to confer legitimacy on the régime and provoked an internal debate in the guerrilla movement. But in the final analysis, what probably counted for most was a bloody campaign of 'white terror' carried out both by the security forces and by paramilitary groups and right-wing societies. The Guatemalan régime managed to contain the violence of the left. But it showed neither the capacity nor the desire to curb the greater violence of the far right. That is why more than one recent observer has come away with the feeling that the country has turned into a political version of Prohibition Chicago.

Guatemala is a small country of fewer than 5 million people, straddling the waist of the Americas. It has always been marginal to the world economy: it has no important minerals (apart from a little oil) and almost no industry. In the last century, it depended on bananas; today, it still relies heavily on a single primary product, coffee. It is still essentially a peasant society, and also one of the most 'Indian' societies in Latin America. Only about half the population speaks Spanish. Guatemala's statistics make depressing reading. Three-quarters of the population earn about twenty cents a day. Many peasants are landless, since 2 per cent of the population hold around 70 per cent of the cultivated land. The illiteracy rate stands at more than 65 per cent, and is actually rising. And the problem of illiteracy is only one aspect of the general lack of communications. The northern province of Alta Verapaz has no roads capable of bearing wheeled traffic. Goods are moved on the backs of the Indians, as in the centuries before the Spanish conquest.

These figures may shock western readers, but they do not add up to a reason for revolt *in themselves*. Rebel leaders have always had trouble in trying to make recruits amongst an Indian population that has to be addressed in its own varying dialects and is deeply suspicious of city-bred radicals. Many of the peasant communities share a static and fatalistic view of the world inherited from their Mayan ancestors. And most Indian youths also have to undergo army discipline: it is much harder for a peasant boy to evade the draft than for an urban *ladino*,[14] and it is symptomatic that more than 62 per cent of army conscripts are illiterate.[15] On the other hand, the seasonal movement of agricultural labour from the northern provinces to the coffee and cotton plantations of the south has aroused higher expectations and deep resentment against employers who often pay less than the wages that were promised. But the most important factor is the memory of the 'revolutionary' decade between 1944 and 1954.

Guatemala is unique in Latin America, not because a radical reformist régime was overthrown by a military coup (backed by the Central Intelligence Agency) in 1954, but because those who seized power promptly set out to put the national clock back by ten years. Colonel Jacobo Arbenz' Agrarian Reform Law of 1952 had provided for the development of the peasant private economy through the re-distribution of land. In comparison with later land reform projects in Chile and Peru, it was a fairly moderate venture. Its basic proposals were to eliminate feudal systems of land tenure, to abolish forced labour and to bring unused or under-utilised estates into production. The law provided for the expropriation of idle lands; but the owners were to be compensated with interest-bearing bonds, and the beneficiaries of land reform were obliged to pay for their new plots on the instalment system.[16]

By the time that Colonel Castillo Armas marched his tiny invading force over the Honduran border and persuaded Arbenz to resign early in 1954, about 100,000 peasant families had already benefited from the land reform.[17] Under pressure from the United Fruit Company and the big landowners, Castillo Armas then proceeded to commit a social and political blunder without parallel in Latin American experience: he returned all the expropriated lands to their former owners. Landowners were licensed to use guns to defend their properties. At a single stroke, Castillo Armas set out to resurrect the social structures that prevailed under Ubico, the dictator deposed in 1944. But Castillo and his successors discovered that a decade of history cannot be erased overnight. It has been alleged that 8,000 peasant organisers were murdered during Castillo's three years in office.[18] The rationale for this official violence was a primitive and hysterical form of anti-communism, that identified the real 'defence against communism' with the interests of a narrow clique of landowners and army colonels.

Castillo's political legacy was a very shaky structure of government: Ydígoras Fuentes was elected to the presidency in 1958, but set up an almost wholly military cabinet after the 1962 strikes and was overthrown by an army junta on the eve of a second election in 1963. Ydígoras was elbowed aside by his own minister of defence, who enforced a 'state of siege' during thirty of his thirty-nine months in office. On 1 July 1966, to everyone's surprise, a civilian took office after a relatively clean election. But President Julio César Méndez Montenegro's reformist intentions were sabotaged from the start by a powerful lobby of hardliners in the army and local finance. He was finally replaced by another military man, Colonel Arana Osorio, after the 1970 elections.

The fact that two elections have been held since 1966 does not alter the fact that the army is the real basis of government in Guatemala. Most state governors, for example, are drawn from the ranks of the army. Under a 'pact' concluded with Méndez Montenegro shortly before he assumed office in 1966, the army has the right of veto over ministerial appointment. But it would be wrong to start out with the idea that the Guatemalan army is a monolithic group. As in other countries where the man on horseback is the master of power, the normal cut-and-thrust of political debate has tended to move inside the barracks. The beginnings of political insurrection in Guatemala in 1960 were a dramatic illustration of the rifts within the armed forces.

The first guerrilla leaders were drawn from the ranks of the idealistic young officers who attempted a putsch against Ydígoras on 13 November 1960. Turcios Lima, Yon Sosa, Luís Trejo and Alejandro de León—all of them lieutenants at the time—were among their number. Most of these men had passed through the Escuela Polytechnica, an institution that reflected the broader horizons and increasing professionalisation of the Guatemalan officer corps and had produced some of Arbenz' most enthusiastic military supporters in the years before 1954. Many of them had also been trained in counter-insurgency techniques by the Americans. Turcios Lima had been to Fort Benning in Georgia and Yon Sosa had gone to Fort Gulick in the Panama Canal Zone.

The motives of the fifty-odd officers who joined the coup were varied.[19] There was widespread resentment among young nationalists at the fact that President Ydígoras was allowing the Americans to train Cuban exiles on Guatemalan soil. Many of the younger officers saw a new, paternalistic role for the army as an instrument of national development and social change. But the coup was badly organised. The rebels stole arms from the Matamoros base outside the capital and occupied the Zacapa base and the town of Puerto Barrios on the Atlantic coast, but within four days, Ydígoras had mastered the situation. The rebels took flight into neighbouring Honduras and El Salvador, to linger on as exiles or return as guerrillas.

What followed between 1960 and 1962 was a process of convergence between these soldier-rebels and other political groups opposed to the Ydígoras régime. The Guatemalan Communist Party (PCT) had always been divided between the 'armed struggle' and the 'peaceful coexistence' schools. Although the party adopted armed struggle in theory after the 1954 coup, no action was taken to carry out this policy—as the secretary-general of the PGT later admitted.[20] The party leaders remained distrustful of the soldier-guerrillas who had founded the Movement of November 13 (MR-13) in 1961. But after a separate communist attempt to found a guerrilla front failed dismally, they decided to hitch their wagon to MR-13, and in December 1962, a united front called the Rebel Armed Forces (FAR) was set up.

Before the FAR was formed, the guerrilla campaign had already been launched with the murder of the secret police chief, Ranulfo González, in January 1962. The MR-13 group set up bases in the east of Guatemala in the Sierra de las Minas and in Izabal state in the following months, and this area was to become the main focus for the rural campaign over the next five years. César Montes, who later became the leader of the FAR, described the terrain in the following term :

We have a very special type of mountain. The Sierra de las Minas runs parallel to the highway that is most important for export, along which products move to the Atlantic ports. So the army can put as many troops as it likes along the whole length of the highway and of the Sierra, and send them up the mountains when it chooses. It isn't like other ranges—for example in Santa Cruz, Bolivia—where the mountains are difficult of access in that part of the Ñancahuanzu gorge, or the Sierra Maestra which is at the tip of Cuba with the road stopping short of there. Here, paths lead up into the Sierra from the highway itself, greatly easing the strain on the army.[21]

The lie of the land made it easy to pour troops into the mountains when a serious government offensive was mounted at the end of 1966.

The guerrilla campaign developed on two fronts. In the northeast, Turcios Lima's 'Edgar Ibarra Front' and Yon Sosa's MR-13 (originally united but increasingly hostile before they formally separated in 1965) set out to coax and coerce peasant support and liquidate alternative leaders in the villages. Both Turcios and Yon Sosa placed great stress on 'armed propaganda'. They took over whole villages in order to deliver speeches and impose a communist cell structure on the villagers. Yon Sosa's group, which was increasingly coming under the influence of Trotskyist ideas, set up a perilously vulnerable 'self-defence' system. Pro-government elements were assassinated and openly replaced by guerrilla sympathisers. When the army took the offensive, this made it very easy to root out the guerrillas' supporters. According to the Declaration of Sierra de las Minas, issued over the joint signatures of Yon Sosa and Turcios Lima, but reflecting the former's ideas:

> The guerrilla front has organized village and farm committees, elected by the peasants themselves. These function clandestinely and give aid to the guerrilla army as well as resolving problems raised within their own communities. In some areas these committees have created their own militia, made up of peasants who continue their daily work on the land but also participate in specific guerrilla actions although they are not part of the regular forces. Many wealthy landowners have been forced to withdraw repressive measures and to abolish the payment of rent on some estates. Other landowners have fled and military agents have been brought to justice.[22]

Turcios' Edgar Ibarra Front laid much greater emphasis on constant movement and secrecy. Turcios did not share Yon Sosa's faith in popular spontaneity, and he later claimed that for Yon Sosa, 'guerrilla warfare is a stimulant used to alter the political

situation. For us, guerrilla warfare is basic, and that's what brings
us against the communists, who are often timid and cautious.'[23]
These disagreements over tactics led to a formal rift between the
two guerrilla leaders in 1965. At Turcios' instigation, the communists helped to form a 'new' FAR excluding Yon Sosa's group
which was supposed to pursue a more aggressive military line. But
Turcios never succeeded in enlisting as much support from the
city-based communists as he was angling for.

In Guatemala City, the urban terrorist campaign, spearheaded by
Turcios Lima and the communist youth cadres, was intensified
after Colonel Peralta Azurdia seized power in 1963. In 1965, there
was a wave of murders and kidnappings in the capital. Colonel
Harold Houser, the chief of the American military mission, was
assassinated in February, and the Guatemalan deputy minister of
defence was killed in May. At the end of the year, there was a series
of kidnappings of prominent local citizens which Turcios tried to
rationalise in the following terms:

> We place the Government in ridicule whenever we want to . . .
> The bourgeoisie paid little attention or seemed rather indifferent
> to our first kidnapping. But when we intensified this type of
> action, the situation changed and this very bourgeoisie demanded
> that the Government guarantee their lives and properties, and
> practically threatened the Government with an economic boycott
> if those guarantees were not granted. Then Peralta Azurdia, self-
> styled Head of State, put into effect the death penalty for kid-
> napping. But the day after the law came into effect we demanded
> ransom for another kidnapping, the victim being no less than the
> son of a bank president and owner of the building in which the
> Yankee Embassy is located. While Mr Peralta talked about the
> guarantee his régime offered to the bourgeoisie, we were demand-
> ing the above-mentioned ransom, and the newspapers published
> this headline: 'While the Head of State Talks About Guarantees,
> the Revolutionaries Collect Ransom for a kidnapping.' The people
> were pleased; when there's a kidnapping, everybody says: ' . . . at
> last they're laying hands on the millionaires.' These happenings
> provoke political crisis.[24]

Although Turcios believed that revolution would only come to
Guatemala through a peasant uprising he also played a leading role
in setting up the terrorist network in Guatemala City. An FAR

leader called José López Ruiz (who had been educated in Cuba before taking charge of the urban guerrillas' explosives section) revealed some of the details of the cell-system after he was captured by the police in 1968. López Ruiz disclosed that ten terrorist cells, each with between three and six members were carrying out sabotage and propaganda activities in Guatemala City.[25] A similar confession from a student guerrilla revealed that there had been a concerted drive to make recruits on campus. He claimed that he had been recruited by his sociology professor, and that guerrilla leaders regularly visited San Carlos university.[26]

The rift between Yon Sosa and Turcios Lima was followed by more bickering in 1966. Yon Sosa continued to attack the communist line as 'a programme of compromise with capitalism', but he also turned against the Trotskyist Fourth International after he discovered that three Trotskyist agents in the MR-13 had been channelling funds back to their master in Buenos Aires. And Turcios Lima and his deputy, César Montes, fell out with the communists over the question of how to play the 1966 election. Three candidates had presented themselves as candidates for the March elections: two (inevitable) colonels, and Julio César Méndez Montenegro, a former law professor fielded by the cautiously reformist Revolutionary Party. Turcios was deeply suspicious of the ballot-box. 'To the revolutionaries,' he declared, 'it must be obvious that their efforts should not be wasted in increasing the number of deceived workers.'[27] But the communists voted to support Méndez as presidential candidate while Turcios was away in Havana. He did not forgive them.

Méndez' victory at the polls marked the parting of the ways between the guerrillas and the communists although the split was not formalised until early in 1968. Under military pressure, Méndez modified his original offer of an amnesty for guerrillas so that it really amounted to an eight-day ultimatum to surrender. The army offensive against the rural guerrilla bases was launched at the end of the year. The guerrillas were caught badly off balance. They had been weakened by the loss of Turcios, who was killed in a mysterious road accident on October 2. The army campaign of 1966–67 was an almost total success. Civic action schemes, despite government publicity, played only a very minor role in the destruction of the rural guerrillas.[28] The triumph of the counter-insurgency operation formally launched on 1 February 1967 under the command of Colonel Arana Osorio really hinged on intelligence, firepower, and counter-terror. The offer of an amnesty and cash rewards for guerrillas who were ready to become informers led to several important defections. An ex-army sergeant nicknamed 'El Gallo' who had risen to a prominent position in the Edgar Ibarra Front gave away the whole courier system of the rural FAR. Colonel Arana ringed the Sierra with troops (who were trained and sometimes guided by Green Berets and American Rangers) and sorties were flown against the guerrillas from American bases in Panama.[29] The guerrillas were easily isolated from their logistics bases in the towns. And the network of peasant committees that had been set up in the north-eastern states was a fairly supine victim to brutal repression.

The most sinister aspect of the counter-insurgency campaign was the use of paramilitary groups and 'death squads' like Mano Blanca (the 'White Hand'), the New Anti-Communist Organisation (NOA) and the Anti-Communist Council of Guatemala (Codeg). Mano Blanca's existence had first been announced a month before Méndez took office. A leaflet was printed showing a white hand over a red circle ringed with black, with the inscription: 'This is the hand that will eradicate renegades and traitors to their country.' The secret societies proceeded to carry out a bloody purge of opposition elements, including thousands of people who had no connection with the guerrillas or the PGT. They were also active in collecting 'dirty' intelligence by torture, and the Guatemalans have proved inventive in devising new forms of cruelty: common forms of torture in the backblocks included tying a rubber band around a man's throat and pulling both ends to break his thyroid (making speech and eating difficult) or pushing a bag filled with insecticide over his head.[30] Estimates of the numbers of people killed in the eastern provinces by vigilante groups between 1967 and 1968 range from 2,000 up to 6,000. An American priest has alleged that the three 'white terrorist' groups mentioned were responsible for the deaths of 'more than 2,800 intellectuals, students, labour leaders and peasants' over a period of eighteen months.[31] It was significant that some of the men who were most active in the secret societies had switched their allegiances from the guerrillas. A notorious example was a young Zacapa landowner, Oliveiro Castañeda, who became the leader of the Mano Blanco with Arana's backing and later entered congress as a member of Arana's party, the National Liberation Movement (MLN).

The government found it difficult to call off the savage mastiffs it had unleashed. The whole country was shocked when right-wing terrorists followed up the sexual assault and murder of a former Miss Guatemala reputed to be a guerrilla sympathiser with the kidnapping of the archbishop of Guatemala early in 1968. Méndez was finally galvanised into action and, with American backing, posted Colonel Arana to Nicaragua as Guatemalan ambassador, and sacked his defence minister and police chief. In an interview with the journalist Norman Gall, Mario Sandoval Alarcón, the secretary-general of Arana's party, the MLN, argued 'that the terrorism of the guerrillas, which has resulted in the death of many of our people, has forced the government to adopt a plan of complete illegality, but this has brought results.'[32] It has already been argued in this book that there is a symbiotic relationship between extremists that can lead to a vicious spiral of violence and counter-violence. But for a government to resort to 'a plan of complete illegality' is for it to abrogate any claim to legitimacy. It has even been asserted that in Guatemala 'a system of institutional terror' has been constructed that chooses its victims from 'a zone of terror' embracing all opposition groups, democratic or not.[33] The victims have included prominent academics, lawyers, journalists, union leaders, and opposition deputies.

Defeat in the countryside led the Guatemalan guerrillas to concentrate on an urban offensive from the end of 1967—although guerrilla fronts still survive in the north-east and there was systematic arson of haciendas in the southern provinces of San Marcos and Escuíntla after 1968. Yon Sosa's forces and the FAR reunited briefly late in 1968, but fell apart again in 1969. Yon Sosa was hunted across the border into the Mexican state of Chiapas where he was gunned down by a Mexican army patrol early in 1970.[34] César Montes survived at the head of the FAR's urban campaign.

FAR terrorism since 1967 has included systematic arson of company buildings and murder or abduction of American advisers, policemen, landowners and foreign businessmen. They killed an American ambassador, John Gordon Mein, after an abortive attempt to kidnap him in 1968. After they abducted the West German ambassador, Count von Spreti, early in 1970 and President Méndez tried to call their bluff by turning down their demand for the release of all political prisoners, they murdered their hostage in cold blood.

In December 1969, the guerrillas opened a new phase of urban violence as a run-up to the March 1970 presidential elections. They murdered four policemen and the right-wing deputy David Guerra Guzmán in December, and on 27 February 1970, they carried out an operation that was clearly designed to damage the electoral chances of Méndez' chosen successor, Fuentes Pieruccini. They kidnapped the Guatemalan foreign minister, Alberto Fuentes Mohr, and released him two days later in return for an imprisoned FAR member. It was hardly possible to imagine a move better-calculated to humiliate the government. President Méndez was shown to be incapable of protecting his closest friends. The abduction of Fuentes Mohr partly explained why the people of the capital flocked to the polling booths of March 1 to vote for Colonel Arana Osorio, the candidate of the right. One FAR leader was reported to have said on the eve of the election that Arana was the guerrillas' choice for president. They were hoping that a new wave of short-sighted repression would make a reformist solution impossible for Guatemala.

Sporadic terrorism continued through 1970. Even the communists claimed that their new fighting arm, confusingly named the Revolutionary Armed Forces, was responsible for some of the terrorist outrages — including a bomb attack on the offices of the conservative newspaper *La Hora* in September. A new vigilante group, *Ojo por Ojo* ('An Eye for an Eye') emerged on the far right. Terrorism had almost ceased to be selective in Guatemala.

Between them, the extremists of both the right and the left sabotaged the chances for moderate reform in Guatemala and made the results of the elections appear meaningless. Who can have faith in the ballot-box when deputies who dare to voice cautious dissent are gunned down on the steps of congress? The example of Guatemala shows in the starkest possible way that, in the long term, there is no purely military solution for insurgency. By failing to tackle the causes of revolt, the Guatemalan régime has managed to perpetuate it. While most other third world governments (though very belatedly in the case of countries like South Vietnam) have been trying to damp down rural support for rebellion through agrarian reform, the Guatemalans have tried to freeze an unjust and untenable division of land. The Guatemalan case also shows that the kind of myopia that overlooks the threat from the extreme right while hammering the far left can end by substituting one devil for another and defining 'order' as the private interest of a handful of callous men.

9
Brazil: Failure of a Strategy

Middle-class Brazilians are fond of saying that their country is currently undergoing the same process of breathless industrial expansion that Japan experienced under the Meiji Restoration or that carried the United States into the twentieth century. One popular view pictures Brazil approaching the year 2000 in the ranks of the great powers, equipped with space satellites and nuclear weapons and trailing behind a population of 200 million.[1] Whether Brazil will really develop into the Japan or the United States of Latin America remains to be seen. The military governments that have ruled since the 1964 coup have fulfilled their promise to bring 'order and progress'. But their kind of order has weighed heavily on the shoulders of part of the population, and the progress demonstrated by the growth figures has been distributed very unevenly.

On the last day of March 1964, the Brazilian armed forces, supported by local business and most of the middle class, overthrew the régime of João Goulart.[2] Goulart, a reformist president who had succeeded Janio Quadros in 1961, had long been distrusted by the high command. Under his ineffectual leadership, the country drifted towards economic collapse. The rate of inflation soared to 8 per cent *per month*, industrial production sagged, and foreign investors were frightened away. At the same time, his promises of agrarian and social reform, blocked by a hostile congress, raised hopes that he was unable to satisfy. The crisis came at the beginning of March, when Goulart appealed to labour and peasant leaders and to junior army officers to back him in his attempt to ram through reform measures by presidential decree. The armed forces were outraged by his refusal to punish radical sailors and marines who had demonstrated in favour of the reform programme, and there was almost unanimous support amongst the officer corps for the coup as a necessary move to restore discipline. Goulart's régime proved brittle. After two days, all resistance had crumbled away and Marshal Humberto Castelo Branco took over as president.

The Brazilian army had intervened in politics on many previous occasions (and, notably, to remove the populist leader Getulio Vargas in 1945 and 1954). It had traditionally acted as the instrument of conservative business and landowning interests. What made the 1964 coup different was that it turned out to be the preliminary to a period of prolonged military rule unparalleled since the early days of the republic, in which the armed forces imposed a new kind of discipline on the country. Elections have been postponed, put off, or stripped of any real political impact, and the powers of congress have been rigorously curtailed.

Soon after the coup, deputies were forbidden to propose bills that would involve public expense, and congress was allowed only a fixed period in which to delay approval of executive measures. Later moves restricted the right of parliamentary immunity and denied deputies the right to demand information from ministers. Only two parties, the official Arena (or National Reforming Alliance) and the opposition MDB (Brazilian Democratic Movement) were licensed to contest elections, although there were moves by Pedro Aleixo, a former vice-president, to establish a new party early in 1971. It remained clear to everyone that the real power lay in the barracks, although the generals drew on the services of talented 'technocrats' like Roberto Campos (finance minister under Castelo Branco) and Delfim Neto and Reis Velloso (ministers of finance and planning respectively under Garrastazú Medici) to manage the economy.

On the economic front, the post-1964 governments cleared the way (after two years of austerity in which real wages dropped and production of consumer goods also fell) for a period of impressive industrial growth.[3] The gross domestic product rose by $9\frac{1}{2}$ per cent in 1970 and it was expected that the official target of a 10 per cent rise in industrial production in 1971 would be surpassed. By a complex process of adjustment and devaluation, the Brazilians learned to live with an annual rate of inflation of around 20 per cent. The planners issued a document late in 1970 entitled 'Goals and Bases for Government Action' that projected annual growth rates of

6 per cent in *per capita* income, 12 per cent in gross fixed investment, and 10 per cent in exports over the 1970–73 period.[4]

These figures were spectacular by Latin American standards, but they masked some long-term problems and structural weaknesses, including the rising burden of debt repayments, the slow development of the domestic market, and the failure to distribute the benefits of rapid growth to the average worker. In 1969, the minimum wage level was the lowest, in real terms, since 1953.[5] And there was the continuing problem of the regions. One Brazilian remarked to me that 'We are running an internal empire here. The *nordeste* is as far from Rio, psychologically, as Uganda was from London in the colonial days.' On a conservative estimate, the people of the south-eastern states, where the fastest economic growth has taken place, are earning four times as much on the average as the people of the north-east. Despite regional development schemes and the activities of development agencies like Sudene, it may take centuries before the *nordestinos* catch up.

Politically, successive military presidents have never formally renounced the idea of an eventual return to civilian rule. In a speech delivered in February 1971, the minister of justice, Alfredo Buzaid, defined the government's political goal as 'social democracy'. That would include freely elected political representation, equality before the law, and personal liberty. He also made it clear that it would take a long time before this came about. In fact there seems to have been a progressive hardening of the Brazilian régime, with some fluctuations. Marshal Castelo Branco, a staff officer, was succeeded by Marshal Costa e Silva, an infantry officer, who suffered a stroke in August 1969 at a moment when he had been talking about liberalising the régime and was replaced by General Garrastazú Medici, a former intelligence officer. At the end of 1968, after a violent year of strikes (especially among the miners of Minas Gerais state), student demonstrations and the beginnings of urban guerrilla warfare in Rio and São Paulo, the generals staged what amounted to a coup within the coup.

Institutional Act No. 5, promulgated on December 13, concentrated all executive powers in the hands of the president and even denied the supreme court the power to judge the constitutionality of government acts. In a document entitled 'Counter-Revolution', issued by Costa e Silva the following week, he justified these extraordinary measures on the grounds that the strikes and terrorist actions 'prove beyond all doubt that the movement of pseudo-students, of many active politicians and persons deprived of their political rights, of the so-called progressive clergymen is exclusively designed to subvert the domestic order and represents an attempt to stage a counter-revolution.'[6]

From this time, repressive measures against liberal students and academics, radical priests and opposition politicians were stepped up. One former opposition deputy has claimed that the generals constructed a 'terrorist state', which he defines in the following terms:

> A terrorist state bases its power on the permanent insecurity of all social classes. Using fear as a political instrument, it places even the bureaucracy, élite administrators, and the repressive apparatus inside the circle of fear. Its legal code is so tenuous that nobody can feel safe or plead 'not-guilty' before the tribunals. Thought control, suspicion, propaganda, manipulation and isolation are its defensive weapons; torture, confiscation, illegal imprisonment and execution and murder are its offensive weapons.[7]

But Brazil is not a totalitarian state. It has been described as a dictatorship without a dictator. The use of torture and other forms of indiscriminate repression have spread, not because of central direction, but because of the absence of sufficient central control over the actions of the various police and intelligence agencies and the absence of legal and institutional curbs on the military tribunals. The *Inqueritos Policais-Militares* have been allowed to function as a parallel judiciary.

The soldiers who have taken it upon themselves to determine the nature of treason started out with only the vaguest perception of the enemy they were pursuing. One of President Medici's personal advisers, Colonel Octavio Costa, explained to me that 'The difference between the soldier and the priest is that the priest looks upon all men as his friends, and thus may be deceived into siding with subversives, while the soldier is trained to divide mankind into friends and enemies, and thus finds it hard to see the difference between liberal critics and subversives.' A mass of evidence has been presented on the use of torture and other forms of official terror in Brazil that shows just how far that logic can lead. One of the rare cases of torture reported in the Brazilian press involved an ordinary housewife who was reported to have been tortured to death at the Barro Banco headquarters of the military police after she had had a quarrel with a policeman's wife.[8] The champion tennis player, Thomas Koch, was badly beaten up by police sadists in 1969, after pausing briefly in a no-parking zone in Santa Cruz.

Incidents of this kind have little to do with a 'political crusade' against any internal enemy, real or imagined. They have a great deal to do with moral corruption and the failure of discipline inside the police apparatus in Brazil. The Brazilian government has promised several times to punish those who abuse their authority. But Colonel Costa also explained that 'We can't afford a My Lai scandal here'. A French correspondent has reported a chilling account of how the hydra-headed intelligence apparatus in Brazil has become tangled up in its own coils. There is a certain rivalry between the naval intelligence organisation, Cenimar, and the military Department of Social and Political Order (DOPS). A former friend of Goulart was arrested by the military police but had the good fortune to pass an admiral he knew well in a corridor as he was being led to the interrogation-room. The admiral secured his release and provided him with a safe-conduct. But he maintained that if he were approached by another intelligence organisation, his only hope would be 'to telephone to the admiral'.[9] The autonomy and the excesses of the security forces have alienated some of the original civilian supporters of the military régime. I spoke with the editor of one of the most important Brazilian papers, who told me that he had been arrested *twenty-five* times by various security agencies. Perhaps that suggests that the act of arrest in itself is not serious. But even in authoritarian states, it would be considered unusual for a police lieutenant to lock up the editor of a major conservative newspaper without a charge, on his own initiative.

Marcio Moreira Alves has argued that 'mounting terror is the only future' for the Brazilian régime.[10] That does not necessarily follow. Brazil has two faces: one is the economic success story, the other the licensed repression. The argument of Brazilian moderates is that in the long run, social reform and political liberalisation will catch up with economic growth.[11] They also point out that there are rival tendencies in the Brazilian armed forces, and that radical change may come from within the military establishment, as in Peru. General Albuquerque Lima, who was transferred to the reserve in March 1971, has identified himself with a group of junior officers who believe that the army should make itself the agent of social transformation and the redistribution of wealth. And Albuquerque Lima did not go down quietly. The government placed a ban on the publication of a highly critical speech he delivered on March 19, protesting against his rustication. The colonels and captains that Albuquerque Lima represents will continue to tug government policy in a more populist and overtly nationalist direction. President Medici himself, who has cultivated a paternal image and won enormous popularity when he appeared with a football in the midst of the 1970 World Cup soccer final, has shown an increasing interest in social reform. In a speech delivered late in 1970, he declared that he planned to ensure 'that the national income is more fairly distributed'.

The government's literacy and housing programmes are a moderately hopeful sign. And although the resistance to change from backward-looking landowners cannot be underrated, their interests are not necessarily the same as those of the 'technocrats' or of modern industrialists. Given Brazil's economic stature, its dependence on foreign capital, its size and diversity, and the strength of its armed forces (200,000 men)[12] it would be safer to bet on change from within the system than on violent revolution.

That, at any rate, was the conclusion of the Brazilian Communist Party (PCB), which clung to the ideal of a 'national bourgeois revolution' and the united front tactics favoured by Moscow after its hopes for riding to power on Goulart's shoulders were disappointed in March 1964. The leadership of the guerrilla movement in Brazil, as in the rest of Latin America, passed into other hands. From the end of 1967, when an attempt to found a rural guerrilla front in the Serra da Caparão was crushed by the security forces, a bewildering variety of guerrilla groups began a campaign of urban terrorism in Rio and São Paulo. This first wave of urban terrorism seemed to have been broken by the end of 1970, when the remnants of the original guerrilla groups dug deeper underground to lick their wounds. But the opening phase of urban guerrilla warfare in Brazil has a broader significance. Its beginning was associated with the first coherent theorist of urban guerrilla warfare, and its bloody ending served as a refutation of some of his central ideas.

MARIGHELLA'S STRATEGY FOR REVOLT

The urban guerrilla movements of Latin America have not yet produced a commanding figure, a human symbol on the model of Che Guevara. They have also failed to produce a revolutionary theorist of any real intellectual stature. That may have something to do with the anonymous character of terrorist operations, and the transience of most of the guerrilla groups. At any rate, the man who came closest to playing both of those leading roles was Carlos Marighella, the chief of the Brazilian *Acão Libertadora Nacional* (ALN). Marighella's career as an urban guerrilla was very brief, but he was an articulate tactician and his main theoretical work, the *Minimanual of the Urban Guerrilla*, has been studied widely outside Brazil. In Marighella's own country, some of the *Minimanual*'s central propositions have already been disproved by events. But the French minister of the interior took its potential influence seriously enough to try to ban its publication in France in 1970.

Unlike most of those he led, Marighella was a veteran political campaigner who had spent most of his adult life in the Brazilian Communist Party. He was fifty-eight on the day he was trapped in a police ambush and shot dead in November 1969. Marighella was born in Salvador, the capital of the state of Bahia on the Atlantic coast, in 1911, the son of an Italian immigrant and—on his mother's side—the descendant of African slaves.[13] Those who fought with him in the ALN later gave him the nickname *o preto* ('the negro'). Marighella was eighteen when the Great Depression began, and the experience of the social crisis in Bahia that came in the wake of the worldwide slump in coffee prices was one of the things that led him to join the local Communist Party. Soon afterwards, he gave up his plans to qualify as an engineer at the Salvador Polytechnic in order to devote himself to full-time political agitation.

Marighella became a Communist at a time when the local party, backed by the Comintern, was preparing for armed revolution. During the 1920s, the Brazilian Communists had systematically infiltrated the armed forces and were fomenting mutinies. At the end of 1934, one communist leader reported that the delegates at a conference of Latin American Communist Parties that 'We now have Communist organisations in the majority of the corps. The army is sympathetic towards strikers.'[14] Marighella had been sent to Rio de Janeiro to take charge of the party's clandestine printing operations a few months before the revolt broke out in November 1935.

Although army units that had transferred their loyalties to the communists managed to seize Natal and Recife in the first hours of the uprising, the revolt was quickly snuffed out in Rio and the other major cities. Luis Carlos Prestes, the communist leader who had been recruited by the Comintern and was famous for his martial exploits as one of the *tenientes* (a rebel movement of young officers who had marched through the country's backblocks in the 1920s) was thrown into jail, along with other key figures. Marighella was arrested for the first time in March 1936.

This early experiment in armed insurrection had a decisive effect on Marighella. After 1935, the Brazilian Communist Party moved towards a different strategy: the pursuit of a popular front, and of change within the system. But Marighella continued to dream of violent revolution, and his later experience deepened his scepticism about the possibilities for peaceful subversion. When he was released from prison on the eve of the 1937 elections, Marighella moved to the rising industrial city of São Paulo, where he became the local party chief and was assigned the task of rooting out the Trotskyists in the local organisation. This was the age of the Stalinist purges; and those who knew Marighella at the time remember him as a ruthless hatchetman with an inquisitor's eye for ideological deviations. Thirty years later, it was his turn to tell the central committee that 'orthodoxy is a matter for the church'.

Marighella was imprisoned for the second time in 1939, and spent the war years on the prison-island of Fernando de Noronha, proselytising among his fellow-inmates. After the war, and the fall of the dictator Getulio Vargas, Marighella was freed under a general amnesty and was elected to congress on the communist ticket in 1946. This was his first, and only, experience of the parliamentary system. He proved himself a vigorous public orator. But in the following year, Brazil broke off diplomatic relations with Moscow and the Communist Party was again driven underground. Marighella again turned his hopes to armed struggle. The year after he was appointed to the Communist Party's central committee in 1952, he made an extended visit to China and studied Maoist strategy and the Chinese experience of 'people's war'. He later became an enthusiastic advocate of Castro's revolution, and was active in organising Brazilian–Cuban solidarity meetings after 1959.

The sequence of events that finally led Marighella to resign from the Brazilian Communist Party began with the schisms of the early 1960s. The issues that divided European Communists in the 1950s— the invasion of Hungary by the Russians, and the reappraisals that followed Stalin's death—had very little impact on the Brazilian party. Things started to fall apart in the wake of the Sino-Soviet rift, and a pro-Chinese faction broke away to form the Communist Party of Brazil (PCdoB) in 1961. Before the left-wing régime of João Goulart (1961–64) was overthrown by the generals, the advocates of armed revolution were fairly rare in Brazil, although two extreme left-wing state governors, Miguel Arraes in the north-east and Leonel Brizola in Rio Grande do Sul, sponsored the formation of para-military groups. Brizola created a network of eleven-man squads (*grupos dos onze*) that were supposed to hold themselves ready to seize key installations and overthrow the government at a given signal. These groups were the backbone of early attempts to set up a guerrilla *foco* in the south after the military coup. But the Brazilian Communist Party calculated on taking over the Goulart government through peaceful subversion. On the eve of the coup, the communist leaders were openly setting their sights on a formal coalition with Goulart. Those hopes collapsed when Marshal Humberto Castelo Branco seized power in April 1964. In his inaugural speech, he promised 'a government of law' and an early return to democracy. 'It is no exaggeration to say,' he added, 'that in this march to the future we shall engage ourselves with ardour in a crusade in which all Brazilians will be called to participate . . . Let the Brazilians come to me and I will go with them.'[15]

The overthrow of Goulart led to the formation of guerrilla groups and sparked off the Brazilian Communist Party's second internal crisis. While the Maoists immediately declared that the only road to power now lay through armed struggle, the Moscow-line communists were hesitant about committing themselves to anything more than the creation of armed 'self-defence' groups in the countryside. Their hesitation cost them some of their support. The Castroites within the party hived off to form the Revolutionary Brazilian Communist Party (PCBR) under the leadership of Mario Alves and Apolonio de Carvalho in 1967.

Marighella had taken his own decision to leave the party a few months earlier. He had been caught up in the street-fighting that immediately followed the coup in April 1964, and joined the mob that tried to invade the Military Club in Rio. A few days later, the police picked him up in a downtown cinema, and he was shot in the stomach while resisting arrest. When he came out of jail for the third time, he found that many of the men who were closest to him in the São Paulo section of the Communist Party shared his disillusionment with the failure of the central committee to give the cue for an insurrection. He decided to step down from the party's executive committee at the end of 1966, and outlined the reasons in a letter sent to the leadership on December 10. He criticised the communist leaders for their estrangement from the party branches and the mood of the country; for practising 'bourgeois' policies and underrating the revolutionary potential of workers and peasants; and for conducting 'ideological intimidation' and exercising a stifling censorship over publications and ideas.

He attacked the idea that the communists could get anywhere by exploring the possibilities for legal opposition in congress or by forming an alliance with Carlos Lacerda (the populist leader who was trying to form a 'broad front' of opposition forces). He argued that 'the era of democratic-liberal solutions is past' and that the future lay in a peasant uprising triggered off by urban guerrilla warfare. And he laid claim to Lenin's ideological legacy:

> The Executive Committee still thinks it can inflict on the dictatorship electoral defeats which will weaken it. It attaches great importance to the Brazilian Democratic Movement [the licensed parliamentary opposition group] as an organisation for the unification of broad forces against the dictatorship . . . Everything is overtly or covertly reduced to an impossible or unacceptable peaceful solution, an illusory redemocratization . . . It seems they did not understand Lenin when, in his work, *Two Tactics*, he states that 'the big problems in the lives of the people can only be resolved by force'. In Brazil, the solution can only be armed struggle.[16]

The final rift between Marighella and the party came in August 1967, when he defied the party ban and accepted an invitation to attend the first Latin American Solidarity Conference (OLAS) in Havana. When the Brazilian Communist Party sent a message to Cuba disowning him, he replied that he had no further wish to remain a member of 'that faculty of fine arts'. But he also told the Cuban youth magazine, *Juventud Rebelde*, that he would always remain a communist. The Havana conference presaged the beginning of a serious guerrilla campaign in Brazil. But José Anselmo dos Santos, the ex-corporal who had formed a short-lived National Liberation Movement, was premature when he forecast that a series of guerrilla *focos* would soon be set up in the countryside and that the movements of the far left were about to unite and establish a mobile headquarters in the mountains. The war of the urban guerrilla took precedence.

Marighella founded the ALN in February 1968. The men who joined him were mainly students and intellectuals in their early twenties, with a sprinkling of ex-soldiers and workers. There were also a number of important recruits from the São Paulo section of the Communist Party, where Marighella had established a firm personal foothold, including Joaquim Câmara Ferreira, a close friend with a similar background who succeeded Marighella after his death in 1969. In the period before Marighella's death, the ALN conducted a series of successful urban guerrilla operations; beginning with 'logistic' exercises (the seizure of arms and money) and progressing through selective assassination and assaults on barracks to the kidnapping of the American ambassador. It entered into a period of decline from the end of 1969.

Although the ALN's activities were confined to urban terrorism, its manifestoes outlined a broader strategy. City operations were regarded essentially as a tactical manoeuvre designed to tie up the government forces and clear the way for a rural guerrilla campaign and, ultimately, for a war of movement in the countryside. At the same time, revolutionary action was supposed to bring the diverse and fragmented guerrilla groups together. As Marighella put it in an interview, 'It is through action that things become clear, that a strategic unity grows stronger and that a unified command will automatically emerge.'[17] From the outset, the organisation was contemptuous of party affiliations and the conventional forms of political agitation. Having renounced one Communist Party of which he had remained a member for the best part of forty years, Marighella was in no hurry to found another. He believed that the ALN would make converts through action: 'Our main activity is not the construction of a party, but the unleashing of revolutionary action.'[18]

Having spurned 'the bourgeois ideology and electoral illusions' of the Brazilian Communist Party, he fell into the opposite trap: an unreasoning faith in the efficacy of violence. Although Marighella criticised the tactics advocated by Debray (the theory of the guerrilla *foco*) he agreed that guerrilla action in itself, detached from a popular movement and unrelated to the social situation in the country, could create the conditions for revolution. That is why his writings fail to discuss crucial questions like political goals and motivation, or techniques of subversion and agitation. They read like manuals of military parade drill, not political manifestoes.

Marighella gives a chillingly technical definition of the urban guerrilla. He writes that 'The urban guerrilla's reason for existence, the basic condition in which he acts and survives, is to shoot.'[19] For Marighella, the terrorist is above all a man with a gun. He recommends that the gun should be a light automatic rifle, easy to carry, that can also be manufactured in a backyard factory. He suggests that the basic form of organisation for an urban guerrilla movement should be the 'firing group' of four or five men, led by the man who is 'the best shot and the one who best knows how to manage the machine-gun'. The political and military commands are one and the same; Marighella does not want to be lumbered with political commissars. And although there must be some form of central direction (co-ordinated by linkmen in each firing group) each terrorist cell must take its own decisions and exercise its own initiative. This can obviously lead to rifts and contradictory tactics (as among the FLQ cells bargaining for the release of their hostages in Quebec). On the other hand, survival in urban conditions depends on quick thinking and split-second timing.

Marighella concedes that the urban guerrilla is at a clear disadvantage in a number of ways. He is bound to be outgunned in an open street-battle, and it is difficult to stay in hiding unless he can count on the sympathy of a large number of collaborators. There is always the problem of keeping up morale in the early stages of a campaign, when a single reverse might spell total disaster. And there is always the besetting fear of informers, the suspicion that sows discord inside any terrorist group. There is evidence to suggest, for example, that Marighella's successor, Joaquim Câmara Ferreira, was betrayed to the São Paulo police by the leader of a dissident faction of another important terrorist group, the *Vanguarda Popular Revolucionaria*. 'Death to spies' is one of the constant refrains of Marighella's *Minimanual*, and he makes some fairly obvious recommendations about security measures, like careful screening of new recruits, oral communications, and rigorous compartmentalisation of functions. ('Each person should know only what relates to his work.')

Marighella argues that the urban guerrilla's only hope of success is to keep up a constant attack. 'Defensive action,' he insists, 'means death to us. Since we are inferior to the enemy in firepower and have neither his resources nor his power base, we cannot defend ourselves against an offensive or a concentrated attack.' The terrorist's job is to hit and run, and Marighella catalogues the things in his favour so long as he restricts himself to pinprick attacks like assassinations, ambushes, kidnappings, sabotage, and raids on banks, prisons, and army installations. The urban guerrilla, like the common criminal, has the advantage of surprise. His problem is to make it clear to the public that he has a political objective. He needs a flawless knowledge of the terrain:

> Familiar with the avenues, streets, alleys, the ins and outs of the urban centres, their paths and shortcuts, their empty lots, their underground passages, their pipes and sewers, the urban guerrilla crosses through irregular and difficult terrain unfamiliar to the police, where they can be surprised in a fatal ambush or trapped at any moment.[20]

This will also enable the terrorist to disrupt the communications of the security forces, to block pursuit by obstructing roads or laying ambushes. Marighella is contemptuous of the usefulness of helicopters in urban counter-guerrilla exercises. He argues that they move too fast to strike at targets moving through crowded streets or dense traffic, and that they are very vulnerable to sniping from below. (He does not observe that helicopters have proved useful to the police in spotting the direction of the quarry.)

Marighella constantly urges decisiveness. His counsel for the terrorist, like Danton's advice for revolutionaries, is really *de l'audace, encore de l'audace et toujours de l'audace.* This reflects his consciousness of what happens to the morale of men who have to hide in city apartments over a long period without the emotional release of action.

Marighella is conscious of the limits of urban guerrilla operations. He defines the tactical goals of the urban guerrilla as, first, to pose a threat to the urban industrial triangle of Brazil (Rio–São Paulo–Belo Horizonte) so that the security forces will be placed on the defensive and tied up in penny packets in their attempt to track down 'a thoroughly fragmented organisation' and to stand guard over the multitude of targets that the modern city presents to terrorists determined to overthrow the system: offices and barracks, ships and aircraft, embassies and industrial plants. Secondly, the urban guerrilla hopes to demoralise the forces of order by a campaign of selective terrorism and by demonstrating their incapacity to track him down. Thirdly, he plans to set an example that will win new recruits and persuade the people that the government is vulnerable to attack and unable even to protect its friends.

For Marighella, urban terrorism is only one element in a broader strategy. He outlines three phases for revolutionary warfare in Brazil, starting with the formation of cadres and the collection of supplies, passing through the stage of guerrilla operations, and culminating with a war of movement in which (in the best Maoist tradition) the countryside would encircle the towns. An ALN manifesto issued in January 1969 conceded that the peasants were in no great hurry to join the revolution and that 'Their struggles have hardly ever transcended the level of brigandage and messianism'.[21] Although successive attempts to start rural guerrilla campaigns in Brazil were snuffed out by the army, Marighella remained insistent that revolution would be impossible without a full-scale peasant uprising.

The central problem for any rebel movement is to win popular support. Marighella saw the urban guerrilla as a catalyst in the process of polarising the political forces in Brazil and creating the conditions for civil war. He believed that, by forcing the government to take increasingly repressive measures to combat terrorism, the guerrillas could win moderate opinion to their side. 'It is necessary,' he wrote, 'to turn political crisis into armed conflict by performing violent actions that will force those in power to transform the political situation in the country into a military situation. That will alienate the masses, who, from then on, will revolt against the army and the police and blame them for this state of things.' He also believed that the success of this strategy of militarisation would trigger off an internal crisis in the régime. It is an argument familiar to all extremists, but it is doubtful whether the cards usually fall the way that Marighella anticipated. Tougher repression in Brazil has alienated some liberal elements. It also seems to have destroyed the urban guerrillas as a military force.

THE FAILURE OF A STRATEGY

How did Marighella's strategy work out in practice? Revolutionary guerrilla warfare is a fairly recent innovation in Brazil. In the three years following the 1964 coup, splinter groups from the Brazilian Communist Party and military rebels united in a series of attempts to set up rural guerrilla bases. There had already been several attempts to organise and politicise the peasants of the north-east and the far south under the Goulart régime. Under the guidance of Francisco Julião and the patronage of Miguel Arraes, the peasant leagues (or *ligas camponesas*) of the north-east had developed from mutual benefit societies concerned with providing money for funerals and other rather unworldly activities into militant unions that attacked the whole structure of labour relations. But they were quickly suppressed after the coup, and one observer commented that 'as a revolutionary instrument, they have been little more than a child's toy'.[22]

In the south, communist dissidents tried to use the 'groups of eleven' (*grupos dos onze*) that had been founded by Goulart's radical brother-in-law, Leonel Brizola, as the basis for a rural guerrilla campaign. An organisation called the MNR (for Nationalist Revolutionary Movement) and directed by the 'revolutionary sergeants' and marines who had sided with Goulart, tried to establish a guerrilla *foco* in the Sierra de Caparão, on the borders of the states of Rio de Janeiro and Espiritu Santo. The MNR were easily suppressed. Cut off from their supply-lines and operating in difficult and unfamiliar terrain, they were encircled by a military strike-force and gave themselves up. This led to the discovery of other guerrilla camps.[23] In 1969, the army uncovered plans for a new series of *focos* and captured a large rebel arsenal in Angra dos Reis.

Guerrilla outposts survive in pockets of rugged terrain, and there have been reports of communist militants and army rebels picking their way through the Amazonian forests to the relative safety of the Mato Grosso. Joaquin Câmara Ferreira, Marighella's successor as leader of the National Liberation Action (ALN), conceded that

> The beginning of a guerrilla unit is quite a delicate operation. The dictatorship is thoroughly convinced of the importance of rural guerrillas and has adopted precautionary measures. It has sent hundreds of informers to the jungle zone, the canefield zone of Pernambuco alone, to keep a close watch on the activities of the workers and report any suspicious moves to the intelligence services.[24]

Like Marighella, Câmara believed that a Brazilian revolution would be possibly only with the support of the peasantry, and he believed that the way to enlist peasant support was through the 'propaganda of the deed':

> Land transfers are rigorously controlled by those same services of espionage. That is why we believe that the first stage of struggle in the countryside should be that of guerrilla actions. Small groups should attack and burn the land registry offices, where the titles to the land owned by the *latifundistas* are registered; attack food warehouses and distribute the food among the people; kill cattle and distribute the beef among the hungry; and, in some cases, arrest and execute US landowners who have kicked the Brazilians off their own land . . . This is what we call carrying subversion to the countryside. [25]

But successive attempts to 'carry subversion to the countryside' in Brazil have failed miserably. Between the 21 April and the 31 May 1970, the People's Revolutionary Vanguard (VPR) maintained a rural guerrilla base in the Ribeira valley. According to the leader of the group, ex-Captain Carlos Lamarca, they took eighteen prisoners and 'put ten soldiers out of action' in the course of three operations. [26] But the camp was betrayed by two VPR defectors, and the armed forces closed in. Some 20,000 troops encircled the valley, using helicopters, T-6 fighter aircraft, bombers and transport planes. Part of the valley was bombed after the peasant population had been evacuated. Most of the guerrillas succeeded in slipping through the army net and making their escape. But the episode was a clear demonstration of the slim chances of survival of a Guevarist movement in the hills in the face of a government able to mobilise overpowering forces at short notice.

Brazil's guerrillas have learned not only that it is simple for the government to isolate and root out rural *focos* but that—given the vast expanse and the great diversity of the country—rural guerrillas do not pose a serious military threat to the 'industrial triangle' of the south-east where wealth and power is concentrated. At the same time, it became clear that spontaneous peasant violence remained essentially *pre-political* in character. The two symbolic figures in Glauber Rocha's films—the *cangaceiro*, or bandit, and the millenarian Christ-figure who leads a deluded flock on an impossible crusade—are still closer in spirit to the *nordestinos* than the guerrilla or the political agitator. The food riots and the occupation of several north-eastern towns by starving peasants after the severe droughts of 1970 were a spontaneous response to disaster that did not carry over into an organised political campaign. Thus the chances of creating the countrywide revolutionary movement that Marighella projected appear very remote.

The Brazilian urban guerrilla groups that proliferated after 1967 were fragmented into a baffling variety of tiny factions. The most important were Marighella's ALN, Lamarca's VPR, the Revolutionary Armed Vanguard-Palmares (VAR-Palmares), the Revolutionary Movement of October 8 (MR-8) and the Communist Workers' Party (POB). There were also a number of Maoist groups (notably the Communist Party of Brazil and Popular Action) that stressed traditional forms of labour agitation as the essential preliminary to a war of national liberation. The urban guerrillas were hamstrung from the very start by these internal divisions and their constant debate about tactics. Was it necessary to set up rural guerrilla bases? The VPR persisted in the attempt despite repeated failures. Was revolutionary warfare possible without a 'vanguard party' to rally mass support and co-ordinate military operations? The ALN and the VPR agreed with Marighella that unity would come in the course of action. But the leaders of the VAR-Palmares (after its rift with the VPR) and the 'Leninist' school thought that it was destructive to resort to isolated terrorist assaults without trying to build up a revolutionary party at the same time. Which was the revolutionary class?

All the urban guerrillas agreed that there could be no compromise with the Brazilian middle class. Their vehement rejection of the Communist Party's search for a 'united front' with middle-class opposition groups was bound up with a personal rebellion against the class from which many of the terrorists sprang. According to General Carlos Muricy, a former chief of staff, 56 per cent of 500 men imprisoned for acts of terrorism and political activities were students or recent graduates—most of them from bourgeois families. However, the urban guerrillas disagreed over the relative importance of the urban working-class, the peasants, and the *lumpenproletariat*. Carlos Lamarca and the VPR swung towards the

202 *The War for the Cities*

idea that the guerrillas would find most support for their goals among the urban slum-dwellers.

But the guerrilla leaders were not strong on theory, and in the last analysis, their divisions owed as much to caution and physical isolation as to purely theoretical squabbles. It is significant that from mid-1970, as the government counter-insurgency programme started to bite deeply, the guerrilla groups drew closer together and there were several attempts at mergers. The reason was simple. Increasingly cut off from the people, the guerrillas were finding it harder and harder to make new recruits. To get the manpower for terrorist operations, they had to draw on each other's resources.

The urban guerrillas also suffered from the fact that they remained estranged from the Brazilian Communist Party (which had in any case declined as a political force after tearing itself apart in a series of internal schisms that began at the time of the Sino–Soviet split and intensified after the 1964 coup). They were also cut off from the other parties of the far left like the Maoist P.C.do Brazil. When the ALN kidnapped the American ambassador, Burke Elbrick, in September 1969, the Communist leader Luis Carlos Prestes observed that 'It is not by spectacular actions, without the participation of the masses, that one can overthrow the dictatorship. Violent actions have no significance in the revolutionary process unless they contribute to heightening the political consciousness and organisation of the masses.'[27] His criticism, echoing the Russian line, was confirmed by events.

The ALN was the spearhead of the urban terrorist campaign during 1968 and 1969. In 1968, its operations were largely confined to building up a stockpile of arms and money through bank-robberies and raids on military arsenals. At this stage, the terrorists were commonly confused with ordinary 'bandits', and they welcomed the confusion as a form of camouflage. But it is interesting to note that Marighella was often said to compare himself wistfully with Lampeão (Virgulino Ferreira) the bandit chief who fought a bloody war for two decades across six states in the north-east.[28] Marighella's group was finally identified as the author of the 1968 attacks after an armoured payroll van was held up in November. That operation brought so much publicity that Marighella later remarked that it had earned him much more than the 120,000 (new) cruzeiros that were stolen, since the publicity his group received would have cost more than 5 million cruzeiros as paid advertisements.[29]

In 1969, the ALN carried out a second series of bank-robberies and selective assassination, culminating in September with the kidnapping of the American ambassador, Burke Elbrick. The abduction was timed to coincide with the official celebration of Independence Day. Fernando Gabeira, an MR-8 militant now living in Algiers who participated in the abduction of Elbrick, has left a detailed account of how the operation was carried out.[30] The kidnapping was planned over a period of two months, during which the terrorists succeeded in infiltrating a female agent ('remarkable for her good looks') into the military intelligence agency, DOPS. From that vantage-point, she managed to collect detailed information about the ambassador's movements. Twelve guerrillas who had already taken part in bank-robberies and other operations set up an ambush for Elbrick, using a rented villa in Marques Street (where the ambassador's residence was located) as their base. The 'grab' was a simple affair. The ambassador's car was halted by another car parked across the road, his chauffeur was thrown out, and he was driven off in his own Cadillac to a place of hiding. Gabeira later tried to justify the crime on the grounds that while 'the ambassador may have been a "liberal", he was a prisoner-of-war none the less.'

The Brazilian government, caught off-balance, agreed to free fifteen political prisoners in exchange for Elbrick. This set the stage for a wave of diplomatic kidnappings in other countries. The style of the abduction also illustrated one of Marighella's favourite tactics for trying to pull the rival terrorist groups closer together. The ALN and the MR-8 wrote out a joint ransom note that demanded the release of Moscow-line communists, student radicals, members of MR-8 and of the National Liberation Command (Colina). This list of names, like later kidnap notes, suggested a degree of unity and harmony among militant opposition groups that was lacking in practice.

Marighella was killed in a gun-battle with São Paulo police in November 1969, after the security forces had extracted information from two Dominican priests connected with the ALN. This was a heavy blow to the guerrilla movement. Marighella's successor, Câmara Ferreira, had a similar background. Like Marighella, he dropped out of the polytechnic where he was studying engineering in the early 1930s, in order to devote himself to the Brazilian Communist Party. After holding a number of important posts in the Communist Party (he was a member of the São Paulo regional committee as early as 1937 and edited the party newspaper between 1947 and 1949) he followed Marighella's lead and dropped out of the party in order to pursue 'armed struggle' after the 1964 coup.

Shortly before his own death, he admitted that the Brazilian guerrilla movement had suffered a number of serious setbacks: 'More than 200 of our front-line comrades are in prison at the moment, and there are 3,000 or 4,000 revolutionaries in prison throughout Brazil.' He is said to have suffered a heart-attack while resisting arrest in São Paulo in October 1970. The real leadership of the urban guerrilla movement had already passed to another organisation, the VPR.

The history of the People's Revolutionary Vanguard (VPR) provides an insight into the world of Brazil's urban guerrillas: a world of fear and betrayal, sudden violence and stormy debates in which a point of doctrine assumes the importance that a woman might have amongst rivals. The VPR was formed in São Paulo in March 1968, by a group of radical students and ex-soldiers. Its first important action, apart from a series of bank-raids and arms robberies, was the murder of an American intelligence agent, Captain Chandler, in October. The movement was divided from the start between the 'Leninists', who wanted to place more emphasis on political agitation, and the 'militarists' who were purely interested in terrorist violence and in trying to set up a camp in the countryside. After the government of Marshal Costa e Silva imposed the Institutional Act No 5 (which equipped the government with extraordinary powers) in December 1968, the 'militarist' faction took control and planned an ambitious offensive operation.[31]

The VPR were in contact with a subversive cell inside the Fourth Infantry Regiment, garrisoned in Quintana, São Paulo. The cell was headed by Captain Carlos Lamarca, a champion pistol-shot and an expert in counter-insurgency techniques. Lamarca's plan was to synchronise a raid on the barracks with a rising from within, in the hope of looting the armoury and making an impressive show of strength. But the VPR over-exposed themselves by mobilising most of their members for the operation, including cadres based in the villages. And the plan was discovered by the army when members of Lamarca's cell were surprised while painting military markings on a getaway van. Lamarca and most of the soldiers in sympathy with him managed to make their escape from the camp with a truckload of automatic weapons early in January 1969. But the four militants arrested by military intelligence broke down under interrogation, and the security forces were able to make a clean sweep of VPR *aparelhos* (or bases) in São Paulo. Within a few days, thirty arrests had been made and the authorities announced that the São Paulo section of the VPR had been wiped out.

These losses intensified the debate about tactics inside the VPR. The 'militarists', under the leadership of Lamarca, again emerged the victors, and their critics were forced to leave the organisation. In July 1969, the VPR merged with another urban guerrilla group, Colina (which was based in the southern states of Guanabara, Rio de Janeiro and Minas Gerais) to form the awkwardly-named Revolutionary Armed Vanguard-Palmares (VAR-Palmares). This was a move towards the revolutionary alliance that Marighella believed would emerge automatically in the course of terrorist action; but the new organisation quickly fell apart after more futile feuding over policy, and the security forces destroyed the rump of the VAR-Palmares in March 1971.

Lamarca tried to breathe life into the new VPR that emerged from this confused process of schism and conciliation by roping in new recruits and by a series of spectacular actions in 1970. On March 11, the VPR abducted the Japanese consul in São Paulo, Nobuo Okichi, and succeeded in getting five political prisoners freed in exchange for his life. The choice of a Japanese diplomat as a victim startled many observers. No doubt the main reason Okichi was picked was that he was exposed; but the choice was also related to the prominence of the Japanese in São Paulo industry and the fact that at least two men in the upper echelons of the VPR were of Japanese origin. At any rate, the VPR went on to show that they were ready to kidnap any diplomat who could be held to ransom. In April, the American consul in Porto Alegre was wounded when the VPR staged an unsuccessful kidnapping attempt; and on June 11 Lamarca's group, operating in harness with the ALN, abducted the West German ambassador, Ehrenfried von Holleben. His car was intercepted a few hundred yards from his home by a team of eight guerrillas who had been waiting at the chosen spot, according to bystanders, for about two hours.

The communiqué left at the scene of the crime declared that the terrorists would no longer confine themselves to kidnapping representatives of major capitalist powers; all foreign diplomats would be considered fair game. They warned that to surround a diplomat with armed guards would only serve to place him in greater danger, since 'we are determined to use as many combatants as are necessary to achieve our ends'. [32] This was tantamount to a declaration of war on the entire international community—with the significant exception of countries like China, Cuba and Algeria, that had never opened diplomatic relations with Brazil. The guerrillas attempted to justify diplomatic kidnapping on the grounds that 'While patriots are undergoing torture and being killed in the prisons, we have no other course of action, although we know that kidnapping endangers the lives of people who have nothing to do with the revolutionary struggle.' [33]

The guerrillas got their price for von Holleben. On June 14, forty political prisoners were freed and flown to Algiers to join the exile community that already included Migual Arraes, the former governor of Pernambuco. The price of a western envoy was clearly going up fast. [34] The policy of the Brazilian government up to this point had been to give in to kidnappers' demands—and then to mount a police dragnet in an attempt to round up the terrorists responsible. That policy was sorely tested when the VPR followed up with another diplomatic kidnapping on 7 December 1970, soon after General Medici's government had won an overwhelming majority in a congressional election. This time, the victim was the Swiss ambassador, Giovanni Bucher, and the price demanded was seventy political prisoners. The security forces countered by rounding up some 8,000 suspects throughout the country, including lawyers, journalists and other professional men as well as students and political activists. Most of them were released after two or three days on the personal instructions of the president.

Although the government finally gave in to the kidnappers' central demand, negotiations got bogged down on a series of marginal issues. The terrorists also called for a 100 per cent rise in wages, free public transport for city workers, the confiscation of Swiss bank deposits and the publication of a singularly violent manifesto. The manifesto promised that 'the armed struggle in the cities and the countryside' would soon be intensified. It called for spontaneous workers' uprisings and described the situation in Brazil in uncompromising terms: 'It is the country that has the highest index of infant mortality and of prostitution in the world, and the most glaring social injustices. Slavery still exists in certain states, the people are exploited, and Brazil has become the favourite hunting-ground of foreign enterprise.'[35] Bucher was finally freed on 16 January 1971, after a group of prisoners had been flown into exile in Chile. But the exchange was by no means an unambiguous propaganda victory for the guerrillas. Three political prisoners refused to leave Brazil and one of them, Irgeu Menegon, a former member of the VPR, made a statement expressing his total disillusionment with the urban guerrillas. 'I joined the VPR,' he said, 'thinking that I could do something for Brazil. But I have been completely deceived. The VPR only uses terror and violence, which horrify me.'[36]

Menegon's *cri de coeur* may have been inspired by the government, but was not an isolated statement. 1970 was a year of frequent defections and heavy losses for the VPR and the other Brazilian guerrilla groups. In June 1970, Massafumi Yoshinaga, a 21-year-old member of the VPR gave himself up and made a television appearance in which he condemned 'the terrorism, selfishness and megalomania of the guerrilla leaders', 'the decadence of their ideals' and 'the gulf between the aspirations of the people and the goals that the revolutionaries are pursuing'. He criticised Lamarca in savage personal terms as a man without leadership qualities, wholly given over to the cult of physical violence.[37] But Yoshinaga's defection was less important for its propaganda effect than for the information that he and his friend Celso Lungaretti carried with them. They revealed the existence of the guerrilla camp in the Ribeira valley. After the army had rooted the rural guerrillas out, Lamarca announced that both informers had been 'condemned to death'. He claimed that they had 'forgotten the class struggle and betrayed their people'.[38]

But by the end of 1970, neither threats nor the isolated drama of the abduction of an ambassador were enough to revive the sagging fortunes of the VPR. Its strength was reported to have dropped from 150 to less than a third that number; Lamarca complained that it had become impossible to persuade men with any military training to venture out into the countryside; and in December, Yoshitame Fujimire, one of his right-hand men, was shot dead. Urban guerrilla operations tailed off in the first half of 1971, when the only significant actions were a series of raids on banks and supermarkets and the murder of a leading businessman, Sr Henning Boilesen, in São Paulo in mid-April. The first wave of urban guerrilla warfare in Brazil had been broken. Carlos Lamarca himself, the last survivor of the 'first generation' of Brazilian guerrilla leaders, was surrounded and killed with two of his comrades in the state of Bahia on September 1971.

It is possible to draw up a balance-sheet for urban terrorism in Brazil. The guerrillas scored some limited successes. For example, they exploited the technique of diplomatic kidnapping to the full and triggered off a process of rampant inflation in the 'price' of diplomatic hostages. The government released 15 prisoners in exchange for an American ambassador; 40 for a West German ambassador; and 70 for a Swiss ambassador. But the kidnappings provoked violent reactions within the régime, and many hardliners opposed the idea of any further bargaining with kidnappers. Marighella's strategy of 'militarisation' worked in so far as terrorist action helped to drive the government farther to the right and provoked an increasingly tough response.

The counter-insurgency campaign had some ugly side-effects that have already been noted, including the indiscriminate use of torture, mass arrests, and the proliferation of right-wing terrorist gangs like the 'death squads' (*escuadrão de morte*).[39] In June 1970, the eleventh episcopal congress, meeting in Brasilia, lent its moral authority to the international protest against the widespread use of torture in Brazil. And it is possible to trace a close connection between mounting guerrilla violence and repressive legislation. After the Elbrick kidnapping, President Medici restored the death penalty (long abolished in Brazil) and introduced a tough new code of penalties for terrorist offences. The police issued a set of instructions to householders requiring each resident to keep a close watch on his neighbours.

But Marighella's strategy failed in the sense that increased repression failed to arouse a broad-based militant opposition to the régime, although it certainly alienated liberal opinion and important sectors of the middle class. On the contrary, the guerrillas provided the régime with the pretext for sweeping curbs on personal liberties and limited the options for a reformist opposition without increasing the chances of a revolution from below.

10

The Tupamaros:
Masters of the Game

Uruguay was always held to be exceptional. *Como el Uruguay no hay* ('There's no place like Uruguay') the saying goes. This little country with a population of under three million and a declining pastoral economy, sandwiched between the giants of South America, Brazil and Argentina, has often been compared with Switzerland. The Uruguayans themselves accepted the comparison as perfectly fitting. The country has a long record of constitutional rule. The only coup that was staged in this century had the support of most bourgeois politicians and was carried out, characteristically, by policemen, not soldiers.

Uruguay was the home of the first social revolution of the twentieth century, and it took place without butchery or burning palaces during the two enlightened presidencies of a mild and prescient man called José Batlle y Ordoñez (1903–1907 and 1911–1915). Batlle gave the people of Uruguay the eight-hour day, a minimum wage, unemployment benefits, old-age pensions and paid holidays. He broke the hold of the church over education and social mores. He legalised divorce, abolished capital punishment and brought in free university education. He extended state control over key sectors of the economy by nationalising major banks, insurance, liquor manufacture, oil, meat-packing and public utilities. He slapped taxes on property and capital gains—though not on income, since he believed that that would dampen private initiative. It was a record of bloodless reform and social integration unrivalled in Latin America, and a good reason to assume that a violent revolution might happen anywhere else in the continent, but not in Uruguay.[1]

So it is paradoxical that it should be in this eminently liberal welfare state that a terrorist movement that calls itself the Tupamaros (or National Liberation Movement) should have perfected the techniques of urban guerrilla warfare and placed the government in a virtual state of siege. In 1965, when the Tupamaros first signed their name to a communiqué protesting against the American involvement in Vietnam, the movement probably contained fewer than fifty active members. A former police chief estimated that by August 1970, the active membership had risen to about 3,000— an enormous figure in a city of some $1\frac{1}{4}$ million people.[2] The Tupamaros displayed a remarkable capacity to survive under urban conditions. In the three years between August 1968, when they committed their first political kidnapping, and August 1971, the Uruguayan police were unable to locate a single hostage. The guerrillas' self-confidence reached the point where they could announce that they were sentencing their victims to 'life imprisonment' in what they rather grandiosely called 'the people's prison', secreted somewhere in Montevideo.

Of course, the Tupamaros were not the first urban terrorists to run rings around the security forces. It is worth remembering that during the Eoka campaign in Cyprus, General Grivas managed to elude capture despite the massive search operations mounted by the British on the small island over the best part of four years. But that was a colonial situation in which the British confronted a cohesive nationalist movement that could command the loyalty of the Greek community through a combination of terror and advocacy of a popular cause. It is hardly comparable with the situation in an independent democratic society where civil violence has been so exceptional in the past that the security forces were caught completely unprepared when the Tupamaros began their campaign.

The degree of support that the Tupamaros have clearly been able to enlist among relatively influential, middle-class sectors of the population in Uruguay suggests that it would be wrong to imagine the downtrodden peasantry as the backbone of revolt in Latin America, or repressive police-states as the places where rebels are most likely to succeed. The Tupamaros are the progeny of an overwhelmingly urban society (about 80 per cent of the Uruguayans live in towns, and half of them live in Montevideo) and they appeal both to romantic middle-class youths, white-collar workers whose

economic expectations have been disappointed, and liberals who
believe that the government has become repressive and abandoned
Batlle's ideals. The Tupamaros, like most of the urban guerrilla
groups in Latin America, are basically a middle-class movement
recruited from the ranks of alienated students, professional men and
minor civil servants.

Captured Tupamaros include Julio Marenales Saenz, professor of
fine arts; Manuel Lluveras and Pedro Almiratti, engineers; Jorge
Candan Grajales, photographer; the children of senators and
prominent businessmen; and a high proportion of students,[3]
journalists and low-level civil servants. At the same time, the
Tupamaros have remained insistent that 'the ideology of the
movement is not dictated by its social composition' and that it is
slowly broadening its membership to include 'cadres recruited from
the working-class, the peasantry, the students, and the armed
forces'.[4] It is true that the Tupamaros retain close links with the
agricultural labourers of the sugar-beet zone in the far north of the
country: the area where the guerrilla movement was originally
conceived.

To understand how a powerful urban guerrilla movement has
emerged in one of Latin America's more enlightened societies and
has managed to erode the social consensus and the bases of government, it is necessary to begin by examining the economic crisis that
has developed in Uruguay over the past decade.[5] Uruguay is a
welfare state that has come upon hard times. Meat and wool
account for about 76 per cent of Uruguay's exports. It is second
only to Argentina in Latin America as a country of cattle-ranchers
and beef-eaters. But since the Korean war, there has been a steady
downhill slide in the world market price of wool, and see-saw
fluctuations in both the price and the production of meat. Despite
the fact that the British health authorities placed a ban on the
import of Uruguayan beef in April 1969, because of 'unsanitary
conditions' in the meat-packing plants, the Uruguayans were able
to raise the value of their meat exports to a record level the following
year—but only because they cut down on local consumption and
decimated the herds, measures hardly likely to allay social unrest
or to solve the economy's structural problems. And outmoded

methods brought a dangerous slump in productivity in other agricultural sectors. In 1969, sugar beet production fell by 55 per cent, and the acreage under wheat shrank by nearly 40 per cent.

The crisis in the export sector was aggravated by the flight of local capital to other countries and a mounting foreign debt. While foreign companies were reluctant to sink money into Uruguay, the government was forced to resort to large-scale borrowing to cover a chronic budget deficit. The size of the foreign debt more than doubled between 1960 and 1965. The upshot of all this was that by 1967, when President Jorge Pacheco Areco took office, Uruguay was the country with the lowest growth rate and the highest level of inflation in Latin America. The peso was devalued seven times in the first eleven months of 1967, and the rate of inflation soared to over 135 per cent. The government's lack of ready cash led to skimping on services and infuriating delays in the payment of civil service salaries, social benefits, and the completion of government projects like the proposed university city.

The overblown bureaucracy, which numbers more than 300,000, was the first to feel the pinch. But the unions were not far behind. President Pacheco's attempts to curb inflation by holding down wages and prices triggered off a series of violent strikes. In 1969, for example, there were fierce clashes with striking bank employees, and the government 'mobilised' some 5,000 of them in order to force them to return to work. It is no accident that the Tupamaros have been able to draw upon first-rate sources of inside information in the major banks, and that is what enabled them to get away with a spectacular series of bank-robberies that culminated in the record haul of more than $6 million in a single operation in December 1970.

The Tupamaros have made it their business to aggravate the economic crisis. They reason that if things get worse, people will blame the government, not them. Hotel waiters in Punta del Este (Montevideo's beach resort) tend to feel differently. The guerrillas launched a systematic campaign to wreck the country's tourist season in 1971 by sending threatening letters to regular foreign visitors, especially Argentinians. The number of tourists visiting Uruguay was said to have dropped by at least 40 per cent over the first half of 1971.

It is against this background of economic decay and mounting social unrest that the Tupamaros evolved from an isolated band of conspirators into a genuine revolutionary force with plans for armed insurrection. The origins of the movement go back to the early 1960s.[6] The far north of Uruguay, a region of sugar and rice plantations, differs from the rest of the country both in its greater poverty (the average per capita income in Uruguay is a comparatively comfortable $600 a year) and in the presence of an increasingly militant 'proletarian' population of day-labourers and landless plantation workers. 'Barbarous north where people starve, get rickets, and children die year after year without knowing milk, fruit, or chocolate.' The news of the Cuban revolution encouraged radical socialists like Raúl Sendic, then a law student in Montevideo, to travel north to try to organise a revolutionary movement among the sugar-growers.

Sendic became the first leader of the Tupamaros. He was active first among the sugar-beet workers of the Department of Paysandu in 1960, and then among the cane-cutters of the Department of Artigas. He was joined by other future Tupamaros like Rodriguez Beletti, a political drifter who had slid further and further to the left, moving from the Communist Youth, to the Maoist Movement of the Revolutionary Left, to the MLN. They helped to found the Union of Artigas Sugar-Workers (UTAA) in 1961. The basic goal of the UTAA was to progress from the redistribution of land to the eventual seizure of power. It began by drawing up a list of 30,000 hectares of land whose owners (many of them widows and spinsters living in Montevideo) had left their estates uncultivated. The UTAA demanded the expropriation of this land, and also demanded that a government inspector should be sent to enforce the eight-hour working day and establish minimal wages. The Minister of the Interior, Storace Arrosa, was accommodating at first, but the union organisers ran into trouble with local landowners and the sugar companies and decided to experiment with more radical tactics.

After occupying the offices of an American sugar company, CAINSA, the UTAA organised 'the march of the hairy ones' to Montevideo on 1 May 1962. Shouting their slogan, *Por la tierra y con Sendic* ('For land and with Sendic'), they marched on the presidential palace, accompanied by radical students carrying crude effigies of Uncle Sam. Stone-throwing and fighting broke out, and the crowd was finally broken up by Republican Guards on horse-back. It was a nasty precedent. The May-day 'march on Monte-video' became an annual ritual, and after the Tupamaros were organised, the UTAA continued to supply grass-roots support and a steady stream of recruits. On 1 May 1968, the UTAA issued a violent manifesto in Montevideo:

> We set out from Bella Unión, in this 'March for Land', with the idea of passing through villages and towns and talking with all the exploited and oppressed . . . We reject dialogue with those who govern us . . . The oligarchy is ready to defend its privileges with blood and fire . . . It would be suicide to place our trust any longer with the ruling classes. We can hope for nothing from dialogue and conciliation. We must fight![7]

This statement ended with the old slogan: 'For land and with Sendic.'

But Sendic himself had drawn two important conclusions from his experience in the north. The first was that his goals would be better served by a clandestine guerrilla movement than by tradi-tional forms of labour agitation. The second was that the real battle would have to be fought in Montevideo. The north was too remote, the pampas (cattle-country) too empty. As a Tupamaro document puts it, 'We have no impregnable strongholds in our country where we can set up a guerrilla base, although there are places that are difficult to attack. On the other hand, we have an enormous city that contains more than 300 kilometres of streets and buildings, ideal for the growth of an urban struggle.'[8]

The Tupamaros were formed between late 1962 and early 1963. The history of those months is still mysterious. They took their name from Tupac Amaru, the celebrated Peruvian Indian leader, who was burned at the stake by the Spaniards in 1782 for organising a revolt against colonial rule. The name had also been used by General José Artigas, one of the heroes of Uruguay's war of inde-pendence, and by an unsuccessful guerrilla movement founded by Guillermo Lobotón in Peru in 1965. The first guerrilla operation organised by Sendic was a raid on the Swiss Rifle Club in July 1963.

Sendic was afterwards identified by the police as the ringleader, and he slipped across the border into Argentina. He returned to Montevideo secretly in the following year. At this stage, the Tupamaros were still anonymous. But they were already taking great pains to try to establish a favourable public image. On Christmas Eve 1963, for example, a 'hunger commando' hijacked a delivery van and handed out presents and packages of food to the poor people of the Aparicio Saravia slums.

The name and the five-pointed red star of the Tupamaros first became public in 1965, when they attempted to justify the bombing of the Bayer chemical plant in Montevideo as a protest against the Vietnam war. In the period up till 1968, the guerrillas were primarily concerned with building up the resources for a major offensive. Their characteristic operations over this period were raids on arms stores, banks and businesses.

They had not yet stolen the initiative from the security forces, and they suffered a number of reverses almost by accident. In March 1965, for example, three cane-cutters associated with the Tupamaros were locked up after they bungled a bank-robbery. In December 1966, the police gave chase to a terrorist group who were caught stealing a station-waggon: one Tupamaro, Carlos Flores, was killed in flight and the police seized on to clues that led them to several guerrilla hideouts. Another guerrilla was killed and several arrested in the raids that followed. And in November 1967, the police stumbled on a terrorist cell while making routine inquiries about a robbery.

After a shooting-match in which both sides lost several casualties, the Tupamaros issued one of their first coherent statements, an attempt to rationalise their use of political violence and their contempt for legal forms of protest:

> We no longer believe in the laws and institutions that 600 privileged people in the political parties and the organs that manipulate public opinion have created (and trample on whenever they like) in order to uphold their interests, impoverishing the people and thrashing them if they resist . . . We are not prepared to stand by without fighting while they sell the patrimony of Artigas to foreigners. There are undoubtedly solutions for the problems of the country, but they will not be achieved without

armed struggle, since they conflict with the interests of very powerful foreigners . . . For all these reasons, we have placed ourselves outside the law. This is the only honest position to adopt when the law is not equal for all; when the law is used to defend the interests of a minority at the expense of the majority . . .[9]

The Tupamaros' language would have been more at home in some other parts of Latin America than in a country where the gap between rich and poor is not extreme by regional standards and foreign dominance of the economy has been limited by Batlle's nationalisation decrees and the simple fact that the country has little to offer to outside investors.

At the same time, a number of prominent politicians have been discredited by evidence of graft and corruption. And above all, the Tupamaros' statement contained an element of self-fulfilling prophecy: their campaign of terrorism drove a weak government, unprepared for civil conflict, to resort to emergency measures that alienated popular support. It has been observed that 'It is an irony of political warfare—and a political fact to be considered and understood—that the rules are not the same for both sides.'[10] The logic of that statement has become clear in Uruguay. A soldier breaking down a door during a search or the accusation that a policeman has tortured a prisoner seems to have aroused a stronger public outcry in Uruguay than the murder of a policeman or the abduction of an ambassador by the Tupamaros.

That may be partly explained by the fact the government is the nominal custodian of the constitution and the country's democratic tradition, and is therefore blamed for any deviation from the norm. It was also due to President Pacheco's increasing isolation and the revelations of corruption and division inside the cabinet. And it had something to do with the guerrillas' very selective tactics and their flair for public relations.

IDEOLOGY AND TACTICS

Like most guerrilla movements in Latin America, the Tupamaros have remained studiously vague about their goals. They have produced very few theoretical statements and until March 1971, the literature of the Tupamaros was largely confined to interviews with stray journalists and commentaries on particular incidents. This apparent indifference to ideology stems from an emotional faith in the primacy of the deed as well as from the desire to appeal to as broad a range of public opinion as possible. One Tupamaro spokesman insisted that 'It is not by carefully elaborating political programmes that one makes the revolution. The basic principles of a socialist revolution have been established and are being carried further in Cuba. It is enough to accept these and to follow the way of armed struggle that will make it possible to put them into practice.'[11] The Tupamaros share the faith of Guevara or Debray in the power of a determined band of guerrillas to create the conditions for revolution—or, in the words of Raúl Castro, to be 'the small motor which starts the big motor of the revolution'. But as the movement evolved and the Tupamaros saw the possibility of increasing their following among the trade unions, they began to talk in more concrete terms about their political goals: nationalisation of basic industries, 'workers' control' in the factories and 'students' control' in the universities, redistribution of land.

The 'Thirty Questions', an interview conducted in mid-1968, provided the first extensive statement of tactics and goals. The Tupamaro mouthpiece declared that 'Revolutionary action in itself, the very act of arming oneself, of preparing oneself, and of pursuing activities which violate the norms of bourgeois legality generates revolutionary consciousness, the organisation, and the conditions for revolution.' He criticised the traditional left for failing to comprehend that 'fundamentally it is revolutionary actions that precipitate revolutionary actions'. The whole dialogue mirrored a highly technical and élitist view of revolutionary warfare. The Tupamaro spokesman argued, for example, that guerrilla actions should be carried out even when the objective conditions for revolution were lacking,

> because an armed movement of the left can be attacked by repression at any stage of its development and should be prepared to defend its existence; remember Argentina and Brazil. Also, because if each activist is not instilled from the beginning with the mentality of the fighter we shall be building other things—a mere structure of support for a revolution that others will make, for example, but not a revolutionary movement in itself.[12]

At the same time, the Tupamaros laid great stress on the need to construct support groups within the unions and to enlist 'the authentic revolutionaries' they believed were present in all parties of the traditional left. The spokesman refused to outline a detailed strategy, on the grounds that changing conditions inspired changing tactics. But he did discuss the situation in the country that the guerrillas had set out to exploit. He pointed out that the economic situation was likely to continue to deteriorate for several years and that the Uruguayan government was trying to maintain order through 'one of the weakest organisations of repression in Latin America'. (At the start of the terrorist offensive in 1968, there were only about 12,000 men in the Uruguayan armed forces, and 22,000 men in the police force—6,000 of them stationed in Montevideo. Very few army officers or policemen had received specialised training on counter-insurgency techniques.)

The Tupamaro spokesman also pointed out that, like Argentina, Uruguay had a large and well-organised trade union movement, and claimed that the guerrillas would be able to turn this to their advantage when the time came to attempt an armed uprising:

> If, admittedly, not all the unions have a high degree of militancy— either because of their composition or because of their leaders— the mere fact that virtually all the basic services of the state (banking, industry and commerce) are organised constitutes of itself a highly positive fact without parallel in Latin America. The possibility of paralysing the state services has created and can create very interesting possibilities if it comes to insurrection because, for example, it is not the same thing to attack a state in the fullness of its strength as to attack one which is half paralysed by strikes.[13]

Two years later, in October 1970, the Tupamaros argued that there were already signs of rising militancy among trade unionists:

> If, confronted with workers' demands for higher wages or with students' demands for university autonomy, the government sends troops into the streets with 'anti-riot' guns and kills students and workers and fills the prisons with them, won't everyone be ready to have done with this government, or another like it, when these same forces, under the leadership of a revolutionary vanguard, set out—as in Guillen's poem—to make he who is first the last and he who is last the first? (*poner el de arriba abajo y el de abajo arriba*).[14]

By this stage, the Tupamaros had built up a network of support groups (*Comités de Apoyo a los Tupamaros*) inside the trade unions and had timed some dramatic terrorist operations to coincide with wildcat strikes—for example, they kidnapped a prominent banker during the 1969 bank employees' work stoppage. But the control of the largest Uruguayan trade union federation, the National Confederation of Workers (CNT) remained firmly in the hands of the Uruguayan Communist Party.

The Tupamaros expanded their ideas about 'the principles of a socialist revolution' in a six-point programme that was issued in March 1971. The programme included proposals for the redistribution of land, the state takeover of commerce, industry and credit institutions, central planning and the seizure of foreign investment without any compensation payments. The proposals for agrarian reform included the following points:

1 The big cattle holdings, plantations, and dairies will be expropriated and placed under worker management.
2 In the understanding that the nation's principal wealth comes from the countryside, it will be capitalised and mechanised to make rapid production increases possible.
3 The small rural enterprises will be respected as regards owner-operators; farm-workers who today have precarious rights to land, such as leaseholders, labourers and share-croppers, will be given effective rights to the land, which must be for those who work it.
4 There will be increased technical assistance for all rural producers, plus fertiliser, seed, wire fencing and other instruments for improved exploitation.[15]

In contrast with the narrowly military focus of earlier Tupamaro statements, the March manifesto represented an attempt to strike a fairly reasonable and 'practical' tone that might appeal to workers and peasant farmers more concerned with their standards of living than with the tenuous dream of a Cuban kind of revolution—hence the down-to-earth talk of fertilisers, and the calculated reassurances for small peasant proprietors (no point in giving them sleepless nights). That also explains why the Tupamaros failed to mention the kind of political system they were planning to introduce, although they had some rather ominous things to say about 'justice' under the new order:

1 The present codes, conceived for the maintenance of private property and the capitalist system in general, will be replaced by others that will take into account essential human values.

. . .

3 The sentences handed down by bourgeois justice on persons convicted of so-called common crimes will be fully reviewed, as will the absolutions of crimes committed by certain friends of the régime.

4 All those who collaborate in the counter-revolution, for example those who have committed murders and other crimes in the service of the present régime or who, making use of the communications media, have helped to spread calumnies and lies against the people's cause, will be sentenced to prison terms in keeping with the gravity of their crimes.[16]

The Tupamaros see themselves as the agents of a continental and global, rather than a purely national, revolution. They have always accepted the possibility that an outside power, probably Brazil or Argentina, would intervene in Uruguay if the country appeared to be on the brink of revolution. Indeed, in the first years that the movement was active, the guerrillas counted on the prospect of foreign intervention as the chance to play the role of the military vanguard in a war of national liberation. The sense of an assault on a world order has led the Tupamaros to exchange cadres, resources and information with similar movements in Brazil, Bolivia and Argentina. The 'triborder' region up in the country's forested northern corner is an easy place to make frontier crossings into either Brazil or Argentina, and petty smugglers and black marketeers have been moving back and forth with relative impunity for many years. Tupamaro sympathisers have occasionally taken a boat across the River Plate from Buenos Aires to join them in a nocturnal escapade. The self-styled 'revolutionary Peronists' in Argentina have been discovered using weapons originally stolen from the Uruguayan security forces, and several Argentine guerrilla groups model themselves closely on the Tupamaros: the Trotskyite People's Revolutionary Army (ERP) even uses the same five-pointed red star as its emblem.

The Tupamaros are organised as cells, or 'firing groups', of four or five men, with the group leader as the link-man with other cells. This is a system familiar to all urban terrorists, and it was one of the keys to the Tupamaros' success in evading the police. The Tupamaros have described the importance of 'compartmentalisation' in the following terms:

> We can say that compartmentalisation and discretion are to the urban guerrilla what a secret camp in the jungle is for his rural counterpart. He does not know more than he needs to know . . . he does not know more places than are necessary for his operations, he does not know more names, including those of his comrades, than is absolutely necessary . . . And compartmentalisation applies not only cells but to columns. Each column has its own combat squads, its own logistic support and infrastructure, and its own links with (broader movements): MLN-people, MLN-unions, MLN-students, MLN-army . . . With this structure, we can say that the Movement is ineradicable.[17]

Maybe. Much of the broader framework of 'columns' and support groups that the Tupamaros often refer to probably exists only on paper, although they have been able to concentrate comparatively large forces for individual operations, such as the occupation of the town of Pando in 1969, and have clearly managed to infiltrate their agents into most branches of the police and the civil service.

One of the striking things about the day-to-day operations of the guerrillas was that they appeared to lack a unified command. The capture of Raúl Sendic and a group of leading Tupamaros in August 1970, for example, did not seem to impair the planning and execution of later guerrilla actions—although there was widespread speculation that Sendic, taking advantage of the liberal conditions in the Montevideo jails, had set up a courier service and was running the movement from behind bars. The Tupamaros have also been fortunate in that there are no important rival guerrilla groups in Uruguay, and so far there have been few signs of the internal schisms in which terrorist movements habitually squander their resources. Only two other guerrilla groups have been active in Montevideo, both of them operating in collusion with the Tupamaros: the Eastern Revolutionary Armed Front (FARO) and the Popular Revolutionary Organisation 33 (OPR 33).

In 1968, the Tupamaros moved over to the offensive against the Pacheco government. By August 1971, there were signs that they were preparing for an armed insurrection, to be synchronised with political strikes—depending on the results of the November presidential elections. Over this period, they succeeded in presenting themselves to the public as a credible military force by maintaining *continuity* of operations. Although they lost their original 'Robin Hood' image as imaginative student pranksters who pilfered from the rich to give to the poor—by systematically murdering policemen as well as an American hostage, Dan Mitrione—they remained very selective in their use of terror.

The Tupamaros have demonstrated, for example, that kidnapping well-known politicians and businessmen and keeping them in hiding for several months can be a more effective way of humiliating a government than shooting down a minister in the street. The Tupamaros experimented with a wide variety of guerrilla techniques between 1968 and 1971. The guerrillas themselves classify their actions as (i) 'propaganda' exercises designed to discredit the government or to fashion a popular image of the MLN; (ii) logistic operations designed to bring in money and arms; and (iii) frontal assault on the government and the forces at its disposal by sabotage, selective assassination and so on. Their strategy depends to a large extent on the way they expect the government to respond. They have tried to drive President Pacheco towards the use of 'counter-terrorism' in the hope that this would excite an outcry from liberal critics at home and abroad and undermine his political position by dividing the cabinet and stirring up trouble in congress—where his partisans were in a minority.[18]

By mid-1971 they had gone some way towards their goals. Some observers were ready to maintain that the Tupamaros had achieved their aim of establishing a 'duel power' situation, in which the government was powerless even to protect its friends, while the terrorists were free to range around the city and enforce what they describe as 'revolutionary justice'. To understand how an urban guerrilla movement operating without the direct support of any of the traditional left-wing parties was able to attain this position of strength in a democratic society, it is necessary to study three of the

Tupamaros' characteristic techniques in detail: 'armed propaganda', subversion and intimidation of the security forces, and political kidnapping.

THE PROPAGANDA OF THE DEED

The guerrilla's central task is to control *people*. To get anywhere in the war for minds, the guerrilla must begin by letting people know he exists; then, through successful armed operations, he must persuade them that he represents a credible military force and that revolution is at least a possibility; and finally, he must find ways of appealing to their interests or winning them to his political goals. Failing that, he must put himself in a position where he can enforce obedience. The first hurdle for the Tupamaros to jump in the effort to get their message across was the strict censorship that the government imposed on news of guerrilla actions. The Montevideo press was forbidden to refer to the Tupamaros by the name they had given themselves, for example; instead, sub-editors resorted to insults or circumlocutions like 'criminals' or, simply, 'the nameless ones'. Soon after he assumed the presidency at the end of 1967, Pacheco Areco closed down two radical newspapers and six extreme left-wing political parties—although the Uruguayan Communist Party is allowed full licence to publish a newspaper and operate a radio station, and the radical weekly *Marcha* continues to print Tupamaro documents.

Shut out of the regular news media, the Tupamaros constructed their own 'counter-media'. To broadcast their own version of events, the guerrillas used a mobile radio transmitter (which was finally confiscated in 1970) and enlisted the help of radio technicians to interrupt regular broadcasts. They have also used the classic form of 'armed propaganda' to communicate their aims. Bands of armed men have occupied cinemas, workers' canteens, and other public meeting places in order to deliver impromptu propaganda talks to a captive audience.

But the great talent of the Tupamaros has been to combine smoothly professional criminal operations with an effort to demonstrate the 'revolutionary justice' of a burglary or a bank-robbery.

From their victims' viewpoint, they have sometimes been embarrassingly successful in turning the right combination. When the Tupamaros broke into the Financiera Monty bank early in 1969, for example, they not only looted cash and securities from the vaults but also unearthed some highly confidential account books that supplied evidence of the misuse of public funds and the secret formation of an illegal cartel. The Liber Arce commando of the Tupamaros afterwards produced a leaflet that claimed to establish, amongst other things, that 'all the activity of the Financiera is illegal. It is prohibited by Law 13,330 of 30/4/65. It consists of: speculation with foreign currencies; illegal export and import of capital; and tax evasion.' The Tupamaros added a list of the names of twenty-two prominent Uruguayan citizens whose names they claimed to have found in the six stolen account-books. Carlos Frick Davies, the minister of agriculture, was forced to resign in the ensuing scandal.

Of course, corruption is nothing new in Latin America. What was new was the attempt by political bank-robbers to prove that theft is a relative idea. Similarly, when a commando group burgled the home of the tobacco magnate, Luis Mailhos Queirolo, early in 1970, they not only got away with gold bullion worth £25,000 but produced evidence that Mailhos had been guilty of tax-evasion on the grand scale. He was later required to pay a record fine of some $2,300,000 (578 million pesos).[19] Neither the Monty nor the Mailhos robberies could have been accomplished without excellent inside information. One of Mailhos' disgruntled former employees provided the guerrillas with a plan of his house and personally guided them on the night of the burglary. The same factor explained the success of spectacular bank-raids like the one in December 1970, that produced a record haul of more than $6 million.

The popular impact of robberies on this scale, quite apart from the question of trying to rationalise the crimes in political terms, was comparable with that of the Great Train Robbery in England. In the minds of the readers of crime magazines and sensationalist tabloids, a kind of aura descended on the men responsible. The sheer love of sensation attracted young hotheads to the Tupamaros and appealed to their latin sense of *machismo*. What the Tupamaros actually did with the money they pocketed in the course of these robberies—the figure may have risen as high as $10 million—is a moot point. Some of it was certainly used to bribe policemen and jailers.

Régis Debray believed that the best form of 'armed propaganda' was an effective, precisely executed, military action. 'The destruction of a troop transport truck,' he maintained, 'is more effective propaganda for the local population than a hundred speeches.' [20] One of the Tupamaros' most successful propaganda exercises was the occupation of the town of Pando, outside Montevideo, on the occasion of the second anniversary of Che Guevara's death on 8 October 1969. That operation was the model for Argentine guerrillas who later took over the town of Garín. In many ways, it was characteristic of the Tupamaros. It illustrated their love of disguises and their penchant for the spectacular. A young couple chosen for their outward respectability hired a funeral cortège on the pretext that an uncle who had died in Buenos Aires was to be buried in a village near Pando. The uncle's 'remains' were said to be inside a large urn that probably contained firearms. The suspicions of the man responsible for the cortège were aroused when the 'nephew' asked him to stop to pick up a crowd of remarkably youthful 'relatives'. By that stage, it was too late. The Tupamaros overpowered the chauffeurs and tied them up.

Once they had reached Pando, they joined forces with another group of guerrillas waiting at the bus depot; about thirty-five Tupamaros took part in the operation. They launched a rapid three-pronged attack. One group occupied the telephone exchange and cut off communications with Montevideo, another invaded the police station, and a third raided three leading banks. The guerrillas were delayed for a few minutes longer than their scheduled quarter of an hour, because an isolated patrolman started a gun-battle inside the Banco de la República. And something more serious went wrong at the last minute. Someone from the town managed to notify a highway patrol of what was happening, and the news was signalled to the capital. Although most of the guerrillas managed to get back to Montevideo safely, the last car was trapped by army patrols. The Tupamaros' losses were heavy: three killed and twenty captured. On the other hand, the guerrillas insisted that the occupation of

Pando was a 'qualitative leap' forward and that, as a result, 'for the first time, a great part of the population saw the guerrilla as a possibility'. [21]

The Tupamaros have also perfected the technique of political kidnapping. Although it is the abduction of foreign envoys that usually draws the chunkiest world headlines, Uruguay's urban guerrillas have used the kidnapping of important local citizens to greater effect as a means of showing up the government's vulnerability. In August 1968, they chose Ulises Pereyra Reverbel—a close friend of the president and the head of the state telephone and electricity corporation, UTE—as their first hostage. Half of the Montevideo police force were promptly detailed to track him down.

Failing to find any trace of the hostage, they invaded the university campus, where they believed that some of the Tupamaros had found sanctuary. (At the beginning of 1971, you could still see the letters MLN—for National Liberation Movement—painted in huge pealing letters on the roof of one of the faculty buildings.) Predictably, the police invasion excited a violent student reaction, and in the rioting that followed a young Communist was killed. He provided the guerrillas with one of their first martyr-figures, and even his name was symbolic, since he was conveniently called Liber Arce (which of course sounds like *liberarse*, 'to free oneself'). Pereyra was set free, crumpled and unshaven but otherwise unharmed, five days after his capture.

The guerrillas followed up their first kidnapping with a similar exercise in September 1969, when they abducted a leading banker, Gaetano Pellegrini Giampetro. They held him for ten weeks. The Pellegrini kidnapping was timed to serve as a show of sympathy with the bank employees who had gone on strike after 182 of their number had been fired. President Pacheco subsequently compelled the bank-clerks to go back to work under the terms of a tough 'militarisation' decree.

The Tupamaros trained their sights on the diplomatic corps after the Brazilians and the Guatemalans had already shown the way. A rash of kidnappings broke out in July 1970, with the capture of a magistrate who had been responsible for the trial of guerrilla prisoners. Then, on the last day of the month, the Tupamaros seized the

Brazilian consul, Aloysio Dias Gomide, and an American police adviser, Dan Mitrione. They captured a third foreign hostage—the American soil expert Dr Claude Fly—at the beginning of August.

The Uruguayan cabinet was divided over how to respond to the Tupamaros' ransom demand for the release of political prisoners and the publication of a manifesto, but the president, backed up by his security ministers, insisted on digging his heels in and refused to bargain. The outcome was the murder of Mitrione. The guerrillas later tried to rationalise that crime, and the comments made by one of their spokesmen (using the *nom de guerre* 'Urbano') to the Cuban Communist Party paper, *Granma*, give an acid taste of the terrorist logic. 'Urbano' claimed that it was necessary to murder Mitrione for two reasons. First, because they had to prove to the government that they were prepared to carry out their threats. Second, because the success or failure of one urban guerrilla group in using diplomatic kidnapping as a form of political blackmail would influence other extremist movements that might be tempted to use the same weapon:

> The execution of our sentence on Mitrione not only involved the responsibility of the Movement before the people (of Uruguay) but also its responsibility to other revolutionary movements in Latin America . . . The logic of the technique of kidnapping to get the release of prisoners has to be followed all the way if it is to remain effective. [22]

That statement showed that the Tupamaros are very conscious of their kinship with other terrorist groups. 'Urbano' concluded, in a chillingly detached way, that the technique of diplomatic kidnapping resembles 'a game of chess in which the capture of one piece forces the other side to change its tactics'. Despite the government crisis in August, during which President Pacheco is reported to have actually written out his resignation on the morning of August 7 and then to have torn it up when he learned that the police had captured Raúl Sendic a few hours later, things have not worked out quite as 'Urbano' anticipated. Pacheco stood his ground—although the ground, as will be later observed, shifted under him.

Dias Gomide was finally released after his wife (who made some moving and emotional appearances on Brazilian television) had collected some $250,000 from sympathisers in her own country to pay his ransom. The Tupamaros made the humane but politically disingenuous gesture of 'pardoning' Dr Fly after he suffered a stroke. They even kidnapped a heart specialist to examine him. He was eventually freed in March 1971.[23]

There were several more important kidnappings in the first half of 1971. The British ambassador, Geoffrey Jackson, was captured while driving to his office down one of Montevideo's narrow one-way streets on January 8. The Tupamaros delayed announcing terms for his release, although a note was discovered in the lavatory of a downtown bar in which they tried to justify the crime as a counter to 'British neo-colonialism'. Jackson was finally set free eight months after his capture. His release was a show of strength as much as a humane gesture. It followed a spectacular jailbreak early in September when 106 guerrillas held prisoner in the Punta Carreras (all of those who had not already escaped, including Raúl Sendic) tunnelled their way to safety. In March, Uruguay's attorney-general, Guido Berro Oribe, had also been kidnapped. According to the Tupamaros' 'Communiqué No. 18', he was interrogated 'on the matter of serious irregularities that have occurred during his term as court prosecutor'. He was set free after he had been made to admit (in tape-recordings circulated to the press) that he had agreed to hand over political prisoners to military tribunals and that he had signed orders for the further detention of prisoners after their original sentences expired.[24] At the end of March, Ulises Pereyra Reverbel was abducted for a second time. The way he was treated by his captors, and President Pacheco's response, threw a spotlight on the greatly increased strength of the Tupamaros. The guerrillas announced that they had sentenced him to life imprisonment in 'the people's prison'. The very idea of keeping a hostage captive in some suburban basement in a nation's capital was a dramatic sign of the Tupamaros' self-confidence. Two months later, Pacheco appointed Juan Fabini to succeed Pereyra as the head of the UTE. This looked very much like a tacit acknowledgement that the president was powerless to help his friend.[25]

For their part, the Tupamaros coolly marked out yet another victim: Frick Davies, the former minister of agriculture, was taken hostage early in May. For the Tupamaros, kidnapping had become something more than a publicity stunt or a means of political blackmail. It was used as a bloodless way of eliminating individual enemies and exposing the government's soft spots: as a terrorist weapon calculated to excite maximal fear and confusion amongst those close to the presidential palace, and minimal horror and revulsion among the public in general in a democratic society.

Selective terror against men in uniform, like kidnapping, has been used by the Tupamaros as a means of isolating their targets. Until late in 1969, the guerrillas avoided bloodshed, and their only victims were gunned down when the police closed in and forced them to fight a street-battle. The first man they assassinated was a police agent, Carlos Ruben Zambrano, who was murdered while sitting in a bus on 15 November 1969. That killing marked a change in tactics, and since then the police have borne the Tupamaros' campaign of selective assassination. In April 1970, Héctor Morán Charquero (a police inspector who had been accused of torturing prisoners) was shot down in a Montevideo street. There were more murders of police agents in June. On June 17, the guerrillas issued an extraordinary communiqué in which they declared that they were willing to observe a truce until early in July. During this period of calm, the government was supposed to reconsider its policy, and policemen and soldiers who had lost their appetite for battle were invited to resign and find new jobs. The impact of this bit of psychological warfare on morale can be gauged by the fact that policemen went on strike a few days later, demanding higher pay and the right to work in civilian clothes in order to make themselves less conspicuous targets. The government arrested sixty-six of them afterwards on charges of insubordination.

The Tupamaros have tried persuasion as well as terror. In April 1971, for example, they sent an open letter to members of the armed forces, calling on them 'not to become accomplices in the arbitrary jailings and corporal punishment of the people of Uruguay'. The guerrillas argued that every time soldiers 'defend the régime, they are defending an antinational and antipopular policy'.[26] Many of the Tupamaros' operations would clearly have been impossible if they had not managed to set up a network of agents inside the police and the armed forces. It was the presence of a man working for the guerrillas in the night watch of the naval training barracks in the capital that enabled the Tupamaros to capture it on the night of 29 May 1970.

That exercise was a good example of Tupamaro methods. After a marine called Fernando Garín had signalled to them by waving his cap, several guerrillas walked up to the sentry, waved forged police identity cards in his face, and asked to speak with the duty officer. While this was happening, a group of rowdy young men appeared and were immediately challenged by the 'policemen'. They said they were students, and were promptly placed under arrest. The whole group was allowed to enter the barracks, where they overpowered the night watch and opened the doors to another seventeen Tupamaros. Within half an hour, the guerrillas were the masters of the entire barracks, and they treated the naval cadets to a political harangue in which they accused some of the officers present of brutality towards prisoners. The guerrillas finally made their escape with 350 rifles, some machine-guns, and large quantities of explosives. They left a memento: copies of a leaflet (probably written by Garín) in which they maintained that members of the armed forces had 'dishonoured their uniform . . . We must choose between a new breed of tyrants and the just and independent Uruguay of the future.'[27]

The Tupamaros have gone on chipping away at the morale of the security forces. A weak and divided army is of course the prerequisite for a successful armed uprising. The guerrillas' initial advantage was that the government forces were inexperienced and thin on the ground, lacking an élite corps for counter-insurgency operations. Since 1968, a special police corps—the Metropolitan Guards—has been set up, and the Americans and the Brazilians have provided training and instructors. But the state of morale in the lower ranks can hardly have been bolstered by the fact that a bitter controversy has taken place among senior officers on the subject of how to cope with the guerrillas. In 1968, General Liber Seregni, who later became the presidential candidate of the left-wing *Frente Amplio*, resigned from his post as the army's inspector-general in protest against official 'repression'. And Police Commissioner Otero was made to resign in 1970 after he had been quoted as making some highly critical remarks about police methods.

Pacheco's government was weakened by its inability to pursue a sustained counter-guerrilla campaign. Each time the police cordoned off a city zone to conduct a major sweep, the public response was a storm of protest. Congress repeatedly refused to extend the emergency powers that Pacheco claimed were necessary to restore order. The crux of the problem, from a purely military viewpoint, was poor intelligence. There were attempts to make landlords responsible for tenants and to introduce identity checks, but the police were unable to supply the troops who were sent into the streets with the kind of information they needed—probably because the Tupamaros were getting plenty of forewarning of major raids through their own network of informers. The government resorted to desperate expedients: a suppressed senate report discussed the use of torture by the police. Violent and indiscriminate repression was hardly the way to deal with urban guerrillas who had little to learn about marksmanship.

TOWARDS REVOLUTION?

The continued guerrilla successes baffled and divided the Uruguayan government and posed a threat to President Pacheco's own position. Pacheco was a rather shadowy figure as vice-president under General Gestido, familiar to most of his countrymen largely through his prowess as an amateur boxer. He was catapulted into the presidency by Gestido's sudden death at the very moment that the Tupamaros were preparing to move over to a frontal attack. He fought the guerrillas with a boxer's doggedness but without imagination. His four-year term was littered with disasters. He found himself confronting an increasingly hostile congress, popularly blamed for his country's misfortunes. That was partly the result of his own heavy-handed tactics. For example, in the face of mounting high school militancy (the notion of 'student power' is no more a monopoly of undergraduates in Uruguay than in western societies) Pacheco tried to set up a centralised executive council to take charge of secondary education and dismissed the existing committees of teaching staffs as the work of 'communist agitation'. In June 1971, after a series of student strikes and school shut-downs, he agreed to back down in the face of strong opposition from congress and the supreme court. The Uruguayans were simply not ready to accept the idea that school pupils needed to be regimented, however sympathetic to the Tupamaros some of them seemed to be.

Pacheco became an increasingly lonely figure, unable to rally the conservative forces. According to General Liber Seregni, the conflict between the government and the Tupamaros came to resemble 'a football match in which the people feel themselves to be spectators'. A commentator in the radical weekly *Marcha* wrote that 'Thanks to Pacheco, Uruguay has at last definitively become a part of Latin America . . . What we see now is the paternal state turning itself into the police-state.' That was a cruel judgment, and a partial one, since what was taking place was a two-way process in which Pacheco was on the receiving end. Caught off-balance, floundering in the face of a well-organised guerrilla campaign, his government resorted to a programme of repression that the country, psychologically still immersed in a healthier, more peaceful age, was just not ready to accept.

Pacheco started out in a precarious political position. His Colorado Party held 16 of the 30 seats in the senate and 50 of the 90 seats in the lower house, but it was formally split into factions, and he could count on the steady support of only sixteen deputies at most. His attempts to renew the emergency powers, or *medidas prontas de seguridad*, were frequently blocked, and in 1971 he resorted to using his power of presidential decree. The security crisis, and Pacheco's lumbering way of tackling it, exacerbated the argument in congress and tore his cabinet apart. One minister of the interior after another handed in his resignation after failing to score a decisive success against the guerrillas. General Francese stepped down after the Jackson kidnapping, and Santiago de Brum Carbajal followed suit in May (although the immediate cause of his resignation was a nasty incident in which a gang of right-wing thugs, led by an off-duty policeman, invaded an upper-class grammar school and assaulted students). The problem of how to respond to kidnappers' demands led to a division between hardliners and 'compromisers'.

But the government was weakened by two issues distinct from the security problem. The first was a series of scandalous exposures of corruption in high places that ended with the resignation of three cabinet ministers in quick succession (they included César Charlone, the finance minister, and Peirano Facio, the foreign minister) after the Banco Mercantil was declared bankrupt at the end of March 1971. Opposition spokesmen in congress claimed that the government had tried to bail out its friends, and the directors of the bank were charged with misappropriating some $7 million in foreign currency. It was patently difficult for men caught up in scandals of this magnitude to command any real measure of public backing. The second divisive issue was Pacheco's determination to run as a candidate for a second presidential term. The secretary-general of the Colorado Party, General Nelson Constanza, resigned his post in November 1970, in protest at Pacheco's manœuvres and the party formally split into a new series of factions at a congress held a few months later, where the president also came under fire for his financial policies.

The issue that dominated Uruguayan politics from the end of 1970 was the presidential election scheduled for November 1971. In a published manifesto at the end of 1970, the organisers of the *Frente Amplio*, or 'broad front', called for an electoral alliance of left-wing parties, and promised that 'no group would be excluded because of its views'. The outcome of this was a popular front modelled on Salvador Allende's *Unidad Popular* alliance. The Uruguayan front that held its first meeting on 5 February 1971, contained some fourteen parties and *groupuscules* of the left, ranging from the Trotskyist Workers' Revolutionary Party (PRT) to the Christian Democratic Party, led by Juan Pablo Terra.[28]

The most important political forces represented in the *Frente Amplio* were Rodney Arismendi's Uruguayan Communist Party, the Socialist Party, and two splinter groups that had broken away from the two traditional parties, the Blancos and the Colorados, that had divided power in Uruguay throughout most of the country's history: Senator Zelmar Michelini's 'List of 99' (a splinter from Pacheco's Colorado Party) and Senator Rodriguez Camusso's 'Popular and Progressive Blanco Movement' (a breakaway from the opposition

Blanco Party). General Liber Seregni, a liberal nationalist of mildly socialist views, was chosen as the *Frente Amplio*'s presidential candidate. Choosing a former general as a figurehead was a shrewd move.[29] Seregni had been one of the leaders of the anti-*golpista* (that is, pro-civilian-rule) faction in the armed forces. His military background and his moderate image were calculated to deter attempts at a right-wing coup in the event of his election.

At the outset, there was widespread scepticism about the *Frente Amplio*'s chances. Uruguay's election laws are weighted in favour of the two traditional parties, since they provide that any number of rival candidates can be presented by the Blanco and Colorado Parties, and that all the votes pulled in by the party ticket (or *devisa*) will go to the candidate who scores best. That partly explained why the left-wing parties had never managed to pull in as much as 10 per cent of the total vote in a previous election. But a series of public opinion polls conducted in Montevideo early in 1971 suggested that the left-wing alliance could count on getting between 25 and 37 per cent of the votes—possibly enough to win if the traditional parties failed to join forces.[30] And the foreign press reported that the *Frente Amplio*'s mass rally on March 26 drew crowds of over 150,000. There was an even bigger turnout on July 26, when General Seregni led a funeral procession to commemorate the death of a 17-year-old student, Heber Nieto, who had been killed during a clash between students and police.

The *Frente Amplio* quickly developed into a major political force, and this presented a tactical problem for the guerrillas as well as for the leaders of the Colorado and Blanco Parties, who were wrangling over who should be allowed to try his luck in the election. The Tupamaros published a communiqué in January in which they insisted that 'the people can only win power ·through armed struggle' but welcomed the popular front as a means of creating a broad-based mass movement:

> We maintain our differences with the organisations composing the front over methods and over the tactical assessment of the front's immediate objective—the elections. Nonetheless, we are willing to offer our support to the *Frente Amplio*. The fact that the front's immediate objective is to participate in the elections

does not cause us to forget that it represents an important attempt to unite the contingents struggling against the oligarchy and foreign capital . . . In offering our support to the *Frente Amplio*, then, we do so with the understanding that its principle task must be to mobilise the toiling masses and that its work in this regard will not begin and end with the elections.[31]

Later in 1971, the Tupamaros started thinking more seriously about what would follow if the *Frente Amplio* came to power. Their faith in 'armed struggle' made them as reluctant as the Chilean *miristas* had been to accept the idea that a revolution could take place through the ballot-box. According to one reported statement, the Tupamaros later declared that 'We will be patient as long as the process is truly democratic and one of transformation. But if the *Frente Amplio* becomes bureaucratic and fence-straddling and begins the customary "political" manœuvres and deals; if the hour of transformation is thus postponed, we'll go back to the armed struggle.' Thus the guerrillas were setting themselves up the guardians of the revolution, as a kind of priestly elect who alone could signal the correct way forward.

Their attitude to the popular front was bound up with the general problem of the relations between the guerrilla movements and the traditional left in Latin America. Rodney Arismendi, the leader of one of the continent's most powerful traditional communist parties, tried to act as a mediator between the Castroites and Moscow. At the OLAS conference in Havana in 1967, for example, he searched for a compromise formula that the communists and the guerrillas could agree on—along the lines that armed struggle is one of the higher forms of revolutionary activity, but not the only one. He was even ready to concede that while all communist parties belong to 'the revolutionary vanguard', they no longer necessarily dominate it (something that may have been obvious enough, but was never accepted by most of his Moscow-line colleagues in other countries).

During a visit to Rome in April 1971, Arismendi again rejected the idea that a violent revolution was possible in Uruguay, but praised the Tupamaros for their 'courage and sincerity'. He concluded that 'We will make the revolution by other means.'[32] The Uruguayan Communists were bound to be influenced by the fact that they had enjoyed a pretty easy ride in Montevideo (running a radio station, for example) and that, even in the teeth of the security crisis, President Pacheco allowed them to hold rallies and mass meetings. The Tupamaro leaders have closer links with the Uruguayan Socialist Party (Sendic himself was a lapsed Socialist) which, like its Chilean counterpart, represents a less cautious and more militant political force than the orthodox Communists. Mounting Russian hostility to the Latin American guerrilla movements was also bound to influence Arismendi. In March 1971, for example, a Russian writers' journal denounced the Tupamaros as 'rollicking, loud-mouthed thugs' pursuing 'gangster tactics'.[33]

The outcome in Uruguay is still in doubt. The elections held on November 28, 1971, were a triumph for the traditional parties. The Uruguayans were confronted with three basic possibilities. The first was another Colorado government. President Pacheco went ahead with his plan to propose himself for re-election, but he never stood much of a chance, since under the constitution he required a clear majority of all votes cast to be eligible for a second term. It was arranged that, if he were disqualified, votes cast in his favour would be passed on to his chosen 'alternative', Juan Maria Bordaberry, the minister of agriculture and a wealthy landowner who was also a staunch partisan of Pacheco's policies. The Colorados presented themselves as the only barrier to communism and civil war in Uruguay. They also set out to appeal to the voter's pocket by announcing some hefty wage rises and 100 per cent increases in pensions in the months prior to the elections.

Secondly, there were the candidates of the opposition Blanco Party. Most notable among them was Wilson Ferreira Aldunate, whose election promises bore some resemblance to those of the *Frente Amplio*; he called for the nationalisation of key sectors of the economy and pointed an accusing finger at the signs of corruption in government circles. Finally, there was General Liber Seregni's *Frente Amplio*, closely modelled on Allende's Popular Unity coalition in Chile. Liber Seregni said he would take over the meat-packing industry, the banking system and the conduct of foreign trade. He also said that he would carve up the big estates and decree a general amnesty for political prisoners. He planned to use the executive powers of the presidency in the best Allende style by parking government inspectors in the banks and the major private companies.

But when it came to the point, the Uruguayan voters rejected the left-wing alternative. The final voting figures gave the ruling Colorados the victory by a narrow lead of less than 10,000 over the Blancos. They polled just under 595,000 votes to the Blancos' 584,000, with the *Frente Amplio* trailing behind as a poor third with a score of only some 276,000 votes. Since Pacheco failed to get his majority, this made Bordaberry the putative future president of Uruguay—although there were immediately opposition charges of electoral fraud, and the decision to stage a recount of all votes cast delayed the final verdict until early in 1972.

The dismal failure of the left in the Uruguayan elections was probably due to several factors. The *Frente Amplio* had become identified in the minds of many voters with the communists and the Tupamaro guerrillas. The example of Chile, where there were signs of economic recession, mounting political violence, and curbs on the liberty of expression under a popular front government similar to the one that General Liber Seregni was proposing, may also have played a part. And it was partly a matter of ingrained voting habits in a country where the parties of the left had never claimed more than about 10 per cent of the poll, and the Colorados and the Blancos have always enjoyed the right to distribute patronage through the civil service.

The problem is that the defeat of the *Frente Amplio* may presage an attempt at an armed uprising. Sr Bordaberry has promised to uphold President Pacheco's policy of confrontation with the Tupamaros. The question is whether he has the military resources to inflict a defeat on the guerrillas. If the Tupamaros decide to attempt an insurrection, and the communists choose to lend their support to such a venture, the Tupamaros' chances of success would look rather better than those of the Venezuelan terrorists in 1962— unless an outside power decided to intervene. There were persistent scare stories in Montevideo in mid-1971 that the Brazilians had drawn up contingency plans for 'Operation 30 Hours'—the time they estimated it would take to storm Montevideo in a blitzkrieg operation. One of Brazil's two leading newspapers, the *Estado de São Paulo*, showed some sympathy for the idea.

In considering the lessons of the Tupamaros' relative success, it is important to remember the elements in the situation that are unique as well as those that are not. Uruguay is after all a small, vulnerable country where the seizure of a single city, Montevideo, would mean the seizure of the nation as a whole. The government lacks the resources to pursue a major security campaign and economic and social development programmes at the same time. On the other hand, what has happened in Uruguay shows how a country's liberal traditions can work against a government confronted with a major challenge to its authority. The supreme irony was that President Pacheco, driven to suspend constitutional liberties in order to pursue his losing battle with the guerrillas, found himself criticised as an enemy of democracy as bitterly as those who had originally set out to overthrow the democratic system. The full measure of the security crisis in Uruguay became clear in the first half of September, with the spectacular jailbreak from the Punta Carreras prison.

11

The Problems of Response

There can be no purely military solution for urban violence. But governments in search of a compromise formula are often caught in a vicious circle: often it is not until the guerrilla threat has emerged that the ruling élite becomes conscious of the urgent need for reform; but by that time there is often deep reluctance to make political concessions in case they are interpreted as a submission to blackmail. On the other hand, it has been observed in this book that urban terrorism is not peculiar to any specific form of society; that a common range of techniques has been applied both in western democracies and in third world dictatorships; and that, under certain conditions, terrorists can succeed in breaking down the fabric of a democratic society. This makes it important to consider the problems of response, both at a national and an international level. This chapter looks, first, at the problems for the security forces in an urban context, and second, at the chances for some kind of international arrangement to curb 'international crimes' such as hijacking and kidnapping.

In the long term—as has been suggested throughout this book—the survival of a particular political system depends not merely on the balance of forces, but on whether it is able to satisfy legitimate demands for reform. One obviously responds in a different way to terrorists in an agrarian society where 2 per cent of the population own 70 per cent of the land (Guatemala) and an advanced industrial society where a fifth of school-leavers go on to university (America). The urban guerrilla, like the protest marcher and irrespective of his political creed, sometimes shows up the 'blockages' in a particular system: the social grievances that cannot be satisfied without basic structural changes.

At a national level, counter-guerrilla operations in urban areas require good intelligence and above all *restraint*. It is only too easy for soldiers to tread on innocent people's toes while conducting search operations in crowded slums; it is vital to avoid arousing public hostility in order to isolate the guerrillas and cut them off from their potential sources of support. This will require a high level of professionalism in the government forces, including special training in riot control and the formation of armed commando groups capable of moving into a guerrilla hideout or freeing a kidnapped hostage with a minimum of needless bloodshed.

Although it is nearly always possible for a government that can rely on the support of its armed forces to crush an urban uprising by force (on the model of the French in Algiers) counter-guerrilla operations must be seen primarily as a battle for men's loyalties. It is necessary to narrow down the number of people seen as 'the enemy' to an absolute minimum in order not to alienate public opinion or limit the right of legitimate dissent. On the other hand, a shaky and ineffectual government—of whatever political leanings— has only an outside chance of keeping its grip by appealing to reason alone. In the face of an organised terrorist campaign, the first requirement is that the government should show both the resolution and the capacity to respond with the necessary force.

In most democratic societies, the police are the men in the front line. The police face special problems, as the situation in America suggests. In the United States, the police have become prime targets both for black militants and radical demonstrators; they have sometimes responded with a brutality that shocked liberal opinion. The killing of four student protesters at Kent State University by nervous and trigger-happy National Guardsmen in 1970 justifiably excited a storm of protest. Those killings illustrated the psychological (and sometimes class) divide between the police and the National Guard and the political dissidents they are asked to control. As the Skolnik Report observed, the police are recruited from the ranks of less-educated, low-income whites at a time when more and more people are receiving university education in the United States. While the average level of education of the American population in general is rising, that of the police has been declining: 'New police recruits are being taken from an ever-shrinking pool of undereducated persons.' On top of that, policemen's pay has been dropping by comparison with the earnings of other social groups, and their social status has been falling equally fast.

The result is declining recruitment, soaring rates of resignation that are now as high as 20 per cent a year in some state police forces, and bitter frustrations that give rise to racial prejudice and brutality —especially in the face of 'hippies' and student protesters who belong to an alien culture but have enjoyed educational and financial advantages that are closed to the policemen on the beat. Paradoxically, it is often the militants who are most bourgeois, and their scapegoats (the visible arm of authority) relatively underprivileged members of an affluent society. Is it really surprising that off-duty policemen in America sometimes try to get rid of their frustrations by attacking a Black Panther office or campaigning for George Wallace? It is all too easy for well-meaning liberals to decry the behaviour of the police without examining the causes.

A similar situation has arisen in France. The French have always been slightly schizoid about their police. A good example of that was the way the shopkeepers of the Latin Quarter in Paris early in 1971 complained to the minister of the interior that the vanloads of riot police on view around the Sorbonne were scaring away the tourists. The police obligingly agreed to adopt a lower profile. Partly as a result, there was a night of rioting and looting of shops along the Boulevard St-Michel early in June. The shopkeepers and café-proprietors of the area deluged the minister of the interior with complaints that they were not getting enough protection, while the right-wing press complained about 'the weakness of the authorities and the absence of the state'. The immediate consequence of that night of violence was the sacking of a senior policeman, Commissioner Degrange, for not getting his men to the scene of the rioting quickly enough, and for failing to inform the Prefect of what was going on.

The sacking of Degrange was only one of a series of controversies that exposed the French police to much unpleasant publicity and plunged them into the thick of the local political debate. The most notorious incident was the *affaire Jaubert*, which took place at the end of May 1971. Jaubert was a radical academic and part-time journalist who had left the French Communist Party in 1965.

According to his own version of the facts, he was an innocent bystander at a demonstration in the Place Clichy in Montmartre when he saw an injured man being picked up by a police rescue squad. For reasons that he failed to explain, he offered to go with the wounded man to the hospital. He claimed that the six policemen inside the van assaulted him without cause, and that he was later beaten and kicked in the gutter before finally being taken to hospital three-quarters of an hour after leaving Montmartre. It was for the court to decide whether or not Jaubert was telling the truth. He was indicted by the public prosecutor for 'rebellion and violence to officers of the law'. In the private view of senior police officers, Jaubert was an *agent provocateur* and had asked to enter the van in order to start a fight that would stir up publicity. Whatever the truth of the matter, Jaubert got his publicity: all the major French newspapers, from *Le Figaro* to *l'Humanité*, criticised the police for this apparent assault on a journalist. The uproar added to the growing feeling in the ranks of the French police that they had been subjected to a campaign of harassment and intimidation.

Like their American counterparts, the French police are conscious that they are badly-paid and that their social status and their public image have been tarnished over the past few years. Like the American police, they believe that they have been subjected to a campaign of defamation. The image of the French police that has been presented in recent films and books in France is certainly a dismal one. But, predictably, the most violent attacks have come from the extreme left. *Rouge*, the organ of the Trotskyist *Ligue Communiste*, printed a remarkably vicious 'definition' of the French policeman early in 1971: 'The difference between a common murderer and a policeman is well known—it is simply that the cop has a licence.' This kind of thing is just another case of the rhetoric of vilification. It is an incitement to police brutality.

Both the French and the American police are more brutal than their British counterparts—partly because they are operating in much more violent societies and have been exposed to the kind of personal and political vendettas that are without parallel in the United Kingdom. French gendarmes complain of how their children are ostracised by their classmates at the instigation of 'radical

teachers'; after sixteen policemen had been murdered in America in
1970, the head of the Fraternal Order of Police, John J. Harrington,
complained that policemen were being treated like 'fish in a barrel'.
Under these circumstances, it is not enough to blame the police
for brutality. What has to be thought about is the possibility of
ensuring greater professionalism by granting higher salaries as in-
ducements to college graduates and providing special centres for
adult education. As the Skolnik Report concluded, the goal must be
to make policing a profession. In an age of civil violence, the goal is
crucially important, since defence against urban terrorism, and the
image of authority, largely depend on the police. The army is brought
in only as a last resort in democratic societies: when the police have
been overstretched, or when they have overreacted.

At an international level, urban guerrilla activities have challenged
the traditional concept that governments have a monopoly of
'legitimate international violence' and may affect the strategic
balance in indirect ways. Although most of the contemporary urban
guerrilla groups share a theory of global revolution, there has not
been much evidence of the interchange of cadres and resources or the
involvement of outside powers. The North Koreans (sometimes
acting in collusion with the Russians, as in Mexico), the Cubans and
the Palestinian commandos have all provided training for urban
guerrilla groups—most of them from Latin America.

There have been reports that the IRA has supported the Basque
guerrilla movement, the Euzkadi Ta Azkatasuna ('Freedom for the
Basque Homeland') that was involved in bank-robberies, bombings
and a diplomatic kidnapping after 1967. Within Latin America, the
Tupamaros have emerged as the patrons of less successful terrorist
organisations. It is easy to cross over from Brazil through the
jungles of the north, and to slip across the River Plate from Buenos
Aires. Some of the Brazilian political prisoners who were freed in
return for the life of the kidnapped Swiss ambassador in 1971 had
received military training in Uruguay; Argentine guerrillas have
been found using weapons captured from the Uruguayan armed
forces; and the Tupamaros have been publicly thanked for their
help by the Bolivian guerrillas. But these exchanges are really only a
drop in the bucket. The urban guerrillas are largely self-reliant as

far as weapons and supplies are concerned, and the most important form of exchange is probably the borrowing of ideas.

The most spectacular example of that is of course the wildfire spread of diplomatic kidnapping as a technique for extorting political concessions since the Brazilian government agreed to release fifteen prisoners in return for the American ambassador in 1969. The Brazilians consistently gave in to political kidnappers. The result was runaway inflation in the price of diplomatic hostages: it cost the Brazilian régime 15 prisoners to free an American ambassador, but 40 for a West German ambassador and 70 for a Swiss ambassador— a rather steep price rise however sentimental one feels about Switzerland, and a sign that for kidnappers, as for other people, the appetite grows with the eating.

Other régimes experimented with a tougher line. This resulted in a series of casualties when kidnappers refused to allow their bluff to be called, although the Argentine government managed to outstare the terrorists who abducted the Paraguayan consul early in 1970. Others were less fortunate. A West German ambassador, Count von Spreti, was murdered in Guatemala in 1970, and the Israeli consul-general in Istanbul was killed by members of the Turkish People's Liberation Army as the police closed in on their hiding-place in May 1971. A provisional count showed that by this stage, a diplomatic hostage had been killed on four of the nine occasions when a government followed a policy of no concessions. When governments agreed to compromise, the hostage was released on all eleven occasions.

That is one reason why some people argue that there are occasions when governments must bow to kidnappers' demands. For humanitarian reasons alone, it is impossible to dictate a general rule. But there are two arguments commonly used to justify a policy of concessions that are worth analysing. The first is that kidnapping is sometimes the weapon of those opposed to dictatorial and oppressive régimes. It was expressed with some fervour by a British ambassador's wife who wrote anonymously to *The Spectator* in the following terms: 'Where does my and the world's compassion lie if we are ever accredited to a country where justice is a caricature twisted to serve the lust of the ruling power?'

But of course political kidnapping is not peculiar to police-states. If that were the case, it would be one of the daily hazards of life in Russia or South Africa, but not in Canada or Uruguay. And it is important to remember that when guerrillas make diplomats their targets, they are not merely attacking their own governments, but the legal code and the framework of diplomacy on which formal relations between sovereign states depend. The argument that men have the right to rebel when confronted with an intolerable social and political situation cannot be used to sanction an assault on the accepted framework for international relations.

Secondly, the argument is sometimes heard that some governments are so bumbling and ineffectual that they are patently unable to guarantee the security of diplomats and consequently must be prepared to pay the price when an envoy is captured. This argument certainly seems to fit Uruguay, where Mr Geoffrey Jackson, the British ambassador captured in January 1971, was held by the Tupamaros for eight months before his release in September. The problem is that no government is really in a position to guarantee the safety of every member of the local diplomatic corps. When the terrorist net is used to haul in such skinny fish as honorary consuls (as in Argentina in May 1971), it would be overtaxing the resources of most police forces to provide protection for everyone.

The kidnapping of diplomats can happen anywhere. That is why it is necessary to think about whether it is possible to take international precautions against an international crime. The attempts that have been made to limit the hijacking of aircraft by formal agreements in the wake of a series of hijackings by the Palestinian *fedayeen* have not met with much success. A draft treaty (the Hague convention) embodying the principle that hijackers must either be prosecuted in the country they land in or extradited to the country of origin for prosecution was opened for signature under the sponsorship of Russia and the United States. It seemed unlikely that any of the countries that normally provide sanctuary for hijackers (notably Cuba, Algeria and some Arab states) would sign.

The immediate effect of the convention would therefore be to limit the use of hijacking as a means of escape by political dissidents in the Soviet bloc who found sanctuary in western Europe in the early 1960s. It is even harder to see how a formal treaty could be used to limit diplomatic kidnappings—or even how governments would be able to agree to the blanket principle that one cannot bargain with kidnappers. A further problem is that any convention that provides for the extradition of those who commit international crimes for political ends might be viewed as a limitation on the traditional right of political asylum.

Urban terrorism creates other problems for international relations. So long as the 'central strategic balance' between the Nato forces and those of the Warsaw pact remains intact, there are likely to be fewer conventional wars but a wider incidence of low-level violence. Although there have not been many signs so far of outside involvement in urban guerrilla situations, the incitement of civil violence is an obvious means of weakening an enemy or achieving a limited political goal. Under different circumstances, for example, a sponsored urban terrorist campaign (nominally in favour of integration with East Germany or the Chinese mainland) might be used in the attempt to alter the political status of West Berlin or Hong Kong. In a broader sense, it is clear that rising civil violence inside one of the major powers helps to change the strategic balance in the world in general. The trouble in Northern Ireland, for example, drove Britain to transfer troops stationed on the Rhine for limited terms of duty in Belfast and Londonderry. Dissent in America has already imposed constraints on foreign policy; a full-scale minority revolt would cripple the nation's capacity for military intervention in other countries.

From the situations that have been studied in this book, it would seem that the urban guerrilla is often in the position of the sorcerer's apprentice. He unleashes a political force that he is usually unable to control. With the lone exception of Uruguay, none of the contemporary urban guerrilla groups stand any real chance of seizing power. On the other hand, many of them have succeeded in transforming the climate of opinion in their countries in a way that favours those who believe in violent and extreme solutions. For this reason, it could be said that the urban guerrilla is dangerous less for what he does than for what he inspires: the breakdown of the moral consensus in a society, the hardening of the political battle-lines, and a right-wing response that sometimes hits back too hard and too eratically. It is these more diffuse political repercussions that must be controlled and understood. The war of the urban guerrilla is likely to develop into one of the most prevalent forms of political violence in the decade of the 1970s, and it may spread to many western cities that were formerly considered immune to the contagion.

Notes

Notes

Introduction

1 See Robert Williams, 'The Potential of a Minority Revolution', Parts 1 and 2, *The Crusader* (Havana) June 1964 and August 1965.

2 See Peter Paret and John W. Shy, *Guerrillas in the 1960s* (New York 1962) pp 11–15 and Carl von Clausewitz, *On War* trans. O. M. Matthijs Jolles (Washington 1950) Book VI, ch 26.

3 Régis Debray, *Revolution in the Revolution?* (Penguin edition 1968) p 67.

4 Carlos Marighella, 'On Principles and Strategic Questions', reprinted in *Les Temps Modernes*, November 1969. See also *Minimanual of the Urban Guerrilla*, printed as Appendix to Robert Moss, *Urban Guerrilla Warfare* (Adelphi Papers No 79, International Institute for Strategic Studies, London 1971).

1 The City and Revolution

1 Herbert Marcuse, 'Liberation from the Affluent Society' in David Cooper (ed), *The Dialectics of Liberation* (Penguin edition 1968) p 176.

2 See Daniel Singer, *Prelude to Revolution: France in May 1968* (London 1970).

3 Cohn-Bendit argues for mass 'spontaneity'. 'The setting up of any party,' he argues, 'inevitably reduces freedom of the people to agree with the party. In other words, democracy is not suborned by bad leadership but by the existence of leadership . . . We are convinced that the revolutionary cannot and must not be a leader . . . What we need is not an organization with a capital O, but a host of insurrectional cells, be they ideological groups, study groups—we can even use street gangs.' *Obsolete Communism: The Left-Wing Alternative* trans. A. Pomerans (Penguin edition 1969) pp 250–1; 256.

4 See Arrigo Levi, *Pci, la lunga marcia verso il potere* (Etas Kompass 1971).

5 See Lucio Magri, 'Italian Communism Today' in *New Left Review* March–April 1971, p 49.

6 See C. S. Sulzberger in *The New York Times* 21 July 1971.

7 See Herman Kahn, *The Emerging Japanese Superstate* (London 1971)

8 See Bernard Béraud, *La gauche révolutionnaire au Japon* (Paris 1970) pp 131–37.

9 Ronald Segal, *The Struggle Against History* (London 1971) p 15.

10 See *The Economist* 17 April 1971.

11 See Samuel P. Huntington, *Political Order in Changing Societies* (New Haven 1968) pp 53–6 and Ted Robert Gurr, *Why Men Rebel* (Princeton University Press 1970).

12 See James P. Comer, 'The Dynamics of Black and White Violence' in *Violence in America: Historical and Comparative Perspectives*. Report to the National Commission on the Causes and Prevention of Violence (New York 1969) pp 444–63 for a stimulating discussion of the origin and motivation of rioters.

13 The Kerner Commission claimed that between 10 and 20 per cent of the 'potential population' took part in the ghetto riots. See Robert M. Fogelson and Robert B. Hill, 'Who Riots? A Study of Participation in the 1967 Riots' in *Supplemental Studies for the National Advisory Commission on Civil Disorders* (Washington 1968) pp 221–48.

14 See James Hundley, Jr., 'The Dynamics of Recent Ghetto Riots' in Richard A. Chikota and Michael C. Moran (eds) *Riot in the Cities* (Fairleigh Dickinson University Press 1970) pp 137–50.

15 See James C. Davies, 'The J-Curve of Rising and Declining Satisfactions' in *Violence in America*, op. cit., pp 690–729.

16 Brian Crozier, *The Rebel* (London 1960) p 9.

17 See *O Jornal do Brasil* and *O Globo* (Rio de Janeiro) for 12 January 1971.

18 For a lively discussion of the position of Latin American students, see Alistair Hennessy, 'University Students in National Politics' in Claudio Véliz (ed) *The Politics of Conformity in Latin America* (London 1967) pp 119–57.

19 Frantz Fanon, *The Wretched of the Earth* trans. C. Farrington (Penguin edition 1970) p 74.

20 John Gerassi (ed) *Towards Revolution* (London 1971) Vol 2, pp 465–6.

21 Andrew C. Janos, 'Authority and Violence: The Political Framework of Internal War' in Harry Eckstein (ed) *Internal War* (Free Press of Glencoe 1964) p 132.

22 *Time*, 27 April 1970.

2 Terrorism as a Political Tool

1 Tom Hayden, *Rebellion and Repression* (New York and Cleveland 1969) p 14.

2 Saint-Just, *Oeuvres choisies* (Paris 1968) p 327.

3 See Stephen T. Hosmer, *Viet Cong Repression and its Implications for the Future* (RAND Corporation, Lexington, Mass. 1970) pp 63–111 and Douglas Pike, *The Viet-Cong Strategy of Terror* (Saigon 1970).

4 *Violence in America* op. cit., pp 813–14.

5 See Gustavus Myers, *History of Bigotry in the United States* (New York 1943) and *Assassination and Political Violence* Report to the National Commission on the Causes and Prevention of Violence pp 212–19.

6 See Edward Hyams, *Killing No Murder: A Study of Assassination as a Political Means* (London 1970) pp 171–97. On the contrast between Zionist terrorism and the contemporary Palestinian commandos, operating from an outside base with insignificant support inside Israel, see Jon Kimche, 'Israel and the Palestinians' in *The Arab-Israeli Dispute* (Institute for the Study of Conflict Special Report, London 1971).

7 See *The Economist* 5 June 1971.

8 On the VOP, see *Que Pasa?* (Santiago) 17 June 1971.

9 See 'La VOP: Terrorismo sin brujala' in *Punto Final* 22 June 1971; and 'El trafico del terror' in *Ercilla* (Santiago) 23 June 1971.

10 Stepniak, *Underground Russia* (New York 1892) pp 32–257.

11 E. H. Carr, *Michael Bakunin* (New York 1961) pp 115–16. See also George Woodcock, *Anarchism* (Penguin edition 1962) pp 134–70.

12 Carr, ibid, p 395.

13 Peter Kropotkin, *Memoirs of a Revolutionist* ed. J. A. Rogers (New York 1962) p 201.

14 Vera Figner, *Mémoires d'une Révolutionnaire* (Paris 1930) p 102.

15 For an interesting sociological description of the leadership of the Narodnaya Volya, see Roland Gaucher, *Les terroristes* (Paris 1965) pp 25–30.

16 See Feliks Gross, *The Seizure of Political Power* (New York 1957) pp 109–10.

17 Thomas Masaryk, *The Spirit of Russia* (London 1915) vol 2, p 545.

18 See Victor Serge, *Les coulisses d'une sûreté générale* (Paris 1925) p 21.

19 A gripping recent account that assigns primary importance to the German factor is George Katkov, *Russia 1917: The February Revolution* (London 1967).

20 Lenin, 'Letter to Franz Koritschoner' (October 1916) reprinted in *International* (London) January/February 1971.

21 Printed as Appendix A to *The Memoirs of General Grivas* ed. Charles Foley (London 1964).
22 ibid.
23 *Memoirs* p 28.
24 ibid, p 46.
25 See Brian Crozier, *The Rebels* (London 1960) p 112.
26 Cited in *Memoirs of General Grivas*, op. cit., p 38.
27 On Harding's innovations, see Gregory Blaxland, *The Regiments Depart: A History of the British Army, 1945-1970* (London 1971) pp 297-9.
28 *Memoirs of General Grivas* p 105.
29 ibid, pp 173-4.
30 Alex Nicol, *La bataille de l'O.A.S.* (Paris 1963) p 12.
31 For the early history of the FLN and their campaign in France, see Jacques Duchemin, *Histoire du F.L.N.* (Paris 1962) and Serge Bromberger, *Les rebelles algériens* (Paris 1958).
32 Duchemin, op. cit., p 263.
33 See Yacef Saadi, *Souvenirs sur la bataille d'Alger* (Paris 1962) pp 19-21.
34 For a brilliantly written and very detailed history of the OAS, see Paul Henissart, *Wolves in the City* (London 1971).
35 See Raymond Aron, *L'Algérie et la république* (Paris 1958).
36 This is also the argument of Dorothy Pickles in *Algeria and France: From Colonialism to Cooperation* (London 1967) pp 105-6.
37 Peter Paret, *French Revolutionary Warfare from Indochina to Algeria* (London 1964) p 120.
38 *Minimanual of the Urban Guerrilla*, op. cit.
39 Lenin, 'The Collapse of the Second International' (1915) in *Collected Works* (Moscow 1967) vol 21, p 213.
40 'A. Neuberg', *Armed Insurrection* trans. Q. Hoare (London 1970) p 213. First published in German in 1928, this was the classic treatise of the Comintern on insurrectionary theory, and contains sections by Togliatti and Marshal Tukhachevsky. An Italian contribution along the same lines appeared on the eve of the Spanish civil war in 1936. See Emilio Lussu, *Théorie de l'insurrection* trans. A. Theron (Paris 1971).

3 Under Western Eyes

1 Eldridge Cleaver, *Soul on Ice* (London 1969) p 114.
2 *To Establish Justice, To Insure Domestic Tranquility* Final Report to

the National Commission on the Causes and Prevention of Violence.
(New York 1970) p 146.

3 ibid, p 51.

4 *International Herald Tribune* 18 August 1971.

5 Bobby Seale, *Seize the Time* (London 1970) p 405.

6 Col Robert T. Rigg, 'A Military Appraisal of the Threat to U.S.
Cities', *Army*, January 1968. For an even more alarmist view written
from the far left, see Robert Lawrence, *Guerrilla Warfare in the United
States* (Canoga Park, California 1970).

7 Max Stanford, 'Black Guerrilla Warfare: Strategy and Tactics' in
The Black Scholar (San Francisco) November 1970, p 37.

8 'Stormy Weather', *San Francisco Good Times* 8 January 1970.

9 David Horowitz, 'Revolutionary Karma vs Revolutionary Politics',
Ramparts March 1971, p 29.

10 *I. F. Stone's Bi-Weekly* 23 March 1970.

11 See J. Kirk Sale, 'Ted Gold: Education for Violence' in *The Nation*
23 April 1970 and *Time* 30 March 1970.

12 Richard E. Peterson, *The Scope of Organized Student Protest in
1967–68* (Princeton, Education Testing Service, 1968).

13 *New Left Notes* 18 June 1969. Reprinted in Harold Jacobs (ed)
Weatherman (New York 1970) p 53.

14 Jacobs, op. cit., p 219.

15 ibid., p 219.

16 *New Left Notes* 23 August 1969.

17 'Everyone Talks about the Weather' in Jacobs, op. cit., pp 440–7.

18 'Communiqué No 1 from the Weatherman Underground', *The
Berkeley Tribe* 31 July 1970.

19 Jacobs, op. cit., p 355.

20 *San Francisco Good Times* 18 September 1970.

21 *RAT* October 1970.

22 'New Morning—Changing Weather' 10 December 1970 (Liberation
News Service).

23 Horowitz, op. cit.

24 *The Economist* 1 August 1970.

25 *Law and Order Reconsidered*: Report of the Task Force on Law and
Law Enforcement (Washington 1969) p 335.

26 *To Establish Justice*, op. cit., p 60.

27 Philip E. Ennis, *Criminal Victimization in the United States: Report
of a National Survey* (Washington 1967) p 54.

28 Philip S. Foner (ed) *The Black Panthers Speak* (New York 1970).

29 See 'The Robert F. Williams Case' in *Crisis* vol 66 (June–September 1959), pp 352–9; 409–10 and August Meier and Elliott Rudwick, 'Black Violence in the 20th Century: A Study in Rhetoric and Retaliation' in *Violence in America* op. cit., pp 399–400.

30 Williams spent a total of seven years in China, Cuba and Africa.

31 See *The Politics of Protest* Task Force Report Submitted to the National Commission on the Causes and Prevention of Violence (Skolnik Report) (New York 1969) p 152.

32 *An Introduction to the Black Panther Party* (The Radical Education Project, Ann Arbor, Michigan, May 1969) pp 2–3.

33 Foner, op. cit., pp. xviii–xix.

34 *People's World* (San Francisco) 10 February 1968.

35 See Gene Marine, *The Black Panthers* (New York 1969) pp 39–40.

36 *The Black Panther* 18 May 1968.

37 *The Black Panther* 4 May 1968.

38 *The Black Panther* 10 January 1970.

39 *Washington Post* 25 August 1971

40 *Le Monde* 20 April 1971.

41 *New York Times* 26 August 1971.

42 For the Panthers' own allegations, see 'Police Harassment of the Black Panther Party: A Sample of Incidents' in *An Introduction*, op. cit.

43 For a general survey, see *Time* 23 August 1971.

44 See *The Times* (London) 25 May 1971 and *The Guardian* (London) 26 May 1971.

45 *Report of the National Advisory Commission on Civil Disorders* (Kerner Report) (Washington 1968).

46 See the *Report of the National Advisory Commission on Rural Poverty* (Washington 1967). The Rural Poverty Commission observed that 'whites outnumber nonwhites among the rural poor by a wide margin', that most of the rural South had become 'one vast poverty area' and that a common source of complaint among poor whites was the idea that city-dwellers had benefited from the anti-poverty programmes at their expense.

47 See Walter Williams, 'Cleveland's Crisis Ghetto' in Peter H. Rossi (ed) *Ghetto Revolts* (New York 1970) pp 13–30.

48 Grove Press, New York 1970.

49 Wallace Terry 11, 'Bringing the War Home' in *The Black Scholar* November 1970, Table 3.

4 Ulster: The Guns Speak

1 This is broadly the attitude adopted, amongst others, by Russell Stetler in 'Northern Ireland—From Civil Rights to Armed Struggle' *Monthly Review* November 1970 and (in a much more intelligent and sophisticated way) by Liam de Paor, *Divided Ulster* (Penguin edition 1970).

2 Quoted in Tim Pat Coogan, *The IRA* (London 1970) p 295.

3 For general historical background, see J. B. Bell, *The Secret Army: A History of the IRA 1916–1970* (London 1970) and Iain Hamilton, *The Irish Tangle* (Conflict Studies No 6, London 1970) as well as Coogan and de Paor.

4 A survey by Building Design Partnership carried out in 1967 showed that conditions in the Protestant and Catholic slums of Belfast are very similar—with the significant difference that the enemployment rate for Catholics in the Cromac district was twice as high as that for the Protestants of Sandy Row. In more than 90 per cent of the houses in both areas, residents lacked a bath, a hand basin, an indoor WC, and a hot water supply.

5 See the survey of Ulster in *The Economist* 29 May 1971.

6 *The Guardian* 21 August 1971.

7 Quoted in Coogan, op. cit., pp 272–3.

8 *Irish Times* 6 July 1971.

5 Quebec: The Fireworks of Hate

1 For useful general accounts of the FLQ campaigns, see James Stewart and the *Montreal Star*, *The FLQ : Seven Years of Terrorism* (Richmond Hill 1970), Ronald Lebel, 'The Fixed Terror of Quebec', *The Globe Magazine* 19 September 1970.

2 *Le Monde* 20 October 1970.

3 'M. René Levesque: pas de romantisme', *L'Express* 26 October 1970.

4 See P-E Trudeau, 'Separatist counter-revolutionaries' in *Federalism and the French Canadians* (Toronto 1968) p 211; and 'Le nouvel trahison des clercs' in *Cité libre*, April 1962.

5 P-E Trudeau, 'Some Obstacles to Democracy in Quebec', *Canadian Journal of Economics and Political Science* Vol 24, No 3, August 1968.

6 Prières du matin: Elevations matutinales. 20 June 1956. Quoted in Trudeau, supra.

7 Stewart, op. cit.
8 See Dr Gustave Morf, *Le terrorisme québeçois* (Editions de l'Homme, Montreal 1970).
9 Pierre Vallières, *Nègres blancs d'Amérique* (Editions Parti Pris, Montreal 1969) p 118.
10 ibid, pp 24; 232.
11 ibid, p 255.
12 ibid, p 67.
13 Stewart, op. cit.
14 'The FLQ's First Manifesto' in *Canadian Dimension* Vol 7, No 5, December 1970 pp 31–2.
15 See Jean-Claude Leclerc, 'FRAP: Awakening the Powerless' in *Canadian Dimension* Vol 7, No 5 and Victor Rabinovitch, 'Contemporary Narrative: The Class Struggle 1968–1970' in *The Struggle for Quebec* (Spokesman Pamphlet No 13, London 1970) for interpretations from the extreme left.
16 Reprinted in Stewart, op. cit.
17 See Clyde Sanger in *The Guardian* 24 November 1970 and *The Times* 17 November 1970.
18 *Le Journal de Montréal* 16 November 1970.
19 *Le Monde* 22 October 1970.
20 *Le Monde* 20 October 1970.

6 The City and the Countryside

1 Carolina Maria de Jésus, *Beyond All Pity* trans. D. St Clair (London 1970) p 36.
2 See David J. Fox, 'Urbanisation and Economic Development in Mexico' in Fox and D. J. Robinson, *Cities in a Changing Latin America* (London 1969).
3 See D. J. Dwyer, 'Urbanization as a Factor in the Political Development of South-East Asia' (Discussion paper at Pacific Conference, Vina del Mar, Chile, 27 September–3 October 1970) p 6 and T. G. McGee, *The Urbanization Process in the Third World* (London 1971) p 14.
4 See Raúl Prebisch, *Transformación y desarrollo: la gran tarea de la América Latina* (Mexico City 1970) pp 32–3.
5 See Bryan Roberts, 'Migration and Population Growth in Guatemala City' in Roberts and Stella Lowder, *Urban Population Growth and Migration in Latin America* (Liverpool 1970).

6 On urban growth in Vietnam, see Samuel P. Huntington, 'The Bases of Accommodation' in *Foreign Affairs* vol 46, 1968, p 648.

7 See Simon Kuznets, 'Industrial Distribution of National Product and Labour Force'. *Supplement* to Vol 5, No 4, of *Economic Development and Cultural Change* (Chicago, July 1957).

8 Charles Tilly, 'Collective Violence in European Perspective' in *Violence in America*, op. cit., p 33.

9 Marx and Engels, *Selected Works* (Moscow 1950) Vol I, p 584.

10 Frantz Fanon, *The Wretched of the Earth*, op. cit., p 103.

11 See Oscar Lewis, *La Vida: A Puerto Rican Family in the Culture of Poverty* (London 1967) and *The Children of Sánchez* (New York 1961).

12 See Bryan Roberts, 'The Social Organisation of Low-Income Urban Families' in Richard N. Adams, *Crucifixion by Power: Essays on Guatemalan National Social Structure, 1944–1966* (Austin, Texas 1970) pp 479–516.

13 In Calcutta, rural migrants were tangibly worse off than in the villages they came from before the problem was aggravated by the flight of refugees from East Pakistan in 1971. Nonetheless, they tended to support the ruling Congress Party in the state elections of 1952, 1957 and 1962. One observer commented that 'To be discontented with the city, one often has to be integrated into it.' See Myron Weiner, 'Urbanization and Political Protest' in *Civilisations* Vol 17, 1967, pp 44–9.

14 See Mario Menendez Rodriguez, 'Venezuela: Douglas Bravo' in *Sucesos* (Mexico City) 24 December 1966.

15 Eric R. Wolf, 'On Peasant Rebellions' in *International Social Science Journal* Vol 21, 1969, p 286.

16 Average incomes in Caracas, for example, are nearly ten times as high as in the rural areas of Venezuela. See U. N. Economic Commission for Latin America, *The Economic Development of Latin America in the Post-War Period* (New York 1964) p 55.

17 Dwyer, op. cit. See also Dwyer, 'The City in the Developing World and the Example of South-East Asia', *Supplement to the Gazette*, University of Hong Kong, Vol 15, No 6, 20 August 1968.

18 Martin Oppenheimer, *Urban Guerrilla* (Penguin edition 1970) p 42.

19 On the 'swamping' effect, see E. J. Hobsbawm, 'Peasants and Rural Migrants in Politics' in Veliz (ed) *The Politics of Conformity*, op. cit.

20 See John Slimming, *Malaysia: Death of a Democracy* (London 1969) pp 25–60; and Robert Moss, 'The Inseparable Divorcees: A Survey of Malaysia and Singapore' in *The Economist* 30 January 1971.

21 *People's Daily* (Peking) 18 January 1970.
22 *Forum* (Dacca) 7 November 1970.
23 *Times of India* 19 May 1970.
24 *Liberation* February 1970.
25 *Times of India* 19 May 1970.

7 Che Guevara and his Heirs

1 K. S. Karol, *Guerrillas in Power* (London 1971) reassesses the relative importance of the rural and urban wings of the rebel movement in Cuba.
2 Hugh Thomas, 'Middle-Class Politics and the Cuban Revolution' in Veliz (ed) *The Politics of Conformity*, op. cit.
3 Che Guevara, *Reminiscences of the Cuban Revolutionary War* trans. V. Ortiz (London 1968) p 202.
4 See Eric R. Wolf, *Peasant Wars of the Twentieth Century* (London 1971) pp 269–72; Dudley Seers (ed) *Cuba: The Economic and Social Revolution* (Chapel Hill, North Carolina 1964) pp 79–80.
5 Guevara, *Reminiscences*, p 29.
6 Hector Béjar, *Peru 1965: Notes on a Guerrilla Experience*, trans. W. Rose (New York 1970) pp 107–8.
7 Che Guevara, *Guerrilla Warfare* (Penguin edition 1969) p 13.
8 ibid, p 16.
9 ibid, p 45.
10 ibid, p 41.
11 Rodney Arismendi, 'Some Aspects of the Revolutionary Process in Latin America' in *World Marxist Review*, October 1964, pp 15–16.
12 See Boris Goldenberg, 'The Rise and Fall of a Party: The Cuban CP (1925–59)' in *Problems of Communism*, July–August 1970, pp 61–80.
13 *Revolution in the Revolution?* trans. B. Ortiz (Penguin edition 1968) p 75.
14 ibid, p 56.
15 For serviceable general surveys of the rural-based guerrilla movements in Latin America, see V. Bambirra et al., *Diez Años de Insurrección en América Latina* (Santiago 1971) 2 vols; Richard Gott, *Guerrilla Movements in Latin America* (London 1970); and Jean Larteguy, *Les Guérilleros* (Paris 1967).
16 Havana Radio, 13 March 1967.
17 On the OLAS conference, see John Gerassi, 'Havana: A New International is Born' in *Monthly Review*, October 1967. In his speech

Notes

on the closing day, Castro declared that in the long term, armed struggle was the only path for Latin America, criticised the Moscow-line communists implicitly as 'super-theorisers', and also attacked 'the absurd concept that the guerrilla movement could be directed from the cities'. (Reported by Havana Radio, 11 August 1967).

18 See Robert Moss, *Urban Guerrillas in Latin America* (Conflict Studies No 8, London, 1970).

19 *El Siglo* (Santiago) 26 February 1971.

20 For a general guide to shifting communist tactics, see Stephen Clissold (ed) *Soviet Relations with Latin America 1918–68: A Documentary Survey* (London 1970); A. Daniel Faleroni, 'Soviet Strategy in Latin America' in J. Gregory Oswald and Anthony J. Strover (eds) *The Soviet Union and Latin America* (London 1970); and Luis Aguilar, 'Fragmentation of the Marxist Left' in *Problems of Communism* July–August 1970.

21 Monje Molina, 'Las divergencias del P. C. Boliviano con Ché Guevara' in *Punto Final* (Santiago) February 1968.

22 See Rodolfo Ghioldi, *No puede haber una revolución en la revolución* (Buenos Aires 1967).

23 The radical movement in the church is one of the most important phenomena in Latin America today. The 'third world' movement in the church draws its inspiration from the statement issued by a group of bishops who attended the Roman synod in October–November 1967. This reads in part: 'History reveals that some revolutions are necessary and have liberated the world from a state of passing irreligion ... The church is in no way the protector of the big estates ... The rich are like this: they declare themselves the rightful owners of what belongs to all because they were the first to get hold of it.' (Reprinted in *El Siglo*, Santiago, 21 March 1971). Some priests have actually joined the guerrillas. The most famous example was Camilo Torres, who died in battle in Colombia. Catholic conservatives in Brazil have accused the local Dominicans of providing asylum for the guerrillas in their monasteries. Priests have collaborated with the Tupamaros in Uruguay and the 'revolutionary Peronists' in Argentina. For pioneering attempts to analyse the roots of clerical radicalism, see B. Castro Villagrana et. al., *La Iglesia, el Subdesarrollo y la Revolución* (Mexico City 1968); and Alain Gheerbrant, *L'Eglise rebelle d'Amérique latine* (Paris 1969).

24 See René Zavaleta Mercado, 'Bolivia y América Latina' in *Marcha* (Montevideo) 30 May 1969.

262 *Notes*

25 Che Guevara, *Bolivian Diary* trans. Carlos P. Hansen and A. Sinclair
(London 1968) p 136.
26 Béjar, op. cit., p 110.
27 Wolf, *Peasant Wars*, op. cit., p 292.
28 *Military Assistance and Foreign Military Sales Facts* (Office of the
Assistant Secretary of Defence, Washington, March 1970).

8 The Shift to the Cities

1 A series of interviews with Argentine guerrilla spokesmen by the
Cuban journalist Hector Victor Suarez were published at the end of
1970. See *Granma* (Spanish edition) 5 December 10 December
11 December and 14 December 1970.
2 See Prebisch, *Transformación y desarrollo*, op. cit.
3 On the prospects for Peru, see Norman Gall, 'The Master is Dead'
in *Dissent* (New York) June 1971 and Marcel Niedergang, 'Peru 70:
La Puerta Estrecha' in *Comercio Exterior* (Mexico City); on Chile,
see 'The New Machiavelli' in *The Economist* 10 April 1971.
4 'Pre-election climate in Venezuela: an interview with Comrade
Teodoro Petkoff' in *World Marxist Review* April 1968.
5 See Moises Moleiro, *El MIR de Venezuela* (Havana 1967) pp 154-6.
6 Gott, *Guerrilla Movements*, op. cit., pp 120-4.
7 Moises Moleiro, 'Las Enseñanzas de la Guerra Revolucionaria en
Venezuela' in Bambirra et al, *Diez Años de Insurrección*, op. cit.,
p 173.
8 Petkoff, op. cit.
9 On the university, see *Granma* (English edition) 6 June 1971.
10 See Régis Debray, 'Latin America: the Long March' in *New Left
Review*, October–December 1965, pp 46-7.
11 See *Por Que?* (Mexico City) April 1968.
12 Bravo toned down his original criticisms in two interviews published
in *Le Monde* (17 July 1970) and *Marcha* (15 May 1970), but continued
to insist that Castro had declared 'a ceasefire, a truce, a retreat' in
the armed struggle by concentrating on Cuba's internal development.
13 Venezuelan guerrilla leaders have been ready to admit this. One of
Bravo's lieutenants, Francisco Prada, told the Chilean left-wing
magazine *Punto Final* that only some of Debray's ideas were relevant
to the armed struggle in Venezuela and that part of the rebel force
had to be based in Caracas since the main military targets were located
there. (*Punto Final*, 27 January 1969). There was a brief revival of

urban terrorism in Caracas—mainly robberies and bank-raids—after President Caldera assumed office in March 1969.

14 'Ladino' is a term applied to whites and *mestizos* who have adjusted to urban life and western customs as distinct from 'indios' still living the traditional life of the countryside. It denotes a cultural, as much as an ethnic, distinction.

15 See Richard N. Adams, *Crucifixion by Power*, op. cit., pp 247–8.

16 See Inter-American Agricultural Development Committee, *Land Tenure and Socio-Economic Development of the Agricultural Sector in Guatemala* (Washington 1965).

17 A great deal has been written about the coup and its aftermath. See in particular (on the left) G. Torriello, *La batalla de Guatemala* (Santiago 1955) and J. J. Arevalo, *Guatemala, la democracia y el imperio* (Montevideo 1954).

18 See Alvaro Lopez, 'La Crisis Politica y la Violencia en Guatemala' in *Diez Años de Insurrección*, op. cit., Vol 1, p 85.

19 On the putsch, see Adolfo Gilly, 'The Guerrilla Movement in Guatemala' in *Monthly Review* May 1965. The weakness of the conspirators lay in their idea that a purely military revolt could succeed. In the early years, the MR-13 guerrilla organisation continued to base its hopes on the possibility of winning over the armed forces. See Yon Sosa, 'Breves Apuntes historicos del M.R.13' in *Pensamiento Critico* (Havana) April 1968. See also Gott, op. cit., pp 36–8.

20 *World Marxist Review* October 1966.

21 Eduardo Galeano, *Guatemala: Occupied Country* trans. C. Belfrage (New York 1969) p 28.

22 'First Declaration of Sierra de las Minas', dated 12 December 1969. Original version in *Revolución Socialista*. Reprinted in Gerassi, *Towards Revolution*, op. cit., Vol 2.

23 Interview with Marcel Niedergang in *Le Monde* 6 February 1966.

24 *Turcios Lima* (biography and documents) (Havana 1970) p 141.

25 *Diario de Centro América* (Guatemala City) 13 March 1968.

26 *Prensa Libre* (Guatemala City) 6 March 1968.

27 *Turcios Lima*, op. cit., pp 93–4.

28 The army inoculation programme in the state of Izabal had already reached some 30,000 people by the end of 1964. The army also played a leading part in building public works, providing running water, and in a literacy campaign.

29 *Latin America* (London) 15 September 1967.

30 See Galeano, op. cit., pp 59–68.
31 Statement by Father Thomas Melville (suspended as a priest of the Maryknoll Order) in *The National Catholic Reporter*, 31 January 1968.
32 Quoted from typescript of a review-article that has since appeared in *The New York Review of Books*. I am indebted to Mr Gall for much of the information on right-wing terrorist groups in Guatemala.
33 See 'El Terror Institucionalizada en Guatemala' in the Venezuelan Jesuit magazine *SIC* (Caracas) February 1971. According to *SIC*, there is a division of labour in Guatemala between a 'directorate' composed of three cabinet ministers plus the president of congress, who preside over the counter-terror; their middle-men; and the 'knives of the king', often drawn from the ranks of policemen, ex-policemen, and private guards, who actually do the dirty work.
34 *Le Monde* 21 May 1970.

9 Brazil: Failure of a Strategy

1 The Brazilians did not take kindly to Hermán Kahn's forecast that they would find themselves at the end of the century in the ranks of the poorer and weaker countries. For an exuberant piece of local 'futurology', see Mario Henrique Simonsen, *Brasil 2001* (Rio de Janeiro 1969).
2 On the background to the coup, see Henry J. Steiner and David M. Trubeck, 'Brazil—All Power to the Generals' in *Foreign Affairs* April 1971 pp 464–79; Edward Lieuwen, *Generals versus Presidents* (London 1964) pp 69–85; and Luciano Martins, 'Aspectos politicos de la revolucion brasilena' in *Revista latinoamericana de sociología*, 1965.
3 On the recent growth of the Brazilian economy, see Economist Intelligence Unit, *Quarterly Economic Review* (Brazil) Nos 1–3, 1971; First National City Bank, *Brazil: An Economic Survey* (New York, March 1971; and J. C. Petersen, 'Brazil' in *Trade and Industry* (London) 30 December 1970, pp 573–6.
4 See *Metas e Bases para a Ação de Gôverno* (Presidencia da Republica, September 1970).
5 United Nations Economic Commission for Latin America, *Economic Survey of Latin America 1969* (New York 1970) p 126.
6 Ruy Mauro Marini, 'La Izquierda Revolucionaria Brasilena y las Nuevas Condiciones de la Lucha de Clases' in *Diez Años de Insurrección*, op. cit., p 149.

7 Marcio Moreira Alves, 'Brésil: Etat terroriste et guérilla urbaine,' in *Politique Aujord'hui* (Paris) July–August 1971, p 89.

8 *O Jornal do Brasil* quoted in *The Times* 26 March 1971.

9 Marcel Niedergang in *Le Monde* 7 February 1971.

10 op. cit., p 101.

11 Delfim Neto, the Finance Minister, has been quoted as saying that 'We are perfectly aware that the use of torture has a very bad effect on our efforts to foster economic growth and the rationalisation of finance and the monetary system . . . We deplore this upsurge in violence. But we believe that it is impossible to put Brazil on a sound economic footing without a firm régime.' *Le Monde* 24 May 1970.

12 Brazil has a system of one-year conscription and a defence budget of around $600 million. As well as the regular forces, there are paramilitary forces totalling about 120,000. See *The Military Balance 1970–1971* (Institute for Strategic Studies, London 1970) pp 74–5.

13 For Marighella's biography, see *Carlos Marighella* (biography and documents) (Havana 1970) and the introductory essay by Conrad Detrez in Carlos Marighella, *Pour la libération du Brésil* (Paris 1970).

14 Clissold (ed) *Soviet Relations with Latin America*, op. cit., p 152.

15 Paul E. Sigmund (ed) *Models of Political Change in Latin America* (New York 1970) pp 134–5.

16 'Letter of Resignation' in *Carlos Marighella*, op. cit., pp 41–2.

17 'Interview sur la guerre revolutionnaire' in Marighella, *Pour la liberation du Brésil* p 64.

18 'Questions d'organisation' (ALN text) in *Les Temps modernes* November 1969.

19 *Minimanual*, op. cit.

20 ibid.

21 'On Principles and Strategic Questions.' Reprinted in *Temps Modernes*, November 1969.

22 Josué de Castro, *Death in the Northeast* (New York 1969) p 21. See also Francisco Julião, *Que são as ligas camponesas?* (São Paulo 1962).

23 See Mauro Marini, op. cit., pp 139–40.

24 'Last interview with Joaquim Câmara Ferreira,' *Granma*, 8 November 1970.

25 ibid.

26 'Interview avec le capitaine Carlos Lamarca,' in Front brésilien d'information, *Bulletin* (Algiers) No 11, July 1970.

27 See *La Prensa* (Santiago) 29 December 1970.

28 *Carlos Marighella*, op. cit., p 14.

29 ibid, p 16.
30 See interview with Gabeira in 'Les rescapes brésiliens parlent,' *AfricAsia* 6 July 1970, pp 37–8.
31 For a fairly full account of VPR tactics, see João Quartim, 'La guérilla urbaine au Brésil' in *Les Temps Modernes*, November 1970.
32 *Le Monde* 13 June 1970.
33 *The Times* 16 June 1970.
34 *The Financial Times* (London) 11 December 1970.
35 *Le Monde* 11 December 1970.
36 *Le Monde* 27 December 1970. See also *O Globo* 23 July 1970, for similar remarks from two other ex-guerrillas, Marcos Vinicio Fernandez and Romulo Augustus Romero.
37 *Le Monde* 7 July 1970.
38 'Communiqué to the International Press' in Brazilian Information Front *Bulletin* (English edition) September 1970.
39 The number of victims of the 'death squads' has been variously estimated as between 800 and 2,000—mostly petty thieves. The squads date from 1958, when a group of policemen, encouraged by General Amaury Kruel—then the security chief in Rio—set out to avenge the murder of a celebrated policeman, Milton le Cocq. Kruel dissolved the group after a public outcry. But they were revived after 1964. See 'Cosa nostra al reves' (*Ercilla* 1 April 1970) and 'Las cuentas del escuadrón' (*Ercilla* 23 June 1971).

10   The Tupamaros: Masters of the Game

1 On the Batlle period, see Roque Faraone, *El Uruguay en que vivimos* (Montevideo 1969).
2 See the interview with Alejandro Otero in *Ya!* (Montevideo) 14 August 1970.
3 See Robert Moss, 'Urban Guerrillas in Uruguay' in *Problems of Communism*, September–October 1971.
4 See the interview in *Granma*, 8 October 1970.
5 For the economic background, see the Economist Intelligence Unit, *Quarterly Economic Reviews* (Uruguay) Nos 1–4, 1970 and 1–3, 1971; Bank of London and South America, *Review* (London) December 1970; and *Revolución y Cultura* (Havana) December 1970, No 21.
6 On the early history of the Tupamaros, see *Revolución y Cultura*, op. cit., and Alain Labrousse, *Les Tupamaros: guérilla urbaine en Uruguay* (Paris 1971).

7 Reprinted in *Revolución y Cultura*, op. cit.

8 See *Punto Final* 2 June 1968.

9 *Epoca* (Montevideo) 7 December 1967.

10 See Robert Taber, *The War of the Flea* (London 1969).

11 *Punto Final* 2 June 1968.

12 ibid.

13 ibid.

14 *Granma* 8 October 1970.

15 *Latin American Roundup* (Havana) 26 March 1971.

16 ibid.

17 *Granma* 8 October 1970. These ideas were expanded in a 150,000-word document made public by the guerrillas in July 1971. Most of it was reprinted in the left-wing daily, *Epoca*.

18 See Robert Moss, *Uruguay: Terrorism versus Democracy* (Conflict Studies No 14, London 1971).

19 For a detailed, if not wholly reliable, account of the Mailhos robbery, see Jean Stubbs, 'Uruguay: A Role for Urban Guerrillas' in the Trotskyite monthly *International* (London) January–February 1971.

20 *Revolution in the Revolution?* p 51.

21 Maria Esther Gilio, *La guerrilla tupamara* (Havana 1970) pp 167–9.

22 *Granma* 8 October 1970.

23 *Granma* 14 March 1971 and *Latin American Roundup* 8 March 1971.

24 *Granma* 21 March 1971 and *Latin America* 19 March 1971.

25 See Christopher Roper in *The Guardian* 8 May 1971 and *Latin American Roundup* 7 April 1971.

26 *Granma*, 18 April 1971.

27 The leaflet is reprinted in Labrousse, op. cit., pp 127–9. Garín signed himself 'A soldier who has joined the MLN.'

28 For a complete breakdown, see *Intercontinental Press* (New York) 1 March 1971.

29 For Seregni's own political attitudes (liberal-nationalist) see *Visión* (Mexico City) 8 May 1971.

30 See in particular the poll in the Uruguayan Communist Party paper *El Popular* (Montevideo) 24 June 1971.

31 See *Marcha* 8 January 1971.

32 *L'Unità* (Rome) 16 January 1971.

33 D. A. Kunaiev, 'Uruguay—So Near and Yet So Far' in *Prostor* (journal of the Kazakhstan Writers' Union) March 1971.

Select bibliography and index

Select bibliography

ADAMS, Richard N., *Crucifixion by Power: Essays on Guatemalan National Social Structure, 1944–1966* (Austin, Texas 1970).

AGUILAR, Luis, 'Fragmentation of the Marxist Left' in *Problems of Communism* July–August 1970.

An Introduction to the Black Panther Party (Radical Education Project, Ann Arbor, May 1969).

APTER, David E., and JOLL, James (eds) *Anarchism Today* (London 1971).

ARISMENDI, Rodney, 'Some Aspects of the Revolutionary Process in Latin America' in *World Marxist Review* October 1964.

ARON, Raymond, *L'Algérie et la République* (Paris 1958).

Assassination and Political Violence. Report to the National Commission on the Causes and Prevention of Violence. (New York 1970).

BAER, W., and KERSTENETZKY (eds) *Inflation and Growth in Latin America* (New Haven 1970).

BAIX, Aristóbulo, 'Uruguay: An Analysis of the Current Situation' in Bank of London and South America *Review* No 48, December 1970.

BAMBIRRA, V., et al., *Diez Años de Insurrección en América Latina* 2 vols (Santiago 1971).

BÉJAR, Hector, *Peru 1965: Notes on a Guerrilla Experience* trans. W. Rose (New York 1970).

BERAUD, Bernard, *La gauche révolutionnaire au Japon* (Paris 1970).

BELL, J. B., *The Secret Army: A History of the IRA 1916–1970* (London 1970).

BLAXLAND, Gregory, *The Regiments Depart: A History of the British Army 1945–1970* (London 1971).

BOURRICAUD, François, *Power and Society in Contemporary Peru* trans. P. Stevenson (London 1970).

BROMBERGER, Serge, *Les rebelles algériens* (Paris 1958).

BUCKMAN, Peter, *The Limits of Protest* (London 1970).

CADEMATORI, José, *La economía chilena* (Santiago 1968).

CALVERT, Peter, *Revolution* (London 1971).

CARR, E. H., *The Bolshevik Revolution 1917–1923* 3 vols (London 1950–1953; Penguin edition, 1966).

Michael Bakunin (London 1937; Vintage edition, New York 1961).
1917: Before and After (London 1969).

CARTER, April, *The Political Theory of Anarchism* (London 1971).

CASTRO, Josué de, *Death in the Northeast* (New York 1969).

CASTRO VILLAGRANA, B., et al., *La Iglesia, el Subdesarrollo y la Revolución* (Mexico City 1968).

CHAPMAN, Peter, *Police State* (London 1970).

CHIKOTA, Richard A., and MORAN, Michael C., (eds) *Riot in the Cities* (Fairleigh Dickinson University Press 1970).

CLAUSEWITZ, Carl von, *On War* trans. O. M. Matthijs Jollis (Washington 1950).

CLEAVER, Eldridge, *Soul on Ice* (London 1969).

CLISSOLD, Stephen (ed) *Soviet Relations with Latin America 1918–68: A Documentary Survey* (London 1970).

COHN-BENDIT, Daniel, *Obsolete Communism: The Left-Wing Alternative* trans. A. Pomerans (London 1968; Penguin edition 1969).

COOPER, David (ed) *The Dialectics of Liberation* (Penguin edition 1968).

CORREIA DE ANDRANDE, Manuel, *Nordeste, Espaço e Tempo* (Petropolis, Brazil 1970).

A terra e o homem no nordeste (São Paulo 1964).

CROZIER, Brian, *The Rebels* (London 1960).

DEBRAY, Régis, 'América Latina: algunos problemas de estrategia revolucionaria' *Casa de las Americas* July–August 1965.

'Le Castrisme: la longue marche de l'Amérique latine' in *Les Temps Modernes* January 1965.

Conversations with Allende trans. B. Brewster and P. Reglan (London 1971).

Revolution in the Revolution? (Penguin edition 1968).

DE KADT, Emanuel, *Catholic Radicals in Brazil* (London 1970).

DUCHEMIN, Jacques, *Histoire du FLN* (Paris 1962).

DWYER, D. J., 'The City in the Developing World and the Example of South-East Asia' (University of Hong Kong, *Supplement to the Gazette*, Vol XV, No 6, August 1968).

'Urbanization as a Factor in the Political Development of South-East Asia' (Discussion Paper at Pacific Conference, Viña del Mar, Chile, 27 September–3 October 1970).

ECKSTEIN, Harry (ed) *Internal War* (Free Press of Glencoe 1964).

EDWARDS, Stewart, *The Paris Commune 1871* (London 1971).

ELLIOTT-BATEMAN, Michael (ed) *The Fourth Dimension of Warfare* (Manchester 1970).

ESSIEN-UDOM, E. U., *Black Nationalism* (Penguin edition 1966).

FAIRBAIRN, Geoffrey, *Revolutionary Warfare and Communist Strategy* (London 1968).

FANON, Frantz, *The Wretched of the Earth* trans. C. Farrington (Penguin edition 1970).

FARAONE, Roque, *El Uruguay en que vivimos* (Montevideo 1969).

FIGNER, Vera *Mémoires d'une révolutionnaire* (Paris 1930).

FONER, Philip S. (ed) *The Black Panthers Speak* (New York 1970).

FOX, David J., and ROBINSON, D. J., *Cities in a Changing Latin America* (London 1969).

FRANK, André Gunder, *Latin America: Underdevelopment or Revolution* (New York 1969).

FURTADO, Celso, *Le Brésil à l'heure du choix* trans. J. Chouard (Paris 1964).
Diagnosis of the Brazilian Crisis trans. S. Macedo (Berkeley and Los Angeles 1968).

GALEANO, Eduardo, *Guatemala: Occupied Country* trans. C. Belfrage (New York 1969).

GARAUDY, Roger, *The Turning-Point of Socialism* trans. P. and B. Ross (London 1970).
The Whole Truth trans. P. and B. Ross (London 1971).

GAUCHER, Roland, *Les terroristes* (Paris 1965).

GERASSI, John 'Havana: A New International is Born' in *Monthly Review* (New York) October 1967.
(ed) *Towards Revolution* 2 vols (London 1971).

GHEERBRANT, Alain, *L'Eglise rebelle d'Amérique latine* (Paris 1969)

GHIOLDI, Rodolfo, *No puede haber una revolución en la revolución* (Buenos Aires 1967).

GIAP, Vo Nguyen, *The Military Art of People's War* ed. R. Stetler (New York 1970).

GILIO, Maria Esther, *La guerrilla tupamara* (Havana 1970).

GILLY, Adolfo, 'The Guerrilla Movement in Guatemala' in *Monthly Review* May 1965.

GOLDENBERG, Boris, 'The Rise and Fall of a Party: The Cuban CP (1925–59)' in *Problems of Communism* July–August 1970.

GOTT, Richard, *Guerrilla Movements in Latin America* (London 1970).

GREENE, Lt-Col T. N. (ed) *The Guerrilla—and how to fight him* (New York 1967).

GRIVAS, General, *The Memoirs of General Grivas* ed. Charles Foley (London 1964).

GROSS, Felix, *The Seizure of Political Power* (New York 1957).

GUEVARA, Ernesto 'Che', *Bolivian Diary* trans. C. P. Hansen and A. Sinclair (London 1968).

Guerrilla Warfare (Penguin edition 1969).

Reminiscences of the Cuban Revolutionary War trans. V. Ortz (London 1968).

HAMILTON, Iain, *The Irish Tangle* (Conflict Studies No 6, Institute for the Study of Conflict, London 1970).

HARKABI, Y., *Fedayeen Action and Arab Strategy* (Adelphi Papers No 53, Institute for Strategic Studies, London 1968).

HAYDEN, Tom, *Rebellion and Repression* (New York 1969).

HENISSART, Paul, *Wolves in the City: The Death of French Algeria* (London 1971).

HOBSBAWM, E. J., 'Chile: Year One' Supplement to *New York Review of Books* 23 September 1971.

Primitive Rebels (New York 1965).

HORNE, Alistair, *The Fall of Paris* (London 1965).

HOROWITZ, David, 'Revolutionary Karma vs Revolutionary Politics' in *Ramparts* March 1971.

HOROWITZ, Irving L., Castro, Josué de, and Gerassi, John (eds) *Latin American Radicalism* (London 1969).

HOSMER, Stephen T., *Viet Cong repression and its implications for the future* (RAND Corporation, Lexington, Massachusetts 1970).

HUNTINGTON, Samuel P., *Political Order in Changing Societies* (New Haven 1968).

HYAMS, Edward, *Killing No Murder: A Study of Assassination as a Political Means* (London 1970).

JACKSON, George, *Soledad Brother: The Prison Letters* (New York 1970. Jointly published by Jonathan Cape and Penguin Books, 1971).

JACOBS, Harold (ed) *Weatherman* (New York 1970).

JELLINEK, Frank, *The Paris Commune of 1871* (London 1937).

JULIÃO, Francisco, *Que são as ligas camponesas?* (São Paulo 1962).

KAROL, K. S., *Guerrillas in Power* (London 1971).

KATKOV, George, *Russia 1917: The February Revolution* (London 1967).

KENNAN, George, *Democracy and the Student Left* (London 1969).

KIMCHE, John, 'Israel and the Palestinians' in *The Arab-Israeli Dispute* (Institute for the Study of Conflict, London 1971).

KROPOTKIN, Prince Peter, *Memoirs of a Revolutionist* ed. J. A. Rogers (New York 1962).

LABROUSSE, Alain, *Les Tupamaros: guérilla urbaine en Uruguay* (Paris 1970).

LANGLOIS, Denis, *Les dossiers noirs de la police française* (Paris 1971).
LARTEGUY, Jean, *Les guérilleros* (Paris 1967).
LAWRENCE, Robert, *Guerilla Warfare in the United States* (Canoga Park, California 1970).
Law and Order Reconsidered. Report of the Task Force on Law and Law Enforcement. (Washington 1969).
LEBEL, Ronald, 'The Fixed Terror of Quebec' in *The Globe Magazine* 19 September 1970.
LENIN, V. I., *Collected Works* (Moscow 1967).
LESTER, Julius, *Look Out Whitey, Black Power's Gon' Get Your Mana* (London 1968).
LEVI, Arrigo, *Pci, la lunga marcia verso il potere* (Rome 1971).
LEWIS, Oscar, *The Children of Sanchez* (New York 1961).
La Vida: A Puerto Rican Family in the Culture of Poverty (London 1967).
LIEUWEN, Edward, *Generals versus Presidents* (London 1964).
LUSSU, Emilio, *Théorie de l'insurrection* trans. A. Theron (Paris 1971).
MAGRI, Lucio, 'Italian Communism Today' in *New Left Review* March–April 1971.
MARIGHELLA, Carlos, 'Minimanual of the Urban Guerrilla' in *Tricontinental* (Havana) January–February 1970.
Pour la libération du Brésil (Paris 1970).
Carlos Marighella (biography and documents) (Havana 1970).
MARINE, Gene, *The Black Panthers* (New York 1969).
MARX and ENGELS, *Selected Works* (Moscow 1950).
MATTHEWS, Herbert L., *Castro: A Political Biography* (London 1969).
McGEE, T. G., *The Urbanization Process in the Third World* (London 1971).
MENENDEZ RODRIGUEZ, Mario, 'Venezuela: Douglas Bravo' in *Sucesos* (Mexico City) 24 December 1966.
MERCIER VEGA, Luis, *Guerrillas in Latin America* (New York 1969).
Metas e bases para a acão de gôverno (Presidencia da Republica, Brazil, September 1970).
MOLEIRO, Moises, *El MIR de Venezuela* (Havana 1967).
MOREIRA ALVES, Marcio, 'Brésil: Etat terroriste et guérilla urbaine' in *Politique Aujord'hui* (Paris) July–August 1971.
MORF, Gustave, *Le terrorisme québecois* (Montreal 1970).
MOSS, Robert, 'The Inseparable Divorcees: A Survey of Malaysia and Singapore' (*The Economist*, 30 January 1971).
Revolution in Latin America (Economist Brief Books No 24).

Urban Guerrilla Warfare (Adelphi Papers No 79, London 1971).
Urban Guerrillas in Latin America (Conflict Studies No 8 London 1970).
Uruguay: Terrorism versus Democracy (Conflict Studies No 14 London 1971).
(with Iain Hamilton) *The Spreading Irish Conflict* (Conflict Studies No 17 London 1971).
NEUBERG, A., *Armed Insurrection* trans. Q. Hoare (London 1971).
NICOL, Alex, *La bataille de l'OAS* (Paris 1965).
NISBET, Charles T. (ed) *Latin America: Problems in Economic Development* (New York 1969).
NUNEZ, Carlos, *The Tupamaros: Urban Guerrillas of Uruguay* (Times Change Press, New York 1970—reprinted from *Tricontinental*).
Tupamaros, la unica vanguardia (Montevideo 1969).
O'BALLANCE, Edgar, *The Algerian Insurrection 1954-1962* (London 1969).
OPPENHEIMER, Martin, *Urban Guerrilla* (Penguin edition 1970).
OSWALD, J. Gregory and STROVER, Anthony J. (eds) *The Soviet Union and Latin America* (London 1970).
PARET, Peter, *French Revolutionary Warfare from Indochina to Algeria* (London 1964).
PARET, Peter and SHY, John W., *Guerrillas in the 1960s* (New York 1962).
PICKLES, Dorothy, *Algeria and France: From Colonialism to Cooperation* (London 1967).
Politics of Protest, The Task Force Report submitted to the National Commission on the Causes and Prevention of Violence (New York 1967).
POSNER, Charles (ed) *Reflections on the Revolution in France: 1968* (Penguin edition 1970).
PREBISCH, Raúl, *Transformación y desarrollo: La gran tarea de América latina* (Mexico City 1970).
QUARTIM, João, *Dictatorship and Armed Struggle in Brazil* trans. D. Fernbach (London 1971).
'La guérilla urbaine au Brésil' in *Les Temps Modernes* November 1970.
QUATTROCCHI, Angelo and NAIRN, Tom, *The Beginning of the End: France, May, 1968* (London 1968).
Report of the National Advisory Commission on Civil Disorders (Kerner Report) (Washington 1968).

Report of the National Advisory Commission on Rural Poverty (Washington 1967).

Revolución y Cultura (Havana) No 26, December 1970 (special issue devoted to the Tupamaros).

ROBERTS, Bryan and LOWDER, Stella, *Urban Population Growth and Migration in Latin America* (Liverpool 1970).

ROSENCOF, Mauricio, *La rebelión de los cañeros* (Montevideo 1967).

ROSSI, Peter H. (ed) *Ghetto Revolts* (New York 1970).

RUDÉ, George, *The Crowd in the French Revolution* (Oxford 1959).
Paris and London in the Eighteenth Century: Studies in Popular Protest (London 1970).

SAADI, Yacef, *Souvenirs sur la bataille d'Alger* (Paris 1962).

SEALE, Bobby, *Seize the Time* (London 1970).

SEGAL, Ronald, *The Race War* (London 1966; Penguin edition 1967).
The Struggle against History (London 1971).

SERGE, Victor, *Les coulisses d'une sûreté générale* (Paris 1925).

SIGMUND, Paul E. (ed) *Models of Political Change in Latin America* (New York 1970).

SIMONSEN, Mario Enrique, *Brasil 2001* (Rio de Janeiro 1969).

SINGER, Daniel, *Prelude to Revolution: France in May 1968* (London 1970).

SLIMMING, John, *Malaysia: Death of a Democracy* (London 1969).

SPENDER, Stephen, *The Year of the Young Rebels* (London 1969).

STANFORD, Max, 'Black Guerrilla Warfare: Strategy and Tactics' in *The Black Scholar* (San Francisco) November 1970.

STEINER, Henry J., and TRUBEK, David M., 'Brazil—All Power to the Generals' in *Foreign Affairs* April 1971.

STEPNIAK, *Underground Russia* (New York 1892).

STETLER, Russell, 'Northern Ireland—From Civil Rights to Armed Struggle' in *Monthly Review* November 1970.

STEWART, James and the *Montreal Star*, *The FLQ : Seven Years of Terrorism* (Richmond Hill, Canada 1970).

THOMAS, Hugh, *Cuba, Or the Pursuit of Freedom* (London 1970).

THOMPSON, Sir Robert, *Defeating Communist Insurgency* (London 1966).
Revolutionary War in World Strategy (London 1970).

To Establish Justice, To Insure Domestic Tranquility. Final Report to the National Commission on the Causes and Prevention of Violence (New York 1970).

TRUDEAU, Pierre E., *Federalism and the French Canadians* (Toronto 1968).

Turcios Lima (biography and documents) (Havana 1970).

United Nations Economic Commission for Latin America, *The Economic Development of Latin America in the Post-War Period* (New York 1964). *Economic Survey of Latin America 1969* (New York 1970).

VALLIÈRES, Pierre, *Nègres blancs d'Amérique* (Montreal 1969).

VELECILLOS, Raymundo, 'Los Tupamaros' in *Elite* (Caracas) 27 August 1970.

VELIZ, Claudio (ed) *The Politics of Conformity in Latin America* (London 1967).

Violence in America: Historical and Comparative Perspectives. Report to the National Commission on the Causes and Prevention of Violence (New York 1969).

WILSON, James O. (ed) *The Metropolitan Enigma* (New York 1970).

WOLF, Eric R., 'On Peasant Rebellions' in *International Social Sciences Journal* Vol 21, 1969. *Peasant Wars of the Twentieth Century* (London 1971).

WOMACK, John Jr, *Zapata and the Mexican Revolution* (London 1969).

WOODCOCK, George, *Anarchism* (Penguin edition 1962).

Index

DATE DUE